Contents

HUMAN
RESOURCE
MANAGEMENT
ESSENTIAL PERSPECTIVES

5E

HUMAN RESOURCE MANAGEMENT

ESSENTIAL PERSPECTIVES

5E

ROBERT L. MATHIS

University of Nebraska at Omaha

JOHN H. JACKSON

University of Wyoming

SOUTH-WESTERN
CENGAGE Learning

Australia • Brazil • Japan • Korea • Mexico • Singapore • Spain • United Kingdom • United States

SOUTH-WESTERN
CENGAGE Learning

Human Resource Management: Essential Perspectives, 5e
Dr. Robert L. Mathis
Dr. John H. Jackson

Vice President of Editorial, Business:
Jack W. Calhoun

Vice President/Editor-in-Chief:
Melissa S. Acuna

Executive Editor: Joe Sabatino

Senior Developmental Editor:
Susanna C. Smart

Marketing Manager: Clint Kernen

Marketing Coordinator: Sarah Rose

Content Project Manager: Corey Geissler

Media Editor: Rob Ellington

Editorial Assistant: Ruth Belanger

Senior Frontlist Buyer, Manufacturing:
Doug Wilke

Production Service: Pre-PressPMG

Senior Art Director: Tippy McIntosh

Internal and Cover Designer: Craig Ramsdell,
Craig Ramsdell Design

Cover Painting: Tippy McIntosh

Library of Congress Control Number: 2008930229

ISBN-13: 978-0-324-59241-2

ISBN-10: 0-324-59241-8

South-Western Cengage Learning
5191 Natorp Boulevard
Mason, OH 45040
USA

Cengage Learning products are represented in Canada by Nelson Education, Ltd.

For your course and learning solutions, visit **academic.cengage.com**

Purchase any of our products at your local college store or at our preferred online store **www.ichapters.com**

Printed in Canada
1 2 3 4 5 6 7 12 11 10 09 08

Dr. Robert L. Mathis

Dr. Robert Mathis is a Professor Emeritus of Management at the University of Nebraska at Omaha (UNO). Born and raised in Texas, he received a BBA and MBA from Texas Tech University and a Ph.D. in management and organization from the University of Colorado. At UNO he received the university's "Excellence in Teaching" award.

Dr. Mathis has co-authored several books and published numerous articles covering a variety of topics over the last twenty-five years. On the professional level, Dr. Mathis has held numerous national offices in the Society for Human Resource Management and in other professional organizations. He also served as President of the Human Resource Certification Institute (HRCI) and is certified as a Senior Professional in Human Resources (SPHR) by HRCI.

He has had extensive consulting experiences with organizations of all sizes in a variety of industries. He has extensive specialized consulting experience in establishing or revising compensation plans for small and medium-sized firms. Internationally, Dr. Mathis has consulting and training with organizations in Australia, Lithuania, Romania, Moldova, and Taiwan.

Dr. John H. Jackson

Dr. John H. Jackson is a Professor of Management at the University of Wyoming. Born in Alaska, he received his BBA and MBA from Texas Tech University. He then worked in the telecommunications industry in human resources management for several years. After that, he received his Ph.D. in management and organization at the University of Colorado.

During his academic career, Dr. Jackson has authored six other college texts and more than fifty articles and papers, including those appearing in *Academy of Management Review, Journal of Management, Human Resources Management,* and *Human Resource Planning.* He has consulted with a variety of organizations on HR and management development matters and served as an expert witness in a number of HR-related cases.

At the University of Wyoming he has served three terms as department head in the Department of Management and Marketing. Dr. Jackson received the university's highest teaching award and worked with two-way interactive television for MBA students. Two Wyoming state governors have appointed him to the Wyoming Business Council and the Workforce Development Council. Dr. Jackson is also president of Silverwood Ranches, Inc.

Preface

The importance of human resource issues for managers and organizations is evident every day. As indicated by frequent headlines and news media reports on downsizing, workforce shortages, employee discrimination, union activity, and other topics, the management of human resources is growing in importance in the United States and the world. Many individuals are affected by HR issues; consequently, they will benefit by becoming more knowledgeable about HR management and the nature of various activities. Every manager's HR actions can have major consequences for organizations. This book has been prepared to provide an essential overview of HR management for students, HR practitioners, operating managers, and others in organizations.

A need exists for an overview of HR management that both HR practitioners and students can use. The positive reception of the previous editions of *Human Resource Management: Essential Perspectives* confirmed this need. Consequently, we are pleased to provide an updated version. In addition, this book presents information in a way that is useful to various industry groups and professional organizations. Finally, this condensed view of HR management also addresses the interest in U.S. practices of HR management in other countries, making it a valuable resource for managers worldwide.

As authors, it is our belief that this book will continue to be a useful and understanding means for those desiring a concise discussion of the important issues and practices in HR management. It is our hope that it will contribute to more effective management of human resources in organizations.

Robert L. Mathis, Ph.D., SPHR
John H. Jackson, Ph.D.

Appendices

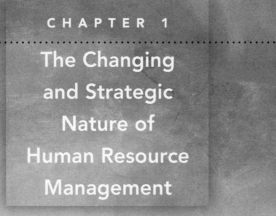

The Changing and Strategic Nature of Human Resource Management

HR—MEETING MANAGEMENT CHALLENGES

Human resource (HR) management is changing to contribute more to organizational results. Key issues include:

- Why HR management is transforming from primarily administrative to being more strategic
- How workforce changes are affecting organizational success and the importance of HR actions
- What HR must do in HR planning and measuring its organizational contributions

In all organizations there are many resources that affect organizational performance. One of the most crucial is human resources, the individuals with talents, capabilities, experience, professional expertise, and their relationships. The human resources are the "glue" that holds all the other assets together and guides their use to achieve results. Certainly, the cashiers, supervisors, and other employees at Wendy's or Lowe's or the doctors, nurses, receptionists, technical professionals, and other employees at a hospital allow all the other assets of their organization to be used to provide customer or patient services. This chapter highlights the factors affecting HR changes that must be addressed in organizations of all types.

Nature of Human Resource Management

As a field, human resource management is undergoing significant transformation. **Human resource (HR) management** is having management systems to ensure that human talent is used effectively and efficiently to accomplish organizational goals. Whether employees are in a big company with 10,000 positions or a small non-profit agency with 10 positions, employees must be recruited, selected, trained, and managed effectively. They also must be adequately and competitively compensated, and many will be given a range of benefits. Additionally, appropriate and legal HR systems are needed to comply with numerous legal requirements. In an environment in which the workforce keeps changing, laws and the needs of employers change too. Therefore, HR management activities continue to change and evolve.[1]

HR Activities

HR management can be thought of as seven interlinked activities taking place within organizations, as depicted in Figure 1-1. Additionally, external forces—legal,

FIGURE 1-1 HR Management Activities

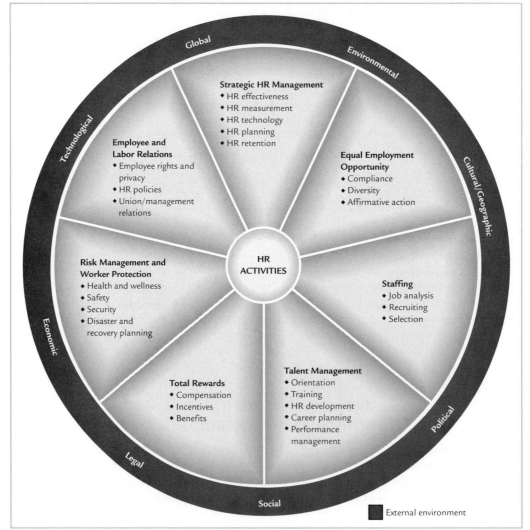

economic, technological, global, environmental, cultural/geographic, political, and social—significantly affect HR activities and how they are designed, managed, and changed. The HR activities are:

- **Strategic HR Management:** As part of maintaining organizational competitiveness, *HR effectiveness* can be increased through the use of *HR measurement* and *HR technology*. Through *HR planning*, managers anticipate the future supply of and demand for employees. An additional strategic HR concern is the *retention* of employees.

- **Equal Employment Opportunity:** *Compliance* with equal employment opportunity (EEO) laws and regulations affects all other HR activities. The *diversity* of a workforce creates additional challenges. For instance, a company must have sufficient diversity to meet *affirmative action* requirements.

- **Staffing:** The aim of staffing is to provide a sufficient supply of qualified individuals to fill jobs in an organization. *Job analysis* lays the foundation for staffing by identifying what people do in their jobs. These analyses are used when *recruiting* applicants for job openings. The *selection* process is concerned with choosing qualified individuals to fill those jobs.

- **Talent Management and Development:** Beginning with the *orientation* of new employees, talent management and development includes different types of *training*. Also, *HR development* of employees and managers is necessary to prepare for future challenges. *Career planning* identifies paths and activities for individual employees as they move within the organization. Assessing how well employees perform their jobs is the focus of *performance management.*

- **Total Rewards:** *Compensation* in the form of *pay, incentives,* and *benefits* rewards people for performing organizational work. To be competitive, employers develop and refine their basic *compensation* systems and may use *variable pay programs* such as gainsharing and productivity rewards. The rapid increase in the cost of benefits, especially for health-care benefits, will continue to be a major issue for most employers.

- **Risk Management and Worker Protection:** Employers need to address an increasing number of workplace risks to ensure worker protection. For decades employers have had to meet legal requirements and be more responsive to concerns for workplace *health* and *safety*. Also, workplace *security* has grown in importance along with *disaster and recovery planning.*

- **Employee and Labor Relations:** The relationship between managers and their employees must be handled effectively. *Employee rights* and *privacy* issues must be addressed. It is important to develop, communicate, and update *HR policies and procedures* so that managers and employees alike know what is expected. In some organizations, *union/management relations* must be addressed as well.

Managing Human Resources in Organizations

In a real sense, *every* manager in an organization is an HR manager, and their effectiveness depends in part on the success of organizational HR systems. However, it is unrealistic to expect a nursing supervisor or an engineering manager to know about the nuances of equal employment regulations or how to design and administer a compensation and benefits system. For that reason, many organizations have people in an HR department who specialize in these activities.

Smaller Organizations and HR Management.   In the United States and worldwide, the number of small businesses continues to grow. In surveys over several years, the issues identified as the greatest concerns in small organizations are consistently: (1) shortages of qualified workers, (2) increasing costs of benefits, (3) rising taxes, and (4) compliance with government regulations.[2] Notice that three of the top four concerns have an HR focus, especially when governmental compliance with wage/hour, safety, equal employment, and other regulations are considered. As a result, for many smaller organizations HR issues are often significant.

HR Management Roles

Several roles can be fulfilled by HR management. The nature and extent of these roles depend on both what upper management wants HR management to do and what competencies the HR staff have demonstrated. Three roles are typically identified for HR:

- *Administrative:* Focusing on HR clerical administration and recordkeeping
- *Operational and employee advocate:* Managing most HR activities in keeping with the strategy that has been identified by management and serving as employee "champion"
- *Strategic:* Helping to define the strategy relative to human capital and its contributing to organizational results

The administrative role traditionally has been the dominant role for HR. However, as Figure 1-2 indicates, a significant transformation in HR is occurring. The HR pyramid is being turned upside down so that significantly less HR time and fewer HR staff are used for clerical administration. Notice in Figure 1-3 that the percentage of emphasis on the operational and employee advocate role is remaining constant. The greatest challenge is for HR to devote more emphasis to strategic HR management.

Administrative Role of HR

The administrative role of HR management has been heavily oriented to processing and recordkeeping. This role has given HR management in some organizations the reputation of being staffed by paper shufflers who primarily tell managers and employees what cannot be done. If limited to the administrative role, HR staff are seen primarily as clerical and lower-level administrative aides to the organization. Two major shifts driving the transformation of the administrative role are greater use of technology and outsourcing.

FIGURE 1-2 Changing Roles of HR Management

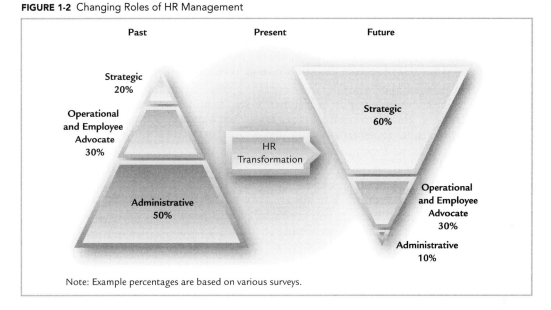

Note: Example percentages are based on various surveys.

Technology Transforming HR.   To improve the administrative efficiency of HR and responsiveness of HR to employees and managers, more HR functions are becoming available electronically or are being done on the Internet. Web-based technology is reducing the amount of HR administrative time and staff needed. Technology is being used in all HR activities, from employment application and employee benefits enrollment to e-learning using Internet-based resources.

Use of technology through human resource management systems serves two major purposes in organizations. One relates to administrative and operational efficiency, the other to effectiveness. The first purpose is to improve the efficiency with which data on employees and HR activities are compiled.

FIGURE 1-3 Fastest Growing Jobs to 2014

Percentage Increase in Jobs		Increase in Job Numbers	
Medical assistants	59%	Retail sales workers	736,000
Network analysts	57%	Registered nurses	703,000
Social service assistants	49%	Post-secondary teachers	524,000
Physician's assistants	49%	Customer service representatives	471,000
Home health aides	48%	Janitors	440,000
Medical records technicians	47%	Waiters/servers	376,000

If automated, many HR activities can be performed more efficiently and quickly and with less paperwork.

An increasing number of firms have HR technology systems that allow employees to access Web-based 401(k) information, and employees and managers are able to make changes to their own data without the assistance of an HR professional.

The second purpose of HR technology is more strategic and related to HR planning. Having accessible data enables HR planning and managerial decision making to be based to a greater degree on information rather than relying on managerial perceptions and intuition.

Outsourcing of HR. Increasingly, many HR administrative functions are being outsourced to vendors. The HR areas most commonly outsourced are employee assistance (counseling), retirement planning, benefits administration, payroll services, and outplacement services.

The primary reasons why HR functions are outsourced is to save money on HR staffing, to take advantage of specialized vendor expertise and technology, and to be able to focus on more strategic HR activities. Such contracting for HR services is an evolving practice that promises to change the administrative HR functions for many employers.

Operational and Employee Advocate Role for HR

HR often has been viewed as the "employee advocate" in organizations. HR professionals spend considerable time on HR "crisis management" dealing with employee problems that are both work and non-work related. Employee advocacy helps ensure fair and equitable treatment for employees regardless of personal background or circumstances.

The operational role requires HR professionals to cooperate with operating managers, to identify and implement needed programs and policies in the organization. This role typically includes many of the HR activities discussed earlier in the chapter.

Strategic Role for HR

Differences between the operational and strategic roles exist in a number of HR areas. The strategic HR role requires that HR professionals be proactive in addressing business realities for the workforce and focusing on future business needs, such as workforce planning, compensation strategies, and the performance of HR. Many executives, managers, and HR professionals increasingly see the need for HR management to become a greater strategic contributor to the "success" of organizations.

The role of HR as a *strategic business partner* is often described as "having a seat at the table," and contributing to the strategic directions and success of the organization. That phrase means HR is involved in *devising* strategy in addition to *implementing* strategy.[3] However, even though this role of HR is recognized, many organizations still need to make significant progress toward fulfilling it.

....

HR Management
Competencies and Careers

As HR management becomes more complex, greater demands are placed on individuals who make HR their career specialty. Even readers of this book who do not become HR managers and professionals will find it useful to know about the competencies required for effective HR management. One area of focus is on ethics and HR management.

Ethics and HR Management

Closely linked with the strategic role of HR is the way HR management professionals influence the organizational ethics practiced by executives, managers, and employees. On the strategic level, organizations with high ethical standards are more likely to meet long-term strategic objectives and profit goals. Differences in legal, political, and cultural values and practices in different countries often raise ethical issues for global employers. HR plays a key role in ensuring ethical behavior in organizations. The number of incidents of employees reporting ethical misconduct has grown in the past decade, primarily because of corporate scandals such as the Enron scandal and others. When the following four elements of ethics programs exist, ethical behavior is likely to occur:

- A written code of ethics and standards of conduct
- Training on ethical behavior for all executives, managers, and employees
- Means for employees to obtain advice on ethical situations they face, often provided by HR
- Systems for confidential reporting of ethical misconduct or questionable behavior

HR Ethics and Sarbanes-Oxley.   The Sarbanes-Oxley Act (SOX) was passed by Congress to make certain that publicly traded companies followed accounting controls that would reduce the likelihood of illegal and unethical behaviors. A number of HR facets must be managed in line with SOX. The biggest issues are linked to executive compensation and benefits.

HR Competencies

The transformation of HR toward being more strategic has implications for the competencies needed by HR professionals. The results of a study have been summarized to identify five basic sets of HR competencies:[4]

- Strategic contribution
- Business knowledge
- HR delivery
- HR technology
- Personal credibility

HR Management as a Career Field

There are a variety of jobs within the HR career field, ranging from executive to clerical. As an employer grows large enough to need someone to focus primarily on HR activities, the role of the HR generalist emerges—that is, a person who has responsibility for performing a variety of HR activities. Further growth leads to the addition of HR specialists, or individuals who have in-depth knowledge and expertise in limited areas of HR.

The broad range of issues faced by HR professionals has made involvement in professional associations and organizations important. For HR generalists, the largest organization is the Society for Human Resource Management (SHRM). Public-sector HR professionals tend to be concentrated in the International Personnel Management Association (IPMA). Other major specialized HR organizations include the International Association for Human Resource Information Management, (IHRIM), the WorldatWork Association, and the American Society for Training and Development (ASTD).

One of the characteristics of a professional field is having a means to certify the knowledge and competence of members of the profession. The CPA for accountants and the CLU for life insurance underwriters are examples. The most well-known certification programs for HR generalists are administered by the Human Resource Certification Institute (HRCI), which is affiliated with SHRM. One way of staying current on HR is to tap information available in current HR Internet resources, as listed in Appendix A.

· ·

Current HR Management Challenges

As the way HR is managed in organizations changes, some challenges are affecting all employers. The environment faced by organizations and their managers is also changing. A look at some of the challenges and changes follows.

Globalization of Business

The internationalization of business has proceeded at a rapid pace. The globalization of business has shifted from trade and investment to the integration of global operations, management, and strategic alliances, which has significantly affected the management of human resources. The HR profession is changing under the force of globalization. Moving jobs to countries with lower labor rates, such as China, Thailand, or India, is another indication of the globalization of HR. Whenever international outsourcing occurs, HR management should be involved to ensure the appropriate consideration of various laws, cultural factors, and other issues.

A current global challenge for international employers is the threat of terrorism, and HR management must respond to such concerns as part of transnational operations and risk management efforts.

Economic and Technological Changes

Economic and technological changes have altered occupational and employment patterns in the United States and other countries. Several changes are discussed next.

Occupational Shifts.   A major change is the shift of jobs from manufacturing and agriculture to service and telecommunications. In general, the U.S. economy has become predominantly a service economy, and that shift is expected to continue. More than 80% of U.S. jobs are in service industries, and most new jobs created by 2014 will also be in services.[5] Projections of growth in some jobs and decline in others illustrate the shifts occurring in the U.S. economy. Figure 1-3 lists occupations that are expected to experience the greatest growth in percentage and numbers for the period ending in 2014.

Workforce Availability and Quality.   Many parts of the United States face significant workforce shortages that exist due to an inadequate supply of workers with the skills needed to perform the jobs being added. It is not that there are too few people—only that there are too few with necessary skills being demanded. Unless major improvements are made to U.S. educational systems, U.S. employers will be unable to find enough qualified workers for the growing number of skilled jobs of all types.

Contingent workers (temporary workers, independent contractors, leased employees, and part-timers) represent more than 20% of the U.S. workforce. The use of contingent workers has grown inpart due to workforce flexibility, but also because many contingent workers are paid less and/or receive fewer benefits than regular employees. Omitting contingent workers from health-care benefits saves some firms 20% to 40% in labor costs.

Technological Shifts and the Internet.   Globalization and economic shifts have been accelerated by technological changes, with the Internet being a primary driver. The explosive growth in information technology and in the use of the Internet has driven changes in jobs and organizations of all sizes. Technology also enables more people to work from home, at night, and during weekends, causing them to always be available.

Workforce Demographics and Diversity

The U.S. workforce has been changing dramatically. It is more diverse racially and ethnically, more women are in it than ever before, and the average age of its members is now considerably older. As a result of these demographic shifts, HR management in organizations has had to adapt to a more varied labor force both externally and internally.

Racial/Ethnic Diversity.   Racial and ethnic minorities account for a growing percentage of the overall labor force, with the percentage of Hispanics equal to or greater than the percentage of African Americans. Immigrants will continue to expand that growth. An increasing number of individuals characterize themselves as *multi-racial,* suggesting that the American "melting pot" is blurring racial and ethnic identities.

Women in the Workforce.   Women constitute almost half of the U.S. workforce. Many women workers are single, separated, divorced, or widowed, and therefore are "primary" income earners. Many women who are married have spouses or domestic partners who are also employed. For many workers in the United States, balancing the demands of family and work is a significant challenge. Employers have had to respond to work/family concerns in order to retain employees.

Aging Workforce.   In many economically developed countries, the population is aging, resulting in a significantly aging workforce. In the United States, during the next decade a significant number of experienced employees will be retiring, changing to part-time, or otherwise shifting their employment. Replacing the experience and talents of longer-service workers is a growing challenge facing employers in all industries.

Organizational Cost Pressures and Restructuring

An overriding theme facing managers and organizations is to operate in a "costless" mode, which means continually looking for ways to reduce costs of all types—financial, operations, equipment, and labor. Pressures from global competitors have forced many U.S. firms to close facilities, use international outsourcing, adapt their management practices, increase productivity, and decrease labor costs in order to become more competitive. The growth of information technology, particularly that linked to the Internet, has influenced the number, location, and required capabilities of employees. In response to organizational-cost pressures and restructurings, as well as the other HR challenges, strategic HR management has become more important.

. . . .
Nature of Strategic HR Management

Strategic HR management refers to the use of employees to gain or keep a competitive advantage. Because business strategies affect HR plans and policies, consideration of human resource issues should be part of the strategic process.

A wide array of data from both academics and consulting firms shows that HR practices really do make a significant difference to business outcomes. Some recognized HR best practices include[6]

- Employment security
- Selective recruiting
- High wages/incentives
- Information sharing/participation

- Training/cross-training
- Promotion from within
- Measurement

The globalization of business has meant that more organizations are operating in multiple countries or have foreign operational links to international suppliers, vendors, and outsourced contributors. Rapid growth of international outsourcing also indicates the linkage between global competitiveness and HR management.

Organizational Culture and HR Strategic Management

The ability of an organization to use its human capital strategically depends at least in part on the organizational culture that is operating. Organizational culture consists of the shared values and beliefs that give members of an organization meaning and provide them with rules for behavior. These values are inherent in the ways organizations and their members view themselves, define opportunities, and plan strategies. Much as personality shapes an individual, organizational culture shapes its members' responses and defines what an organization can or is willing to do.

Organizational culture should be seen as the "climate" of the organization that employees, managers, customers, and others experience. This culture affects service and quality, organizational productivity, and financial results. Critically, it is the culture of the organization, as viewed by the people in it, that affects the attraction and retention of competent employees. Alignment of the organizational culture and HR strategy help affect such aspects as merger success, productivity, and whether human capital can indeed be a core competency.

HR management plays a significant strategic role in organizations where there are identifiable core competencies that relate to people. Strategic HR management plays a significant role in the following areas:

- Organizational productivity
- Customer service and quality
- Financial contributions

Organizational Productivity

Productivity can be a competitive advantage because when the costs to produce goods and services are lowered by more effective processes, lower prices can be charged. Better productivity does not necessarily mean more output; perhaps fewer people (or less money or time) are used to produce the same amount.

Productivity at the organizational level ultimately affects profitability and competitiveness in a for-profit organization and total costs in a not-for-profit organization. Perhaps of all the resources used for productivity in organizations, the most closely scrutinized is human resources. Many strategic HR management efforts are designed to enhance organizational productivity, as Figure 1-4 indicates.

Customer Service and Quality Linked to HR Strategies

In addition to productivity, customer service and quality significantly affect organizational effectiveness. Having managers and employees focus on customers contributes significantly to achieving organizational goals and maintaining

FIGURE 1-4 Approaches to Improving Organizational Productivity

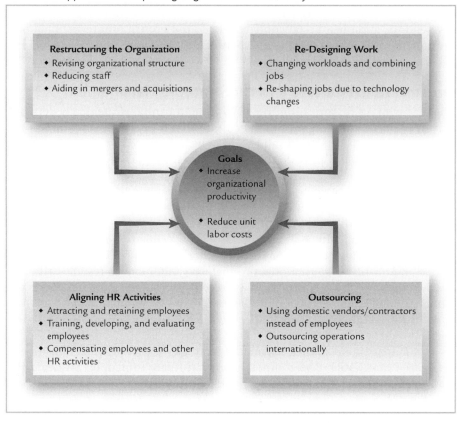

a competitive advantage. In most organizations, service quality is greatly influenced by the individual employees who interact with customers. Delivering high-quality services and/or products can significantly influence organizational effectiveness, because a firm must consider how well its products and services meet customer needs.

HR Effectiveness and Financial Performance

During the past several years, HR management has given significant attention to working more effectively with financial executives to make certain that HR is a financial contributor to organizational effectiveness. The return on investment (ROI) of all resources and expenditures in organizations can be calculated, including the ROI of human expenditures. There are many different ways of measuring the financial contributions of HR and many difficulties associated with doing so. Later in this chapter, the discussion of HR metrics will highlight some specific HR measurement approaches.

. . . .

Human Resource Planning

Human resource planning is the process of analyzing and identifying the need for and availability of human resources so that the organization can meet its objectives. The focus of HR planning is to ensure the organization has the *right number of human resources*, with the *right capabilities*, at the *right times*, and in the *right places*. In HR planning, an organization must consider the availability of and allocation of people to jobs over long periods of time, not just for the next month or even the next year.

This level of planning requires knowledge of expansions or reductions in operations and any technological changes that may affect the organization. Additionally, as part of the analyses, HR plans can be made for shifting employees within the organization, laying off employees or otherwise cutting back the number of employees, retraining present employees, or increasing the number of employees in certain areas. Factors to consider include the current employees' knowledge, skills, and abilities in the organization and the expected vacancies resulting from retirements, promotions, transfers, and discharges. In summary, doing HR planning right requires significant time and effort by HR professionals working with executives and managers.

HR Planning Process

The steps in the HR planning process are shown in Figure 1-5. Notice that the HR planning process begins with considering the organizational objectives and strategies. Then HR needs and supply sources must be analyzed both externally and internally and forecasts must be developed. Key to assessing internal human resources is having solid information accessible through a human resource management system.

Once the assessments are complete, forecasts must be developed to identify the relationship between supply and demand for human resources. Management then formulates HR strategies and plans to address imbalances, both short-term and long-term.

Specific strategies may be developed to fill vacancies or deal with surplus employees. For example, a strategy might be to fill 50% of expected vacancies by training good lower level employees and promoting them into anticipated needed openings—a promotion from within strategy.

Finally, specific HR plans are developed to provide more specific direction for the management of HR activities. The most telling evidence of successful HR planning is a consistent alignment of the availabilities and capabilities of human resources with the needs of the organization over a period of time.

Scanning the External Environment

At the heart of strategic planning is environmental scanning, a process of studying the environment of the organization to pinpoint opportunities and threats. The external environment affects HR planning in particular because each organization must draw from the same labor market that supplies all other organizations, including competitors. Indeed, one measure of organizational effectiveness is the

FIGURE 1-5 HR Planning Process

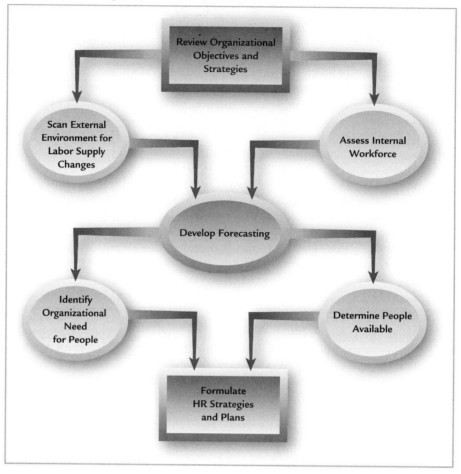

ability of an organization to compete for a sufficient supply of human resources with the appropriate capabilities. All elements of the external environment—government influences, economic conditions, geographic and competition issues, and workforce changes—must be part of the scanning process.

When considering these factors, it is important to analyze how they affect the current and future availability of workers with specific capabilities and experience. For instance, in a number of industries, the median age of engineers is over 50 years, and the supply of engineering graduates is not sufficient to replace such employees as they retire.

Assessing the Internal Workforce

Analyzing the jobs that will need to be done and the skills of people who are currently available in the organization to do them is the next part of HR planning. The needs of the organization must be compared against the labor supply available inside the organization.

Jobs and Skills Audit.   The starting point for evaluating internal strengths and weaknesses is an audit of the jobs being done in the organization. A comprehensive analysis of all current jobs provides a basis for forecasting what jobs will need to be done in the future. The following questions are addressed during the internal assessment:

- What jobs exist now?
- How many individuals are performing each job?
- What are the reporting relationships of jobs?
- How essential is each job?
- What jobs will be needed to implement future organizational strategies?
- What are the characteristics of anticipated jobs?

Organizational Capabilities Inventory.   As HR planners gain an understanding of the current and future jobs that will be necessary to carry out organizational plans, they can conduct a detailed audit of current employees and their capabilities. The basic source of data on employees is the HR records in the organization. Different HR information databases can be used to identify the knowledge, skills, and abilities (KSAs) of employees. The information in those inventories can also provide a basis for determining what additional capabilities will be needed in the future workforce.

Forecasting Organizational HR Supply and Demand

The information gathered from scanning the external environment and assessing internal strengths and weaknesses is used to predict HR supply and demand in light of organizational objectives and strategies. Forecasting uses information from the past and the present to identify expected future conditions. Projections for the future are, of course, subject to error. Fortunately, experienced people usually are able to forecast with enough accuracy to benefit long-range organizational planning.

HR forecasting should be done over three planning periods: short range, intermediate range, and long range. The most commonly used planning period of six months to one year focuses on *short-range* forecasts for the immediate HR needs of an organization. Intermediate- and long-range forecasting are much more difficult processes. *Intermediate-range* plans usually project one to three years into the future, and *long-range* plans extend beyond three years.

The demand for employees can be calculated for an entire organization and/or for individual units in the organization. Demand for human resources can be forecast by considering specific openings that are likely to occur. The openings (or demands) are created when new jobs are being created or current jobs are being reduced. Additionally, forecasts must consider when employees leave positions because of promotions, transfers, turnovers, and terminations. The overall purpose of the forecast is to identify the needs for human resources by number and type for the forecasting period.

Once human resources needs have been forecast, then availability of human resources must be identified. Forecasting the availability considers both *external* and *internal* supplies. Although the internal supply may be somewhat easier to calculate, it is important to calculate the external supply as accurately as possible.

External Supply.   The external supply of potential employees available to the organization needs to be identified. Extensive use of government estimates of labor force populations, trends in the industry, and many more complex and interrelated factors must be considered. Such information is often available from state or regional economic development offices.

Internal Supply.   Estimating internal supply considers the number of external hires and the employees who move from their current jobs into others through promotions, lateral moves, and terminations. It also considers that the internal supply is influenced by training and development programs, transfer and promotion policies, and retirement policies, among other factors. In forecasting the internal supply, data from the replacement charts and succession planning efforts are used to project potential personnel changes, identify possible backup candidates, and keep track of attrition (resignations, retirements, etc.) for each department in an organization.

Succession Planning

One important outcome of HR planning is succession planning, which is a process of identifying a long-term plan for the orderly replacement of key employees. In larger organizations, the aging of the workforce has significant implications for HR planning and succession planning. One common flaw in succession planning is that too often it is limited to key executives. It may be just as critical to replace several experienced mechanical engineers or specialized nurses as to plan for replacing the CEO. Succession planning is discussed more in Chapter 5.

Workforce Realignment

With all the data collected and forecasts done, an organizational plan can be developed. Such a plan can be extremely sophisticated or rather rudimentary. Regardless of the degree of complexity, the ultimate purpose of the plan is to enable managers in the organization to match the available supply of labor with the demand that is expected given the strategies of the organization. If the necessary skill levels do not exist in the present workforce, the organization can train employees in the new skills or undertake outside recruiting. If the plan reveals that the firm employs too many people for its needs, a human resource surplus exists; if too few, an HR shortage.

Managing a Human Resources Surplus.   HR planning is of little value if no subsequent action is taken. The action taken depends on the likelihood of a human resources surplus or shortage. A surplus of workers can be managed within an HR plan in a variety of ways. Regardless of the means, the actions are difficult because workforce reductions often are ultimately necessary.

In this era of mergers, acquisitions, and downsizing, many workers have been laid off or had their jobs eliminated due to the closing of selected offices, plants, and operations. To provide employees with sufficient notice of such losses, a federal law was passed, the Worker Adjustment and Retraining Notification (WARN) Act. The WARN Act imposes stiff fines on employers who do not follow the required process and give proper notice.

Methods for handling human resource surplus situations can include a number of means. Common ones are:

- Workforce downsizing
- Attrition and hiring freezes
- Voluntary separation programs
- Early retirement buyouts
- Layoffs
- Outplacement assistance services

Managing a Shortage of Employees. Managing a shortage of employees seems simple enough—simply hire more people. However, there are consequences to hiring full-time employees in terms of costs, benefits, and other factors. Other options are available that should be considered *before* recruiting and hiring to fill a shortage:

- Use overtime.
- Add contingent workers.
- Bring back recent retirees.
- Outsource work.
- Reduce turnover.

HR Planning in Mergers and Acquisitions

HR management can contribute to the success of mergers and acquisitions (M&As). Experience with the failures shows clearly that for M&As to succeed, organizations have to ensure that different organizational cultures mesh. *Cultural compatibility* is the extent to which such factors as decision-making styles, levels of teamwork, information-sharing philosophies, the formality of the two organizations, etc., are similar.

To address organizational culture concerns, HR professionals should be involved before, during, and after M&As.[7] Significant time must be spent identifying the cultural differences, how they are to be addressed, and ways to integrate managers and employees from both entities. The failures of M&As often are attributed to the incompatibility of the different organizational cultures involved. What changes will be made to the organization structure, how employee benefits will be meshed, what jobs and locations will get more or less staff, and many other issues must be decided and communicated. Ultimately, how HR contributes to various aspects of mergers and acquisitions likely affects the overall effectiveness of the newly combined organizations.

. . . .

Measuring Effectiveness Using HR Metrics

A long-standing myth perpetuates the notion that one cannot really measure what the HR function does. That notion is, of course, untrue; HR—like marketing, operations, or finance—must be evaluated by considering the results of its actions and the value it adds to the organization. It is through the development and use of metrics that HR can better demonstrate its value and track its performance.[8]

HR metrics are specific measures tied to HR performance indicators. A metric can be developed using costs, quantity, quality, timeliness, and other designated goals. In fact, most HR activities can be measured and benchmarked. Some examples are shown in Figure 1-6.

Whether determining the cost of turnover, the average time needed to fill job openings, scores on employee satisfaction surveys, or the ratio of payroll expenditures to revenues, metrics provide specific data to track HR performance. Requirements for developing HR metrics include the following:

- Accurate data can be collected
- Measures are linked to strategic and operational objectives
- Calculations can be clearly understood
- Measures provide information expected by executives
- Results can be compared both externally and internally
- Measurement data drive HR management efforts

Measures of Strategic HR Effectiveness

For HR to fulfill its role as a strategic business partner, HR metrics that reflect organizational strategies and actions must be used. Some of the more prevalent measures compare *full-time equivalents* (FTEs) with organizational measures. An FTE is a measure equal to one person working full-time for a year. For instance, two employees, each working half-time, would count as one FTE.

Return on Investment.   A widely used financial measure that can be applied to measure the contribution and cost of HR activities is *return on investment (ROI)*, which is a calculation showing the value of expenditures for HR activities. It can also be used to show how long it will take for the activities to pay for themselves.

Economic Value Added.   Another measure used is *economic value added (EVA)*, which is the net operating profit of a firm after the cost of capital is deducted. Cost of capital is the minimum rate of return demanded by shareholders. When a company is making more than the cost of capital, it is creating wealth for share-

FIGURE 1-6 Examples of Strategic and Operational HR Metrics

Strategic	Operational
• Revenue generated per FTE	• Annual turnover rate
• Net income before taxes per FTE	• Benefits costs as percentage of payroll
• Ratio of managers to non-managers	• Training expenditures per FTE
• Labor costs as percentage of total operating costs	• Average time to fill openings
• ROI of human capital expenditures	• Workers' compensation costs per FTE
• HR department expenses as percentage of total expenses	• Number of applicants per opening
• Payroll/benefits costs as percentage of revenues	• Absenteeism by employee level/department

holders. An EVA approach requires that all policies, procedures, measures, and methods use cost of capital as a benchmark against which their return is judged. Human resource decisions can be subjected to the same analyses.

HR and the Balanced Scorecard.   One effective approach to the measurement of the strategic performance of organizations, including their HR departments, is the *balanced scorecard.* Use of the balanced scorecard stresses measuring the strategic performance of organizations on four perspectives:

- Financial
- Internal business processes
- Customer
- Learning and growth

Organizational measures in each of these areas are calculated to determine if the organization is progressing toward its strategic objectives. Using the balanced scorecard requires spending considerable time and effort to identify the appropriate HR measures in each of the four areas and how they tie to strategic organizational success. Various companies as diverse as Verizon, EDS, and Union Pacific, as well as small firms, are using the balanced scorecard to ensure better alignment of HR measurement efforts and strategic goals.[9]

HR Measurement and Benchmarking.   Another approach to assessing HR effectiveness is **benchmarking**, which compares specific measures of performance against data on those measures in other organizations. HR professionals interested in benchmarking compare their measurement data with those from outside sources, including individual companies, industry sources, and professional associations.

Using benchmarking, HR effectiveness is best determined by comparing ratios and measures from year to year. But it is crucial that the benchmarking look at the strategic contributions HR makes to the organization, not just the operating efficiency measures.

HR Audit.   One general means for assessing HR is through an HR audit, which is similar to a financial audit. An HR audit is a formal research effort that evaluates the current state of HR management in an organization. This audit attempts to evaluate how well HR activities in each of the HR areas (staffing, compensation, health and safety, etc.) have been performed, so that management can identify areas for improvement. An HR audit often helps smaller organizations without a formal HR professional identify issues associated with legal compliance, administrative processes and recordkeeping, employee retention, etc.

Regardless of the time and effort placed on HR measurement and HR metrics, the most important consideration is that HR effectiveness and efficiency must be measured regularly for HR staff and other managers to know how HR is contributing to organizational success.

NOTES

1. Mark Roehling and Patrick Wright, "Organizationally Sensible vs. Legal-Centric Approaches to Employment Decisions," *Human Resources Management,* 45 (2006), 605–627.
2. *Small Business by the Numbers* and other reports from the U.S. Small Business Administration, *www.sba.gov.*
3. Theresa M. Welbourne, "Human Resource Management: At the Table or Under It?," *Workforce Management Online,* August 2006, 1–5, *www.workforce.com.*
4. The summary of the five competencies is based on Wayne Brockbank and Dave Ulrich, *Competencies for the New HR Guidebook* (Alexandria, VA: Society for Human Resource Management, 2003).
5. U.S. Bureau of Labor Statistics, 2006, *www.bls.gov.*
6. Jeffrey Pfeffer, "Producing Sustainable Competitive Advantage Through the Effective Management of People," *Academy of Management Executive,* November 2005, 95–109.
7. Moira Donoghue, "Is Human Resources Ready?" *Workspan,* May 2006, 62-65.
8. Robert Grossman, "Measuring the Value of HR," *HR Magazine,* December 2006, 44–49.
9. Nancy R. Lockwood, "The Balanced Scorecard: An Overview," *SHRM Research,* June 2006, 1–9.

INTERNET RESOURCES

Society for Human Resource Management (SHRM)—SHRM is the largest HR professional organization and its site contains extensive information and resources. Link to its Web site: *http://www.shrm.org.*

HRM Guide—For network of Human Resource and other Web sites containing articles about Strategic Human Resource Management, link to the HRM Guide Web site at: *http://www.hrmguide.net*

SUGGESTED READINGS

Richard Barrett, *Building a Values-Driven Organization,* (Butterworth-Heineman, 2006).

Jeffrey S. Hornsby and Donald Kurathko, *Front-Line HR,* (Thomson Learning, 2005).

Patricia Phillips, et. al. *THE ROI Fieldbook,* (Society for Human Resource Management, 2007).

John C. Scott, Jack E. Edwards, and Nambury S. Raju, (*Evaluating Human Resource Programs,* SHRM/Wiley, 2007).

CHAPTER 2

Organization/ Individual Relations and Employee Retention

HR—MEETING MANAGEMENT CHALLENGES

Retention of employees in many jobs and organizations has become a major concern by a growing number of employers. Key issues include:

- Why employee retention has become so crucial
- How HR handles workforce and job changes is affecting employee retention efforts
- Ways to measure and reduce employee absenteeism and turnover

The long-term economic health of most organizations depends on the efforts of employees with both the appropriate capabilities and the motivation to do their jobs well. Organizations that are successful over time can usually demonstrate that relationships with their employees *do* matter. Key considerations in these relationships include the psychological contract, job satisfaction, and loyalty. This chapter addresses these concerns, which are increasingly affecting employers and employees.

Many employers are facing significant issues that create conflicting pressures and problems, as pointed out in Chapter 1. Two major issues are:

- A limited labor supply of qualified people to replace employees who retire or leave for other reasons.
- Given the difficulties and expenses of replacing good-performing, experienced employees, employee retention is becoming more crucial.

Individual/Organizational Relationships

Relationships between individuals and their employing organizations can vary widely. Both parties may view the employer/employee relationship as satisfactory. Or one may see it as satisfactory and one may not. Or both may be looking for a way to end the relationship. **Job satisfaction** and *commitment* often help determine whether an employee will want to stay or leave. The *individual's performance* is a major part of whether the employer wants the employee to stay. Therefore, individual/organizational relationships are key in order for organizations to maximize the effectiveness of employee performance, motivation, and retention.

The Psychological Contract

One concept that has been useful in discussing employees' relationships with organizations is that of a psychological contract, which refers to the unwritten expectations employees and employers have about the nature of their work relationships. Because the psychological contract is individual and subjective, it focuses on expectations about "fairness" that may not be defined very clearly by either party.

Expectations about both tangible items (such as wages, benefits, employee productivity, and attendance) and intangible items (such as loyalty, fair treatment, and job security) are encompassed by unwritten psychological contracts between employers and employees. Rather than just paying employees to follow orders and put in time, increasingly, employers are expecting them to utilize their knowledge, skills, and abilities to accomplish results. A psychological contract that can help achieve those ends recognizes the following components:

Employers Provide:	**Employees Contribute:**
• Competitive compensation and benefits	• Continuous skill improvement and increased productivity
• Flexibility to balance work and home life	• Reasonable time with the organization
• Career development opportunities	• Extra effort when needed

Much has been written about the differing expectations of individuals in different generations. Rather than identifying the characteristics cited for each of these groups, it is most important here to emphasize that people's expectations about psychological contracts differ between generations, as well as within generations. For employers, the differing expectations present challenges. For instance, many baby boomers and matures are concerned about security and experience. However, younger generation Yers are often seen as the "why" generation, who expect to be rewarded quickly, are very adaptable, and tend to ask more questions about why managers and organizations make the decisions they do. Generational differences are likely to continue to create challenges and conflicts in organizations because of the different expectations inherent in different generations.

Job Satisfaction.   Employees *do* behave as if there is a psychological contract, and hope their employers will honor the "agreement" which affects job satisfaction.

In its most basic sense, **job satisfaction** is a positive emotional state resulting from evaluating one's job experiences. Job *dis*satisfaction occurs when one's expectations are not met. For example, if an employee expects clean and safe working conditions, then the employee is likely to be dissatisfied if the workplace is dirty and dangerous.

Dimensions of job satisfaction frequently mentioned include work, pay, promotion opportunities, supervision, and co-workers. Job satisfaction appears to have declined somewhat in recent years, and elements of the employee/employer relationship have been cited. More demanding work, fewer traditional hierarchical relationships with management, shorter relationships, and less confidence in long-term rewards are frequently cited reasons.[1]

Loyalty and Organizational Commitment

Even though job satisfaction itself is important, perhaps the "bottom line" is how job satisfaction influences organizational commitment, which then affects employee turnover. As Figure 2-1 depicts, the interaction of the individual and the job determines levels of job satisfaction and organizational commitment. Employers find that in tight labor markets, turnover of key people occurs more frequently when employee loyalty is low, which in turn emphasizes the importance of a loyal and committed workforce.

Organizational commitment is the degree to which employees believe in and accept organizational goals and desire to remain with the organization. A related idea is *employee engagement*, which is the extent to which an employee is willing and able to contribute.

FIGURE 2-1 Factors Affecting Job Satisfaction and Organizational Commitment

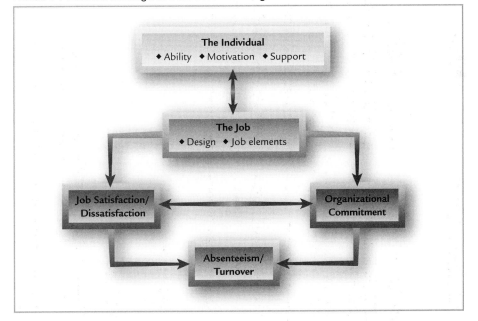

A logical extension of organizational commitment focuses more specifically on **continuance commitment factors**, which suggests that decisions to remain with or leave an organization ultimately are reflected in employee absenteeism and turnover statistics. Individuals who are not as satisfied with their jobs or who are not as committed to the organization are more likely to withdraw from the organization.

. . . .

Individual Employee Performance

The relationship between the individual employee and the organization helps clarify why people might leave a job, as does satisfaction, loyalty, and commitment. But for an employer to *want* to keep an employee, that employee must be performing well. The HR unit in an organization exists in part to analyze and address the performance of individual employees.

Individual Performance Factors

The three major factors that affect how a given individual performs are; (1) individual ability to do the work, (2) effort expended, and (3) organizational support. The relationship among factors is widely acknowledged in management literature as follows:

$$\text{Performance } (P) = \text{Ability } (A) \times \text{Effort } (E) \times \text{Support } (S)$$

Individual performance is enhanced to the degree that all three components are present with an individual employee, and diminished if any of these factors is reduced or absent. For instance, assume that several production workers have the abilities to do their jobs and work hard, but the organization provides outmoded equipment or the management style of supervisors causes negative reactions by the workers. Individual motivation, one of the variables that affects effort, is often missing from the performance equation.

Individual Motivation

Motivation is the desire within a person causing that person to act. People usually act for one reason: to reach a goal. Thus, motivation is a goal-directed drive, and it seldom occurs in a void. The words *need, want, desire,* and *drive* are all similar to *motive,* from which the word *motivation* is derived. Understanding motivation is important because performance, reaction to compensation, turnover, and other HR concerns are affected by and influence motivation.

Motivation is complex and individualized, and managerial strategies and tactics must be broad based to address the motivation concerns of individuals. For instance, managers must determine whether inadequate individual behavior is due to employee deficiencies, inconsistent reward policies, or low desire for the rewards offered. Many organizations spend considerable money to "motivate" their employees, using a wide range of tactics.

. . . .

Retention of Human Resources

Retention of human resources must be viewed as a strategic business issue. Until a few years ago, the opposite of retention, turnover, was a routine HR matter requiring records and reports, but top management did not get involved. However, what was once a bothersome detail has become a substantial money issue for many employers. There are now fewer qualified and productive people in the workforce, and the high performers are even more in demand. Thus, companies are being forced to study why employees leave and why they stay.

Keeping good employees is a challenge that all organizations share and that becomes even more difficult as labor markets tighten. Unfortunately, some myths have arisen about what it takes to retain employees, including the following:

- Money is the main reason people leave.
- Hiring has nothing to do with retention.
- If you train people, you are only training them for another employer.
- Do not be concerned about retention during a merger.
- If solid performers want to leave, the company cannot hold them.

Conventional wisdom says that employees leave if they are dissatisfied, and that money will make them stay. That greatly oversimplifies the issue. People often leave jobs for reasons that have nothing to do with the jobs themselves. Mergers, unsolicited job offers, family responsibilities, a spouse's relocation, a poor performance appraisal, and administrative changes are all "shocks" that can bring on serious thoughts of leaving, even when people are not dissatisfied with their jobs. Further, people sometimes stay with jobs for non-work reasons. Some factors that limit individuals' willingness to leave the jobs are *links* between themselves and others; compatibility or *fit* with the job/organization/community; and potential *sacrifice*, or what they would have to give up if they left the job.

Those characteristics of the "stay or go" decision are personal and not entirely within the control of an employer. However, there are factors related to those individual decisions that an employer can control. Figure 2-2 shows those factors, and also indicates that they are "drivers" of retention, or forces that an employer can manage to improve retention.

If employees choose to leave an organization for family reasons—because a spouse is transferring, to raise children, etc.—there may be a limited number of actions the employer can take to keep them on the job. However, there are significant actions that an employer *can* do to retain employees in most other circumstances.

Characteristics of the Employer and Retention

A number of organizational characteristics influence individuals in their decisions to stay with or leave their employers. Organizations experience less turnover when they have positive and distinctive cultures, effective management, and recognizable job security.

FIGURE 2-2 Drivers of Retention

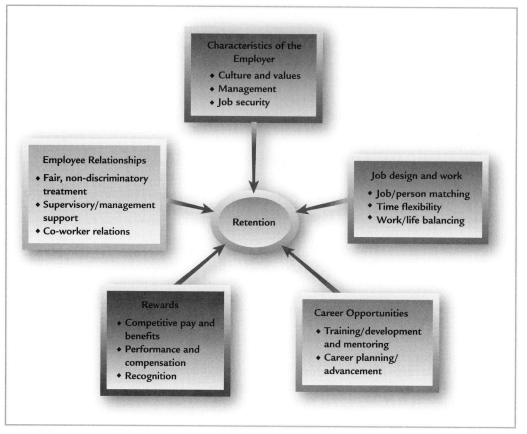

Culture and Values. Organizational culture is a pattern of shared values and beliefs of a workforce. Those items provide organizational members with meaning and rules for behavior. For example, the "100 Best Companies to Work For" have somewhat different cultures and values. Yet their commitment to treating their employees well is a constant in good times and bad.

Management and Retention. Other organizational components that affect employee retention are related to the management of the organization. The attitudes and approaches of management are the key. One factor affecting how employees view their organizations is the visionary quality of organizational leadership. Often, leaders demonstrate their vision by having an identified strategic plan that guides how the firm responds to changes. If a firm is not effectively managed, then employees may be turned off by the ineffective responses and inefficiencies they deal with in their jobs.[2] Further, effective management provides the resources necessary for employees to perform their jobs well.

Job Security. Many individuals have seen a decline in job security during the past decade. All the downsizings, layoffs, mergers and acquisitions, and organizational restructurings have affected employee loyalty and retention. Also, as co-workers experience layoffs and job reductions, the anxiety levels of the remaining employees rise. Consequently, employees start thinking about leaving before they too get cut. On the other hand, organizations in which job continuity and security are high tend to have higher retention rates.

Jobs and Retention

Some jobs are considered "good" and others are thought to be "bad," but not all people agree on which are which. People vary considerably in their preferences for particular job features. As a result, some people like some kinds of work and others like different kinds of work, based on the design of jobs.

Job design refers to organizing tasks, duties, responsibilities, and other elements into a productive unit of work. It addresses the content of jobs and the effect of jobs on employees. Identifying the components of a given job is an integral part of job design. Currently, job design is receiving greater attention for three major reasons:

- Job design can influence *performance* in certain jobs, especially those where employee motivation can make a substantial difference. Lower costs resulting from reduced turnover and absenteeism also are related to the effective design of jobs.
- Job design can affect **job satisfaction**. Because people are more satisfied with certain job configurations than with others, identifying what makes a "good" job becomes critical, which in turn affects employee retention.
- Job design can affect both *physical* and *mental health*. Problems such as hearing loss, backache, and leg pain sometimes can be traced directly to job design, as can stress, high blood pressure, and heart disease.

Approaches to Job Design/Redesign

One approach for designing or re-designing jobs is to simplify the job tasks and responsibilities. Job simplification may be appropriate for jobs that are to be staffed with entry-level employees. However, making jobs too simple may result in boring jobs that appeal to few people, causing high turnover. Several different approaches have been used as part of job design.

Job Enlargement and Job Enrichment. Attempts to alleviate some of the problems encountered in excessive job simplification fall under the general headings of job enlargement and job enrichment. Job enlargement involves broadening the scope of a job by expanding the number of different tasks to be performed.

Job enrichment is increasing the depth of a job by adding responsibility for planning, organizing, controlling, or evaluating the job. Some examples of job enrichment are:

- Giving the employee an entire job rather than just a piece of the work
- Providing the employee more freedom and authority to perform the job as necessary

- Increasing the employee's accountability for work by reducing external control
- Expanding assignments so that the employee can learn to do new tasks and develop new areas of expertise
- Directing feedback reports to the employee rather than only to management

Job Rotation.   One technique that can break the monotony of an otherwise simple, routine job is job rotation, which is the process of shifting a person from job to job. Some argue that job rotation does little in the long run—that although rotating a person from one boring job to another may help somewhat initially, the jobs are still perceived as boring. The advantage of job rotation is that it develops an employee's capabilities for doing several different jobs.

Person/Job Fit

The person/job fit is a simple but important concept of matching characteristics of people with characteristics of jobs. If a person does not fit a job, theoretically either the person can be changed or replaced or the job can be altered. But matching people with jobs they like and fit can be a challenge. Figure 2-3 shows some characteristics of people and jobs that might need to be matched.

If people do not fit their jobs well, they are more likely to look for other employment, so retention is affected by the *selection process*. A number of organizations have found that high turnover rates in the first few months of employment are often linked to inadequate selection screening efforts.

FIGURE 2-3 Some Characteristics of People and Jobs

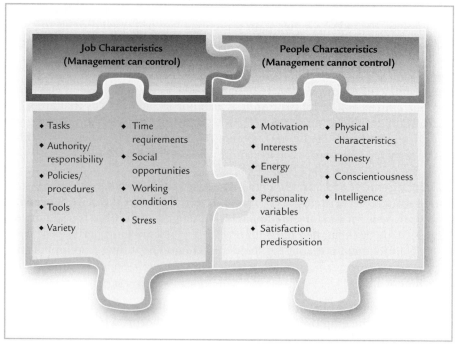

Once individuals have been placed in jobs, other job/work factors affect retention. Because individuals spend significant time on the job, they expect to have modern equipment, technology, and *good working conditions,* given the nature of the work. Physical and environmental factors such as space, lighting, temperature, noise, and layout affect retention of employees.

Additionally, workers want a *safe work environment,* in which risks of accidents and injuries have been addressed. That is especially true for employees in such industries as manufacturing, agriculture, utilities, and transportation, which have higher safety risks than do many service industries and office environments.

Using Teams in Jobs

Typically, a job is thought of as something done by one person. However, where appropriate, jobs may be designed for teams. In an attempt to make jobs more meaningful and to take advantage of the increased productivity and commitment that can follow such a change, more organizations are assigning jobs to teams of employees instead of individuals. Some firms have gone as far as dropping such terms as *workers* and *employees,* replacing them with *teammates, crew members, associates,* and other titles that emphasize teamwork.

The role of supervisors and managers changes with use of teams. An interesting challenge for self-directed work teams involves the emergence or development of team leaders. With more firms operating globally, the use of global teams has increased significantly. Many times, members of global teams seldom or never meet in person. Instead, they "meet" electronically using Web-based systems. The virtual team is composed of individuals who are separated geographically but linked by communications technology. The success of virtual work teams depends on a broad number of factors.

Teams are more likely to be successful if they are allowed to function with sufficient authority to make decisions about their activities and operations. As a transition to work teams occurs, significant efforts are necessary to define the areas of work, scope of authority, and goals of the teams. Additionally, teams must recognize and address dissent and conflict. Contrary to what some might believe, suppressing dissent and conflict to preserve harmony ultimately becomes destructive to the effective operation of a team.

Work Schedules and Retention

The main causes of job-related stress appear to be time pressures, fears of losing a job, deadlines, and fragmented work. The increasing use of technology means that many employees are "always on call" and can "burn out" on work. To aid employee retention by responding to stress and other concerns, employers are using work schedule alternatives and telework. The work schedules associated with different jobs vary. Some jobs must be performed during "normal" daily work hours and workdays, and some jobs require employees to work nights, weekends, and extended hours. The number of work hours in a week varies from country to country. Throughout organizations, many different work scheduling arrangements are being used, including shiftwork, flexible hours, job sharing, and other methods..

Shift Work and the Compressed Workweek.   *Shift work* is a commonly used work schedule design. Many organizations need 24-hour coverage and therefore schedule three 8-hour shifts each day. Many employers provide some form of additional pay, called a *shift differential,* for working the evening or night shift.

One type of shift work is the **compressed workweek**, in which a full week's work is accomplished in fewer than five 8-hour days. Compression simply alters the number of hours an employee works each day, usually resulting in more work hours each day and fewer workdays each week. The use of the compressed workweek illustrates how greater flexibility in work schedules is occurring.

Flexible Scheduling.   Flexible work schedules allow organizations to make better use of workers by matching work demands to work hours. One type of flexible scheduling is flextime, in which employees work a set number of hours a day but vary starting and ending times.

Time Flexibility.   Flexibility in work schedules has grown in importance. Workload pressures have increased because of downsizing. Further, with more Americans living longer, the need for elder care is increasing. Dual-income couples in the "sandwich generation," caring for children *and* aged parents, may find flexible scheduling options very desirable.

Work/Life-Balancing.   Balancing the demands of work with the responsibilities of life, including family and personal responsibilities, is a challenge. Work/life balancing programs commonly used include:

- Different work arrangements
- Leave for children's school functions
- Compressed workweek
- Job sharing
- On-site child/adult care
- Telecommuting
- Employee assistance plans
- On-site health services
- Wellness programs
- Fitness facility

The purpose of all these offerings is to convey that employers recognize the challenges employees face when balancing work/life demands. The value of work/life programs has been well documented as aiding employee retention by reducing employee turnover.

Job Sharing.   Another alternative used to add flexibility and more work/life balancing is job sharing, in which two employees perform the work of one full-time job. For instance, a hospital allows two radiological technicians to fill one job, whereby each individual works every other week. Such arrangements are beneficial for employees who may not want to or be able to work full-time because of family, school, or other reasons. Job sharing also can be effective because each person can substitute for the other when illness, vacation, or other circumstances occur. The keys to successful job sharing are that both "job sharers" must work effectively together and each must be competent in meeting the job requirements.

Telework. The developments in information and communications technology mean that employees can work anywhere and anytime. As a result, a growing number of employers are allowing employees to work from widely varied locations.

Some employees *telecommute*, which means they work via electronic computing and telecommunications equipment. Many U.S. employers have employees who telecommute one or more days a week and who may work from home, a client's facility, an airport conference room, a work suite in a hotel resort, a business-class seat on an international airline flight, or even a vacation condominium. But HR must develop policies regarding teleworkers and must train supervisors and managers on how to "lead" employees who may not be physically present much of the time.

Career Opportunities and Retention

Organizational efforts to aid career development can significantly affect employee retention.[3] Such surveys have found that *opportunities for personal growth* lead the list of reasons why individuals took their current jobs and why they stay there. That component is even more essential for technical professionals and those under age 35, for whom opportunities to develop skills and obtain promotions rank above compensation as a retention concern.

Organizations also increase employee retention through formal career planning efforts. Employees discuss with their managers career opportunities within the organization and career development activities that will help the employees grow. Career development and planning efforts may include formal mentoring programs. Efforts to aid employee retention for careers in a number of ways. Tuition aid programs, typically offered as a benefit by many employers, allow employees to pursue additional educational and training opportunities. These programs often contribute to higher employee retention rates. Also, companies can reduce attrition by showing employees that they are serious about promoting from within.

Mentoring can increase retention because it provides both career opportunities and development. Mentoring can be formal or informal. As the number of contacts grows through mentors or others, it turns into a career networking system, either inside the organization or outside, or perhaps both.

Rewards and Retention

The tangible rewards that people receive for working come in the form of pay, incentives, and benefits. Numerous surveys and experiences of HR professionals reveal that one key to retention is having *competitive compensation practices*. Many managers believe that money is the prime retention factor. Often, employees cite better pay or higher compensation as a reason for leaving one employer for another. However, the reality is a bit more complex.

Competitive Pay and Benefits. Pay and benefits *must be competitive*, which means they must be close to what other employers are providing and what individuals believe to be consistent with their capabilities, experience, and performance. If compensation is not close, often defined as within 10% of the "market" rate, then turnover is likely to be higher. Also, a number of employers have used a wide range of benefits to attract and retain employees.

Performance and Compensation.   Many individuals expect their rewards to be differentiated from those of others based on performance. That means, for instance, that if an employee receives about the same pay increase and overall pay as others who produce less, are absent more and work fewer hours, then that person may feel that the situation is "unfair." This perception may prompt the individual to look for another job where compensation recognizes performance differences.

Recognition.   Employee recognition as a form of reward can be either tangible or intangible. Tangible recognition comes in many forms, such as "employee of the month" plaques and perfect-attendance certificates. Intangible and psychological recognition includes feedback from managers and supervisors that acknowledges extra effort and performance, even if monetary rewards are not given.

Employee Relationships and Retention

A final set of factors found to affect retention is based on the relationships that employees have in organizations. Such areas as the reasonableness of HR policies, the fairness of disciplinary actions, and the means used to decide work assignments and opportunities all affect employee retention. If individuals feel that policies are unreasonably restrictive or are applied inconsistently, then they may be more likely to look at jobs offered by other employers.

....

Managing Retention

The foregoing section summarized that retention is critical because turnover can cause poor performance in otherwise productive units.[4] Now the focus turns toward what managers can do about retention issues. Figure 2-4 shows the keys to managing retention.

Retention Measurement and Assessment

To ensure that appropriate actions are taken to enhance retention, management decisions require data and analyses rather than subjective impressions, anecdotes of selected individual situations, or panic reactions to the loss of key people. Having several *absence and turnover measurements* to analyze is important. Two other sources of information might be useful before analysis is done: employee surveys and exit interviews.[5]

Exit Interviews.   One widely used type of interview is the exit interview, in which individuals are asked to give their reasons for leaving the organization. The information gathered is used to make changes to aid retention. A wide range of issues can be examined in exit interviews. However, departing employees may be reluctant to divulge their real reasons for leaving. A skilled HR interviewer

FIGURE 2-4 Managing Retention

may be able to gain useful information that departing employees may not wish to share with managers and supervisors.

Employee Surveys.   Employee surveys can be used to diagnose specific problem areas, identify employee needs or preferences, and reveal areas in which HR activities are well received or are viewed negatively. For example, questionnaires may be sent to employees to collect ideas for revising a performance appraisal system or to determine how satisfied employees are with their benefits programs. Regardless of the topic of a survey, obtaining employee input provides managers and HR professionals with data on the "retention climate" in an organization.

Retention Management Interventions

The analysis of data mined from turnover and absenteeism records, surveys of employees, and exit interviews is an attempt to get at the cause of retention problems. Analysis should recognize that turnover and absenteeism are symptoms of other factors that may be causing problems.[6] When the causes are treated, the symptoms will go away. Some of the first areas to consider when analyzing data for retention include the work, pay/benefits, supervision, and management systems.

Retention Evaluation and Follow-Up

Once appropriate management actions have been implemented, it is important that they be evaluated and that appropriate follow-up be conducted and adjustments made. *Regular review of turnover data* can identify when turnover increases or decreases among different employee groups classified by length of service, education, department, and gender, etc. *Tracking of intervention results* and *adjustment of intervention efforts* also should be part of evaluation efforts. Evaluation of employee absenteeism and turnover is a key point of retention evaluation and interventions.

Employee Absenteeism

Absenteeism is any failure to report for work as scheduled or to stay at work when scheduled. The cause does not matter when counting someone absent. Being absent from work may seem like a small matter to an employee. But if a manager needs 12 people in a unit to get the work done, and 4 of the 12 are absent most of the time, the work of the unit will decrease some or additional workers will have to be hired to provide results.

Types of Absenteeism

Employees can be absent from work for several reasons. Clearly, some absenteeism is inevitable because of illness, death in the family, and other personal reasons. Such absences are unavoidable and understandable. Many employers have sick leave policies that allow employees a certain number of paid days each year for those types of *involuntary* absences.

However, much absenteeism is avoidable, or *voluntary*. Often, a relatively small number of individuals are responsible for a disproportionate share of the total absenteeism in an organization. One problem is that a number of employees see no real concern about being absent or late to work because they feel that they are "entitled" to some absenteeism.

Controlling Absenteeism

Voluntary absenteeism is better controlled if managers understand its causes clearly. Once they do, they can use a variety of approaches to reduce it. Organizational policies on absenteeism should be stated clearly in an employee handbook and stressed by supervisors and managers. The disciplinary approach is the most widely used means for controlling absenteeism, with most employers using policies and punitive practices. Figure 2-5 shows what actions that employers may use to control employee absenteeism.

Employee Turnover

Some people contend that turnover and absenteeism are different reactions to the same problems. That may be true—both can be classified as organizational withdrawal. Absenteeism is temporary withdrawal and turnover is permanent withdrawal. Like absenteeism, turnover is related to job satisfaction

FIGURE 2-5 Employee Absenteeism Control Actions

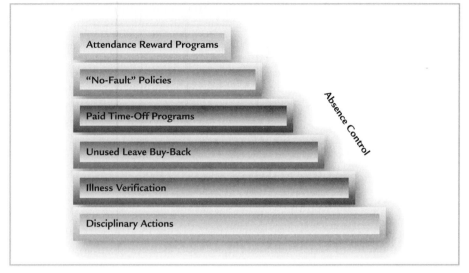

and organizational commitment. Turnover occurs when employees leave an organization and have to be replaced. Many organizations have found that turnover is a costly problem. In many service industries, the turnover rates and costs are frequently very high.

Types of Employee Turnover

Turnover is classified in a number of ways. Each of the following classifications can be used, and the various types are not mutually exclusive:

- **Involuntary Turnover**
  Employees are terminated for poor performance or work rule violations

- **Voluntary Turnover**
  Employees leave by choice

- **Functional Turnover**
  Lower-performing or disruptive employees leave

- **Dysfunctional Turnover**
  Key individuals and high performers leave at critical times

- **Uncontrollable Turnover**
  Employees leave for reasons outside the control of the employer

- **Controllable Turnover**
  Employees leave for reasons that could be influenced by the employer

Employees quit for many reasons that cannot be controlled by the organization. These reasons include: (1) the employee moves out of the geographic area, (2) the employee decides to stay home with young children or elder relatives, (3) the employee's spouse is transferred, and (4) the employee is a student worker who graduates from college.

Even though some turnover is inevitable, many employers today recognize that reducing turnover is crucial. Therefore, they must address turnover that is controllable. Organizations are better able to retain employees if they deal with the concerns of employees that are leading to this type of turnover.

It appears that the amount of money an organization invests in its employees is one of those concerns because it increases the costs of turnover. With respect to turnover and expense, firms that have invested significantly in employees have had lower turnover rates and their profits are affected positively. Tactics for adapting to ongoing turnover include simplifying jobs, outsourcing, and cross training.

....

HR Metrics: Measuring Absenteeism and Turnover

A major step in reducing the expense of absenteeism and turnover is to decide how the organization is going to record those events and what calculations are necessary to maintain and benchmark their rates. A number of considerations are required.

Measuring Absenteeism

Controlling or reducing absenteeism must begin with continuous monitoring of the absenteeism statistics in work units. Such monitoring helps managers pinpoint employees who are frequently absent and departments that have excessive absenteeism. Various methods of measuring or computing absenteeism exist. One formula suggested by the U.S. Department of Labor is as follows:

$$\frac{\text{Number of person-days lost through job absence during period}}{\text{(Average number of employees)} \times \text{(Number of workdays)}} \times 100$$

(This rate also can be based on number of hours instead of number of days.)

- *Incidence rate:* The number of absences per 100 employees each day
- *Inactivity rate:* The percentage of time lost to absenteeism
- *Severity rate:* The average time lost per absent employee during a specified period of time (a month or a year)

Measuring Turnover

The turnover rate for an organization can be computed in different ways. The following formula from the U.S. Department of Labor is often used; in it, *separations* means departures from the organization.

$$\frac{\text{Number of employee separations during the month}}{\text{Total number of employees at midmonth}} \times 100$$

Common turnover rates range from almost 0% to more than 100% a year and vary among industries. Often a part of HR management systems, turnover data can be gathered and analyzed in a number of different ways, including the following categories:

- Job and job level
- Department, unit, and location
- Reason for leaving
- Length of service
- Demographic characteristics
- Education and training
- Knowledge, skills, and abilities
- Performance ratings/levels

Determining Turnover Costs. Determining turnover costs can be relatively simple or very complex, depending on the nature of the efforts and data used. Figure 2-6 shows a simplified costing model. In this model, if a job pays $20,000 (A) and benefits cost 40% (B), then the total annual cost for one employee is $28,000. Assuming that 20 employees quit in the previous year (D) and that it takes three months for 1 employee to be fully productive (E), the calculation in (F) results in a per person turnover cost of $3,500. Overall, the annual turnover costs would be $70,000 for the 20 individuals who left. In spite of its conservative and simple nature, this model makes the point that turnover is costly. For instance, if the job is that of a teller in a large bank where more than 150 people leave in a year, the conservative model produces turnover costs of more than $500,000 a year. More detailed and sophisticated turnover costing models consider a number of factors. Some of the most common areas considered include the following:

- *Separation costs:* Includes HR staff and supervisor time and salaries to prevent separations, exit interview time, unemployment expenses, legal fees for separations challenged, accrued vacation, continued benefits, etc.
- *Replacement costs:* Includes recruiting and advertising expenses, search fees, HR interviewer and staff time and salaries, employee referral fees, relocation and moving costs, supervisor and managerial time and salaries, employment testing costs, reference checking fees, pre-employment medical expenses, etc.

FIGURE 2-6 Simplified Turnover Costing Model

Job Title: _____

A. Typical annual pay for this job _____
B. Percentage of pay for benefits multiplied by annual pay _____
C. Total employee annual cost (add A + B) _____
D. Number of employees who voluntarily quit the job in the past 12 months _____
E. Number of months it takes for 1 employee to become fully productive _____
F. Per person turnover cost (multiply [E ÷ 12] × C × 50%*) _____
G. Annual turnover cost for this job (multiply F × D) _____

*Assumes 50% productivity throughout the learning period (E).

- *Training costs:* Includes paid orientation time, training staff time and salaries, costs of training materials, supervisors' and managers' time and salaries, co-worker "coaching" time and salaries, etc.
- *Hidden costs:* Includes costs not obvious but that affect lost productivity, decreased customer service, other unexpected employee turnover, missed project deadlines, etc.

NOTES

1. Dean B. McFarlin, "Hard Day's Work: A Boon for Performance But a Bane for Satisfaction?" *Academy of Management Perspectives,* November 2006, 115–116.
2. Richard Florida and Jim Goodnight, "Managing for Creativity," *Harvard Business Review,* July/August 2005, 124–131.
3. "Professional Development Opportunities Key to Retaining Talented Employees," *www.shrm.org/press.*
4. K. Michele Kacmar et al., "Sure Everyone Can Be Replaced . . . But at What Cost?

Turnover as a Predictor of Unit-Level Performance," *Academy of Management Journal,* 49 (2006), 133–144.
5. "America's Fast-Growth Companies Spend Half Their Budget on Workforce But Few Spend on Employee Retention," *World at Work,* September 12, 2006, 1–2, *www. worldatwork.com.*
6. M. R. Barrick and R. D. Zimmerman, "Reducing Voluntary, Avoidable Turnover through Selection," *Journal of Applied Psychology,* 90, 2005, 159–166.

INTERNET RESOURCES

CCH Incorporated—CCH Incorporated conducts an Annual Unscheduled Absence Survey. For information on the rate and financial impact of employee absenteeism, visit its Web site at: *http://hr.cch.com*

Talent Keepers—This organization offers Web-based employee retention details, data, and examples. Link to its Web site at: *http://www.talentkeepers.com*

SUGGESTED READINGS

G. Michael Barton, *Recognition at Work,* 2nd ed., (WorldatWork Press, 2006).

Andrea Burgio-Murphy and Mark Murphy, *The Deadly Sins of Employee Retention,* BookSurge, 2006.

Rodger Griffeth and Peter Hom, *Innovative Theory and Empirical Research on Employee Turnover,* (Information Age Publishing, 2004).

S.P. Hundley, Frederic Jacobs, and Marc Drizin, (*Workforce Engagement,* WorldatWork Press, 2007).

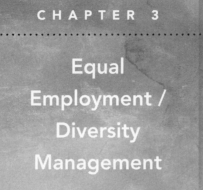

Equal Employment / Diversity Management

HR—MEETING MANAGEMENT CHALLENGES

Equal Employment Opportunity (EEO) and diversity represent major issues for HR in most organizations. EEO is the law and managing diversity is the challenge that accompanies it. To understand why this is the case, this chapter considers:

- The basic legal underpinnings of EEO
- How to manage diversity
- Why affirmative action is controversial

Nature of Equal Employment Opportunity

Inequality in the treatment of people with different backgrounds has been a concern for years. Some countries have "castes" where individuals in some groups are treated better or worse based on race, ethnicity, religion, or other factors. In the United States, slavery was a major concern until amendments to the U.S. Constitution gave all citizens rights to due process (Fifth Amendment), freedom from slavery (Thirteenth Amendment), and equal protection under the law (Fourteenth Amendment). Despite these protections, discrimination in employment has a long history. Women and men working in similar jobs sometimes have been paid differently; African Americans and Latinos/Hispanics simply have not been considered for some jobs even if they are qualified, or they have been treated differently or terminated unfairly.

The civil rights movement of the late 1950s and 1960s influenced public attitudes toward members of racial minorities and women. That influence ultimately resulted in four decades of legislation designed to level the playing field in employment. Beginning in 1963 with the Equal Pay Act and then the Civil Rights Act of 1964, numerous Title VII provisions, Executive Orders, regulations, and interpretations by courts and administrative agencies continue to affect every part of HR management.

At the core of equal employment is the concept of discrimination. Objectively, the word *discrimination* simply means "recognizing differences among items or people." For example, employers must discriminate (choose) among applicants for a job on the basis of job requirements and candidates' qualifications. But when discrimination is based on race, gender, or some other factors, it is illegal and employers face problems.

The following bases for protection have been identified by various federal, state, and/or local laws:

- Race, ethnic origin, color (including multi-race/ethnic backgrounds)
- Sex/gender (including pregnant women and also men in certain situations)
- Age (individuals over age 40)
- Individuals with disabilities (physical or mental)
- Military experience (military status employees and Vietnam-era veterans)
- Religion (special beliefs and practices)
- Marital status (some states)
- Sexual orientation (some states and cities)

Discrimination in employment has been a growing concern as the U.S. workforce becomes more diverse. There are two types of illegal employment discrimination: disparate treatment and disparate impact.

Disparate Treatment

The first main type of illegal discrimination occurs with employment-related situations in which either: (1) different standards are used to judge different individuals, or (2) the same standard is used, but it is not related to the individuals' jobs. Disparate treatment occurs when members of a protected class are treated differently from others. Figure 3-1 illustrates the differences between disparate treatment and disparate impact.

Disparate Impact

The second type of employment discrimination that has been legally supported focuses on the proportion of protected-class members in the workforce of employers.

FIGURE 3-1 Illegal Employment Discrimination

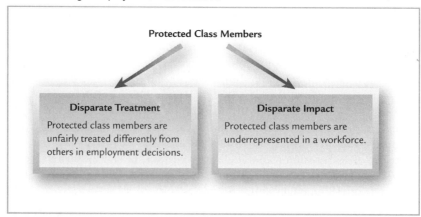

Disparate impact occurs when members of a protected class are substantially under-represented as a result of employment decisions that work to their disadvantage.

Equal Employment Opportunity Concepts

Several basic EEO concepts have been applied as a result of court decisions, laws, and regulatory actions. The four key areas discussed next have evolved to clarify how disparate treatment and disparate impact have been interpreted and enforced.

Business Necessity and Job Relatedness.   A business necessity is a practice necessary for safe and efficient organizational operations. Business necessity has been the subject of numerous court decisions. Educational requirements often are based on business necessity. However, an employer who requires a minimum level of education, such as a high school diploma, must be able to defend the requirement as essential to the performance of the job. For instance, equating a degree or diploma with the possession of math or reading abilities is considered questionable.

Bona Fide Occupational Qualification (BFOQ).   Title VII of the 1964 Civil Rights Act states that employers may discriminate on the basis of sex, religion, or national origin if the characteristic can be justified as a "bona fide occupational qualification reasonably necessary to the normal operation of the particular business or enterprise." Thus, a bona fide occupational qualification (BFOQ) is a characteristic providing a legitimate reason why an employer can exclude persons on otherwise illegal bases of consideration.

What constitutes a BFOQ has been subject to different interpretations in various courts across the United States. Legal uses of BFOQs have been found for hiring Asians to wait on customers in a Chinese restaurant or Catholics to serve in certain religious-based positions in Catholic churches.

Burden of Proof.   Another legal issue that arises when discrimination is alleged is the determination of who has the **burden of proof**, which is what individuals who file suit against employers must prove in order to establish that illegal discrimination has occurred.

Based on the evolution of court decisions, current laws and regulations state that the plaintiff charging discrimination:

- must be a *protected-class member* and
- must prove that *disparate impact* or *disparate treatment* existed.

The employer then must show that the bases for making employment-related decisions were specifically job related and consistent with considerations of business necessity.

Non-Retaliatory Practices.   Employers are prohibited by EEO laws from retaliating against individuals who file discrimination charges. Retaliation occurs when employers take punitive actions against individuals who exercise their legal rights. For example, a construction company was ruled to have engaged in retaliation when an employee who filed a discrimination complaint had work hours reduced, resulting in a loss of pay, and no other employees' work hours were reduced in order to avoid retaliation the following actions are recommended for employers[1]:

- Train supervisors on what retaliation is and what is and is not appropriate.
- Conduct a thorough internal investigation and document the results.
- Take appropriate action when any retaliation occurs.
- Review any HR or job-related changes when taking actions involving individuals who have filed EEO complaints.

. . . .

Major Equal Employment Laws

Even if an organization has little regard for the principles of equal employment opportunity, it must follow federal, state, and local EEO laws and some affirmative action regulations to avoid costly penalties. Numerous federal, state, and local laws address equal employment opportunity concerns.

Civil Rights Act of 1964, Title VII

Although the first civil rights act was passed in 1866, it was not until passage of the Civil Rights Act of 1964 that the keystone of anti-discrimination employment legislation was put into place. The Equal Employment Opportunity Commission (EEOC) was established to enforce the provisions of Title VII, the portion of the act that deals with employment.

Title VII of the Civil Rights Act states that it is illegal for an employer to:

1. *fail or refuse to hire or discharge any individual, or otherwise discriminate against any individual with respect to his compensation, terms, conditions, or privileges of employment because of such individual's race, color, religion, sex, or national origin, or*

2. *to limit, segregate, or classify his employees or applicants for employment in any way that would deprive or tend to deprive any individual of employment opportunities or otherwise adversely affect his status as an employee because of such individual's race, color, religion, sex, or national origin.*

Those organizations that meet one or more of the following criteria include:

- All private employers of 15 or more persons who are employed 20 or more weeks a year
- All educational institutions, public and private
- State and local governments
- Public and private employment agencies
- Labor unions with 15 or more members
- Joint labor/management committees for apprenticeships and training

Executive Orders 11246, 11375, and 11478

Changing laws during the last 30 years have forced employers to address additional areas of potential discrimination. Several acts and regulations apply specifically to government contractors. These acts and regulations specify a minimum number of employees and size of government contracts. The requirements primarily come from federal Executive Orders 11246, 11375, and 11478. Many states have similar requirements for firms with state government contracts.

Civil Rights Act of 1991

The Civil Rights Act of 1991 requires employers to show that an employment practice is *job related for the position* and is consistent with **business necessity**. The act clarifies that the plaintiffs bringing the discrimination charges must identify the particular employer practice being challenged and must show only that protected-class status played *some role.*

Sex/Gender Discrimination Laws and Regulations

A number of laws and regulations address discrimination based on sex or gender. Historically, women experienced employment discrimination in a variety of ways. The inclusion of sex as a basis for protected-class status in Title VII of the 1964 Civil Rights Act has led to various areas of protection for women.

Pregnancy Discrimination.   The Pregnancy Discrimination Act (PDA) of 1978 requires that any employer with 15 or more employees treat maternity leave the same as other personal or medical leaves. Closely related to the PDA is the Family and Medical Leave Act (FMLA) of 1993, which requires that individuals be given up to 12 weeks of family leave without pay and also requires that those taking family leave be allowed to return to jobs. The FMLA applies to both men and women. Courts have generally ruled that the PDA requires employers to treat pregnant employees the same as non-pregnant employees with similar abilities or inabilities.

Equal Pay and Pay Equity.   The Equal Pay Act of 1963 requires employers to pay similar wage rates for similar work without regard to gender. A *common core of tasks* must be similar, but tasks performed only intermittently or infrequently do not make jobs different enough to justify significantly different wages. Differences in pay may be allowed because of:

1. Differences in seniority
2. Differences in performance
3. Differences in quality and/or quantity of production
4. Factors other than sex, such as skill, effort, and working conditions

Sexual Harassment

The Equal Employment Opportunity Commission has issued guidelines designed to curtail sexual harassment. **Sexual harassment** refers to actions that are sexually directed, are unwanted, and subject the worker to adverse employment conditions or create a hostile work environment. Sexual harassment can occur between a boss and a subordinate, among co-workers, and when non-employees have business contacts with employees.

According to EEOC statistics, more than 80% of the sexual harassment charges filed involve harassment of women by men. However, some sexual harassment cases have been filed by men against women managers and supervisors, and for same-sex harassment.

Americans with Disabilities Act (ADA)

The passage of the Americans with Disabilities Act (ADA) in 1990 expanded the scope and impact of laws and regulations on discrimination against individuals with disabilities. The ADA affects employment matters as well as public accessibility for individuals with disabilities and other areas. Organizations with 15 or more employees are covered by the provisions of the ADA, which are enforced by the EEOC, and the act applies to private employers, employment agencies, and labor unions. State government employees are not covered by the ADA, which means that they cannot sue in federal courts for redress and damages. However, they may still bring suits under state laws in state courts.

Who Is Disabled?   As defined by the ADA, a disabled person is someone who has a physical or mental impairment that substantially limits that person in some major life activities, who has a record of such an impairment, or who is regarded as having such an impairment. In spite of the EEOC guidelines, some confusion still remains as to who is disabled. Court decisions have found individuals who have high blood pressure, epilepsy, allergies, obesity, color blindness, and hearing impairments to be disabled. However, various court decisions have narrowed the definition of who is disabled.[2] Figure 3-2 shows the most frequently cited ADA liabilities.

FIGURE 3-2 Most Frequent ADA Disabilities Cited

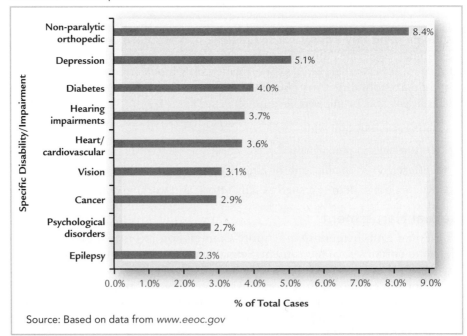

Source: Based on data from *www.eeoc.gov*

Mental Disabilities.   A growing area of concern under the ADA is individuals with mental disabilities. A mental illness is often more difficult to diagnose than a physical disability. Employers must be careful when considering "emotional" or "mental health" factors such as depression in employment-related decisions. They must not stereotype individuals with mental impairments or disabilities but must instead base their evaluations on sound medical information.

ADA and Job Requirements.   Discrimination is prohibited against individuals with disabilities who can perform the essential job functions—the fundamental job duties—of the employment positions that those individuals hold or desire.

For a qualified person with a disability, an employer must make a reasonable accommodation, which is a modification to a job or work environment that gives that individual an equal employment opportunity to perform. EEOC guidelines encourage employers and individuals to work together to determine what are appropriate reasonable accommodations, rather than employers alone making those judgments. The ADA offers only general guidelines in determining when an accommodation becomes unreasonable and places undue hardship on an employer. The ADA contains restrictions on obtaining and retaining medically related information on applicants and employees. Restrictions include prohibiting employers from rejecting individuals because of a disability and from asking job applicants any question about current or past medical history until a conditional job offer is made.

. . . .

Other Types of Discrimination

Age Discrimination in Employment Act (ADEA)

The Age Discrimination in Employment Act (ADEA) of 1967, amended in 1978 and 1986, prohibits discrimination in terms, conditions, or privileges of employment against all individuals age 40 years or older working for employers having 20 or more workers. However, the U.S. Supreme Court has ruled that state employees may not sue state government employers in federal courts because the ADEA is a federal law. The impact of the ADEA is increasing as the U.S. workforce has been aging. Consequently, the number of age discrimination cases has been increasing, according to EEOC reports.

Older Workers Benefit Protection Act (OWBPA).   This law is an amendment to the ADEA and is aimed at protecting employees when they sign liability waivers for age discrimination in exchange for severance packages. To comply with the act, employees must be given complete accurate information on the available benefits. For example, an early retirement package that includes a waiver stating the employee will not sue for age discrimination if he or she takes the money for early retirement must[3]:

- Include a written, clearly understood agreement.
- Offer value beyond what the employee will receive without the package.

- Advise the employee to consult an attorney.
- Allow the employee at least 21 days to consider the offer.
- Allow the employee 7 days to revoke the agreement after signing it.

Immigration Reform and Control Acts (IRCA)

The United States has always had a significant number of immigrants who come to work in this country. The increasing number of immigrants who have entered illegally has led to extensive political, social, and employment-related debates. The existence of more foreign-born workers means that employers must comply with the provisions of the Immigration Reform and Control Acts (IRCA). Employers are required to obtain and inspect I-9 forms, and verify documents such as birth certificates, passports, visas, and work permits. They can be fined if they knowingly hire illegal aliens.

Religious Discrimination

Title VII of the Civil Rights Act identifies discrimination on the basis of religion as illegal. The increasing religious diversity in the workforce has put greater emphasis on religious considerations in work places. However, religious schools and institutions can use religion as a bona fide occupational qualification for employment practices on a limited scale. Also, the employers must make **reasonable accommodation** efforts regarding an employee's religious beliefs.

Military Status and USERRA

The employment rights of military veterans and reservists have been addressed in several laws. The two most important laws are the Vietnam Era Veterans Readjustment Assistance Act of 1974 and the Uniformed Services Employment and Reemployment Rights Act (USERRA) of 1994. Under the latter, employees are required to notify their employers of military service obligations. Employers must give employees serving in the military leaves of absence protections under the USERRA, as Figure 3-3 highlights.

FIGURE 3-3 Uniformed Services Employment and Reemployment Rights Act (USERRA) Provisions

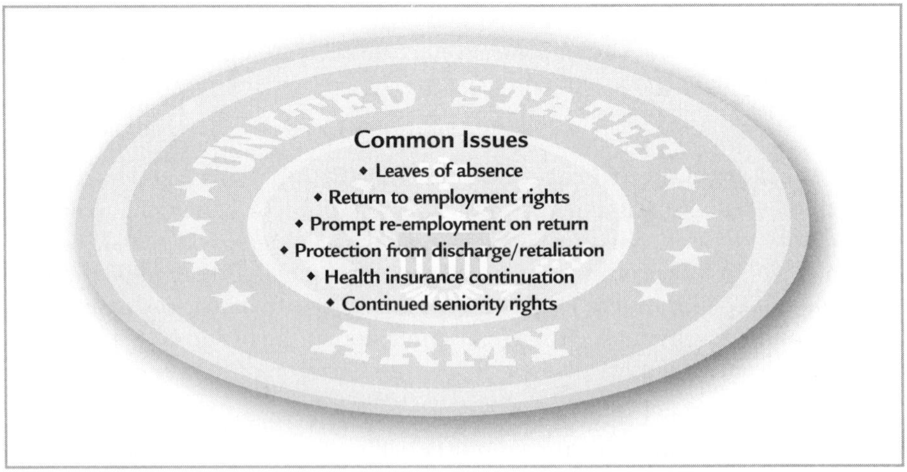

Common Issues
- Leaves of absence
- Return to employment rights
- Prompt re-employment on return
- Protection from discharge/retaliation
- Health insurance continuation
- Continued seniority rights

With the use of reserves and National Guard troops abroad, the provisions of USERRA have had more impact on employers. This act does not require employers to pay employees while they are on military leave, but many firms provide some compensation, often a differential.

Sexual Orientation

Recent battles in a number of states and communities illustrate the depth of emotions that accompany discussions of "gay rights." Some states and cities have passed laws prohibiting discrimination based on sexual orientation or lifestyle. Even the issue of benefits coverage for "domestic partners," whether heterosexual or homosexual, has been the subject of state and city legislation. No federal laws of a similar nature have been passed. Whether gays and lesbians have any special rights under the equal protection amendment to the U.S. Constitution has not been decided by the U.S. Supreme Court.

Appearance and Weight Discrimination

Several EEO cases have been filed concerning the physical appearance of employees. Court decisions consistently have allowed employers to set dress codes as long as they are applied uniformly. For example, establishing a dress code for women but not for men has been ruled discriminatory. Also, employers should be cautious when enforcing dress standards for women employees who are members of certain religions that prescribe appropriate and inappropriate dress and appearance standards. Some individuals have brought cases of employment discrimination based on height or weight. The crucial factor that employers must consider is that any weight or height requirements must be related to the job, such as when excess weight would hamper an individual's job performance.

....

EEO Compliance

Employers must comply with a variety of EEO regulations and guidelines. To do so, it is crucial that all employers have a written EEO policy statement. They should widely communicate this policy by posting it on bulletin boards, printing it in employee handbooks, reproducing it in organizational newsletters, and reinforcing it in training programs. The contents of the policy should clearly state the organizational commitment to equal employment and incorporate a listing of the appropriate protected classes.

Additionally, employers with 15 or more employees may be required to keep certain records that can be requested by the Equal Employment Opportunity Commission, the Office of Federal Contract Compliance Programs, or numerous other state and local enforcement agencies. Under various laws, employers are also required to post an "officially approved notice" in a prominent place for employees. This notice states that the employer is an equal opportunity employer and does not discriminate.

EEO Records Retention.   All employment records must be maintained as required by the EEOC. Such records include application forms and documents concerning hiring, promotion, demotion, transfer, layoff, termination, rates of pay or other terms of compensation, and selection for training and apprentice-ship. Even application forms or test papers completed by unsuccessful applicants may be requested. The length of time documents must be kept varies, but gen-erally *three years is recommended as a minimum.* Complete records are necessary to enable an employer to respond should a charge of discrimination be made.

EEOC Reporting Forms.   Many private-sector employers must file a basic report annually with the EEOC. Slightly different reports must be filed bienni-ally by state/local governments, local unions, and school districts. The following private-sector employers must file the EEO-1 report annually:

- All employers with 100 or more employees, except state and local governments
- Subsidiaries of other companies if the total number of all combined employees equals 100 or more
- Federal contractors with at least 50 employees and contracts of $50,000 or more
- Financial institutions with at least 50 employees, in which government funds are held or saving bonds are issued

In 2007, changes were made in the EEO-1 data collected. Details on employ-ees must be reported by gender, race/ethnic group, and job levels. The most significant change was adding the phrase "two or more races," in order to reflect the multi-diverse nature of a growing number of employees.

Applicant-Flow Data.   Under EEO laws and regulations, employers may be re-quired to show that they do not discriminate in the recruiting and selection of members of protected classes. Because employers are not allowed to collect such data on application blanks and other pre-employment records, the EEOC allows them to do so with a separate *applicant-flow form* that is not used in the selection process. The applicant-flow form is filled out voluntarily by the applicant, and the data must be maintained separately from other selection-related materials. With many applications being made via the Internet, employers must collect this data electronically to comply with regulations on who is an applicant.

....

Diversity Management

The philosophy and legal requirements of equal employment opportunity (EEO) have been discussed earlier in this chapter. Understanding what the laws say is important, but managing human resources for EEO requires significant efforts. EEO is the foundation for HR management in dealing with a varied workforce and legal compliance. Two approaches that are at the forefront of these efforts are: (1) non-discriminatory practices and (2) affirmative action.

Although both of these approaches are controversial at times, they are widely used to ensure that workforce diversity management occurs. Such a broad focus is crucial given the changing composition of the workforce in the United States and other countries. To manage diversity, organizations develop initiatives and take actions that use the capabilities of all people.

FIGURE 3-4 Recent Year Charge Statistics from EEOC

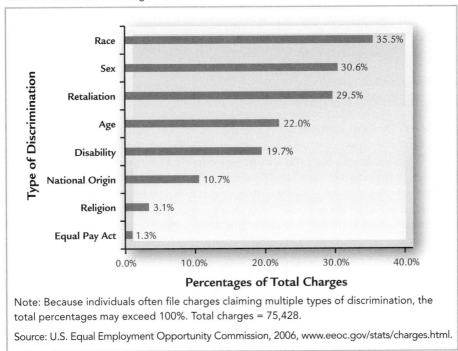

Note: Because individuals often file charges claiming multiple types of discrimination, the total percentages may exceed 100%. Total charges = 75,428.

Source: U.S. Equal Employment Opportunity Commission, 2006, www.eeoc.gov/stats/charges.html.

The original purpose of the Civil Rights Act of 1964 was to address race and national origin discrimination. This concern continues to be important today, and employers must be aware of potential HR issues that are based on race, national origin, and citizenship in order to take appropriate actions. The attention is especially important given the shifting racial/ethnic mix of the U.S. population.

Managing Racial/Ethnic Discrimination

Employment discrimination can occur in numerous ways, from refusal to hire someone because of their race/ethnicity to treatment of those protected class employees. In a recent year, about 35% of the charges filed with the EEOC were on racial complaints, and about 10% were on national origin complaints. Racial discrimination still represents the highest percentage of discrimination complaints, as Figure 3-4 shows.

The area of racial/ethnic harassment is such a concern that the EEOC has issued guidelines on it. It is recommended that employers adopt policies against harassment of any type, including ethnic jokes, vulgar epithets, racial slurs, and physical actions.

In one case there was a clear advantage of taking quick remedial action. In that case an employee filed a lawsuit against an airline because co-workers told racist jokes and hung nooses in his workplace. The airline was able to show that each time any employee, including the plaintiff, reported.

Language Issues and EEO

As the diversity of the workforce increases, more employees have language skills beyond English. Interestingly, some employers have attempted to restrict the use of foreign languages, while other employers have recognized that bilingual employees have valuable skills. Regardless of the HR policies and practices used, the reality is that language issues must be dealt with as part of managing a racially and ethnically diverse workforce.

English-Only Requirements.   A number of employers have policies requiring that employees speak only English at work. These employers contend that the policies are necessary for valid business purposes. For instance, a manufacturer requires that employees working with dangerous chemicals use English to communicate hazardous situations to other workers and to read chemical labels.

The EEOC has issued guidelines clearly stating that employers may require workers to speak only English at certain times or in certain situations, but the business necessity of the requirements must be justified.[4]

Bilingual Employees.   A growing number of employers have found it beneficial to have bilingual employees so that foreign-language customers can contact someone who speaks their language. Some employers do not pay bilingual employees extra, believing that paying for the jobs being done is more appropriate than paying for language skills that are used infrequently on those jobs. Other employers pay "language premiums" if employees must speak to customers in another language.

Requirements for Immigrants and Foreign-Born Workers

Much of the growth in various racial and ethnic groups is due to immigrants from other countries who are here as temporary workers, visitors, students, illegals, etc. For many types of jobs, particularly the lower-skilled jobs in such areas as hospitality and agricultural businesses, workers with limited educational skills are coming from Mexico, Sudan, the Balkan countries, and Latin American and Asian countries.

Employers are required to comply with provisions of the Immigration Reform and Control Acts, as mentioned previously. Foreign-born workers are required to have visas and other documents. It is crucial that employers verify the legal work status of all individuals.

Managing Sex/Gender Issues

The growth in the number of women in the workforce has led to more sex/gender issues related to jobs and careers. A significant issue is related to biology (women bear children) and to tradition (women have a primary role in raising children). A major result of the increasing share of women in the workforce is that more women with children are working. According to the U.S. Bureau of Labor Statistics, about three-fourths of women aged 25–54 are in the workforce. Further, about half of all women currently working are single, separated, divorced, widowed, or otherwise single heads of households. Consequently, they are "primary" income earners, not co-income providers, and must balance family and work responsibilities.

The increasing number of working mothers with children has led employers to take steps to establish compatible policies. Many employers have policies allowing new mothers to leave their work sites during business hours in order to nurse or use breast pumps.

Pay Inequity.   On average, women annually receive about 77% of men's earnings, and that percentage has increased over time. That discrepancy depends to a large extent on differences between jobs, industries, and time spent at work. One study found that when race/ethnicity is considered, the gap widens. However, there is probably a discrimination component to the problem as well. To guard against pay inequities that are considered illegal under the Equal Pay Act, employers should follow these guidelines[5]:

- Include benefits and other items that are part of remuneration to calculate total compensation for the most accurate overall picture.
- Make sure people know how the pay practices work.
- Base pay on the value of jobs and performance.
- Benchmark against local and national markets so that pay structures are competitive.
- Conduct frequent audits to ensure there are no gender-based inequities and that pay is fair internally.

Nontraditional Jobs.   An increasing number of women in the workforce are moving into jobs traditionally held by men. The U.S. Department of Labor defines nontraditional occupations for women as those in which women constitute 25% or less of the total number employed. Even though the nature of the work and working conditions may contribute some to this pattern, many of these jobs pay well, and as more women enter these occupations, women's earnings will rise.

Glass Ceiling.   For years, women's groups have alleged that women in workplaces encounter a glass ceiling, which refers to discriminatory practices that have prevented women and other protected-class members from advancing to executive-level jobs. Women in the United States are making some progress in getting senior-level, managerial, or professional jobs. Nevertheless, women hold only 12% of the highest-ranking executive management jobs in Fortune 500 companies. By comparison, women hold much lower percentages of the same kinds of jobs in France, Germany, Brazil, and many other countries.

Managing Sexual Harassment and Workplace Relationships

As more women have entered the workforce, more men and women work in teams and on projects. Consequently, more employers are facing issues involving the close personal relationships that develop at work.

When work-based friendships lead to romance and off-the-job sexual relationships, managers and employers face a dilemma: Should they "monitor" these relationships to protect the firm from potential legal complaints, thereby "meddling" in employees' private, off-the-job lives? Or do they simply ignore these relationships and the potential problems they present? These concerns are significant, given a survey that found that about 40% of workers have dated co-workers.[6]

Most executives and HR professionals (as well as employees) agree that workplace romances are risky because they have great potential for causing conflict. Many agree that romance must not take place between a supervisor and a subordinate. Some employers have addressed the issue of workplace romances by establishing policies dealing with them.

Sexual Harassment

As noted earlier, sexual harassment most frequently occurs when a male in a supervisory or managerial position harasses women within his "power structure." Also, same-sex harassment has occurred. Court decisions have held that a person's sexual orientation neither provides nor precludes a claim of sexual harassment under Title VII. It is enough that the harasser engaged in pervasive and unwelcome conduct of a sexual nature.

Two basic types of sexual harassment have been defined by EEOC regulations and a large number of court cases. The two types are different in nature and defined as follows:

1. *Quid pro quo* is harassment in which employment outcomes are linked to the individual granting sexual favors.
2. Hostile environment harassment exists when an individual's work performance or psychological well-being is unreasonably affected by intimidating or offensive working conditions.

Employer Responses to Sexual Harassment.   It is crucial that employers respond proactively to prevent sexual and other types of harassment. If the workplace culture fosters harassment, and if policies and practices do not inhibit harassment, an employer is wise to re-evaluate and solve the problem before lawsuits follow.

Only if the employer can produce evidence of taking reasonable care to prohibit sexual harassment does the employer have the possibility of avoiding liability through an affirmative defense. Critical components of ensuring reasonable care include the following:

- Establish a sexual harassment policy.
- Communicate the policy regularly.
- Train employees and managers on avoiding sexual harassment.
- Investigate and take action when complaints are voiced.

Managing Age Issues

The populations of most developed countries—including Australia, Japan, most European countries, and the United States—are aging. These changes mean that as older workers with a lifetime of experiences and skills retire, HR faces significant challenges in replacing them with workers having the capabilities and work ethic that characterize many mature workers. Employment discrimination against individuals age 40 and older is prohibited by the Age Discrimination in Employment Act (ADEA). Therefore, employers must be aware of HR issues associated with managing older workers.

One issue that has led to age discrimination charges is labeling older workers as "overqualified" for jobs or promotions. In a number of cases, courts have ruled that the term *overqualified* may have been used as a code word for workers being too old, thus causing them not to be considered for employment. Also, selection and promotion practices must be "age neutral." Older workers face substantial barriers to entry in a number of occupations, especially those requiring significant amounts of training or ones where new technology has been recently developed.

Workforce Reductions and Additions. In the past decade, many employers have used early retirement programs and organizational downsizing to reduce their employment costs. The Older Workers Benefit Protection Act (OWBPA) was passed to ensure that equal treatment for older workers occurs in early retirement or severance situations. In some cases involving older employees, age-related comments such as "That's just old Fred" or "We need younger blood" in conversations were used as evidence of age discrimination.

To counter significant staffing difficulties, some employers are recruiting older people to return to the workforce through the use of part-time and other scheduling options. During the past decade, the number of older workers holding part-time jobs has increased. It is likely that the number of older workers interested in working part-time will continue to grow. A strategy used by employers to retain the talents of older workers is phased retirement, whereby employees gradually reduce their workloads and pay levels.

Managing Individuals with Disabilities in the Workforce

Employers looking for workers with the knowledge, skills, and abilities to perform jobs often have neglected a significant source: individuals with physical or mental disabilities. At the heart of employing individuals with disabilities is for employers to make reasonable accommodations in several areas. Common means of reasonable accommodation are shown in Figure 3-5. First, architectural barriers should not prohibit disabled individuals' access to work areas or restrooms. Second, appropriate work tasks must be assigned. Satisfying this requirement may mean modifying jobs, work area layouts, or work schedules or providing special equipment.

FIGURE 3-5 Common Means of Reasonable Accommodation

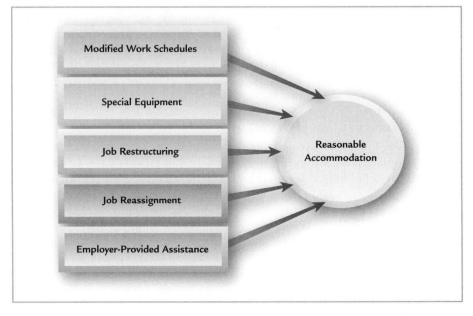

Key to making reasonable accommodations is identifying the essential job functions and then determining which accommodations are reasonable so that the individual can perform the core job duties. Fortunately for employers, most accommodations made are relatively inexpensive. Employers who show a positive interest in making accommodations are more likely to encourage individuals with disabilities to believe that they will receive appropriate considerations for employment opportunities.

Managing Religion and Spirituality in the Workplace

Title VII of the Civil Rights Act of 1964 prohibits discrimination at work on the basis of religion; also, employers are prohibited from discriminating against employees for their religious beliefs and practices. Since the terrorist attacks on September 11, 2001, such considerations have become even more important in protecting Muslim individuals and others from discrimination and harassment.

Some firms have established "holiday swapping pools," whereby Christian employees can work during Passover or Ramadan or Chinese New Year, and employees from other religions work Christmas. Other firms allow employees a set number of days off for holidays, without specifying the holidays in company personnel policies.

One potential area for conflict between employer policies and employee religious practices is dress and appearance. Some religions have standards about appropriate attire for women. Also, some religions expect men to have beards and facial hair, which may violate company appearance policies.

FIGURE 3-6 Various Approaches to Diversity and Their Results

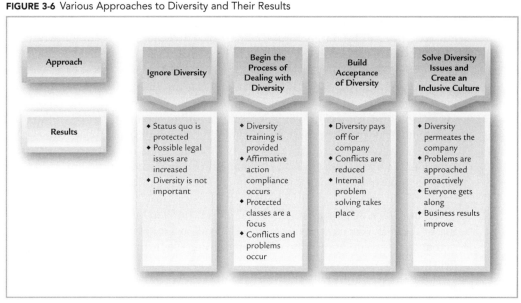

Another issue concerns religious expression. In the last several years, employees in several cases have sued employers for prohibiting them from expressing their religious beliefs at work. In other cases, employers have had to take action because of the complaints by workers that employees were aggressively "pushing" their religious views at work, thus creating a "hostile environment."

Managing Diversity

As the foregoing discussions have shown, the U.S. workforce has become quite diverse. The tangible indictors of diversity that employers must consider means that different organizations approach the management of diversity from several perspectives. As Figure 3-6 shows, the continuum can run from resistance to creation of an inclusive diversity culture. The increasing diversity of the available workforce, combined with growing shortages of workers in many occupations and industries, has resulted in more employers recognizing that diversity must be managed. Organizational experiences and research have indicated that establishing broad responsibility for diversity leads to more effective diversity training, networking, mentoring, and other efforts.[7]

A wide variety of programs and activities have been used in organizations as part of diversity management efforts. Almost half of companies in one survey have a written policy on employee diversity, a significant increase over a 12-year span.[8] That is an essential beginning, but for diversity to succeed, the most crucial component is seeing it as a commitment throughout the organization, beginning with top management. Diversity results must be measured, and management accountability for achieving these results must be emphasized and rewarded. Once management accountability for diversity results has been established, then it is important that policies and activities provide organizational justice and fairness in work treatment for employees. A number of different activities can be implemented as part of a diversity management program, including diversity training.

Diversity Training.   Traditional diversity training has a number of different goals. One prevalent goal is to minimize discrimination and harassment lawsuits. Other goals focus on improving acceptance and understanding of people with different backgrounds, experiences, capabilities, and lifestyles.

Approaches to diversity training vary, but often include at least three components. *Legal awareness* is the first and most common component. Here, the training focuses on the legal implications of discrimination. A limited approach to diversity training stops with these legal "do's and don'ts."

By introducing *cultural awareness,* employers hope to build greater understanding of the differences among people. Cultural awareness training helps all participants to see and accept the differences in people with widely varying cultural backgrounds.

The third component of diversity training—*sensitivity training*—is more difficult. The aim here is to "sensitize" people to the differences among them and how their words and behaviors are seen by others. Some diversity training includes exercises containing examples of harassment and other behaviors.

The effects of diversity training are viewed as mixed by both organizations and participants. A limited number of studies have been done on the effectiveness of diversity training. There is some concern that the programs may be interesting or entertaining, but may not produce longer-term changes in people's attitudes and behaviors toward others with characteristics different from their own.

Some argue that traditional diversity training more often than not has failed, pointing out that it does not reduce discrimination and harassment complaints. Rather than reducing conflict, in a number of situations diversity training has heightened hostility and conflicts. In some firms, it has produced divisive effects, and has not taught the behaviors needed for employees to work well together in a diverse workplace.

This last point, focusing on behaviors, seems to hold the most promise for making diversity training more effective. For instance, dealing with cultural diversity as part of training efforts for sales representatives and managers has produced positive results. Teaching appropriate behaviors and skills in relationships with others is more likely to produce satisfactory results than focusing just on attitudes and beliefs among diverse employees.

Backlash Against Diversity Efforts.   The negative consequences of diversity training may manifest themselves broadly in a backlash against diversity efforts. This backlash takes two main forms. First, and somewhat surprisingly, the individuals in protected groups, such as women and members of racial minorities, sometimes see the diversity efforts as inadequate and nothing but "corporate public relations." Thus, it appears that by establishing diversity programs, employers are raising the expectation levels of protected-group individuals but the programs are not meeting the expectations.

On the other side, a number of individuals who are not in protected groups, primarily white males, believe that the emphasis on diversity sets them up as scapegoats for the societal problems created by increasing diversity. Sometimes white males show hostility and anger at diversity efforts. Those programs are widely perceived as benefiting only women and minorities and taking away opportunities for men and non-minorities.

Trainers emphasize that the key to avoiding backlash in diversity efforts is to stress that people can believe whatever they wish, but at work their values are less important than their *behaviors*. Dealing with diversity is not about what people can and cannot *say*, it is about being *respectful* to others.

Managing diversity training, and indeed diversity itself, must be well thought out and implemented. Diversity is a reality for employers today, and effective diversity management is crucial to HR management.

Affirmative Action

Affirmative action is, in part, a requirement for an employer to document the inclusion of women in its workforce. Through affirmative action employers are urged to hire groups of people based on their race, age, gender, or national origin to make up for historical discrimination. As part of those government regulations, covered employers must submit plans describing their attempts to narrow the gaps between the composition of their workforces and the composition of labor markets where they obtain employees. But affirmative action has been the subject of numerous court cases and an ongoing political and social debate both in the United States and globally.

Generally, the courts have upheld the legality of affirmative action, but recently they have limited it somewhat. The court decisions provided both guidance and confusion, so additional cases are likely to be appealed to various courts. Thus, it is important for HR professionals to monitor both court decisions and political efforts, given the continuing controversies and debate over the fairness of affirmative action.

Debate on Affirmative Action

Employers use affirmative action *goals*, *targets*, and *timetables* to specify how many of which types of individuals they hope to have in their workforces in the future. By specifying these goals, employers say they are trying to "appropriately include protected group members" or "ensure a balanced and representative workforce." These claims and others like them are commonly used to describe affirmative action, which leads to specific debate points.

Debate: Why Affirmative Action Is Needed. Without affirmative action, proponents argue that many in the United States will be permanently economically disadvantaged. Proponents argue for programs to enable women, minorities, and members of other protected groups to be competitive with males and whites. Otherwise, they will never "catch up" and have appropriate opportunities. Specific points made by advocates include the following:

- Affirmative action is needed to overcome past injustices or eliminate the effects of those injustices.
- Affirmative action creates more equality for all persons, even if temporary injustice to some individuals may result.
- Raising the employment level of protected-class members will benefit U.S. society in the long run.
- Properly used, affirmative action does not discriminate against males or whites.
- Goals indicate progress is needed, not quotas.

Debate: Why Affirmative Action Is No Longer Needed.   Opponents of affirmative action believe that it establishes two groups: (1) women, racial minorities, and others in protected classes, and (2) everyone else. For any job, a person will clearly fall into one group or the other. Critics of affirmative action say that regardless of the language used, subsequent actions lead to the use of *preferential selection* for protected-class members over equally qualified white males and others not covered by the EEO regulations. The result may be seen as *reverse discrimination,* which occurs when a person is denied an opportunity because of preferences given to protected-class individuals who may be less qualified. Other points made by opponents include the following:

- Affirmative action penalizes individuals (males and whites) even though they have not been guilty of practicing discrimination.
- Creating preferences of certain groups results in discrimination against others.
- Affirmative action results in greater polarization and separatism along gender and racial lines.
- Affirmative action stigmatizes those it is designed to help.
- Goals become quotas by forcing employers to "play by the numbers."

What studies, surveys, and employer experiences all indicate is that affirmative action is a controversial subject, and it will continue to be so. Despite this, employers must comply with the regulations.

NOTES

1. Jathan Janove, "Retaliation Nation," *HR Magazine,* October 2006, 63–67.
2. John W. Sheffield, "Navigating Current Trends Under the ADA," *Employee Relations Law Journal,* Summer 2005, 3–21.
3. For specifics, see "Older Workers Benefit Protection Act," *Ceridian Abstracts,* July 20, 2005, *www.hrcompliance.ceridian.com.*
4. "English-Only Rules," *HR Compliance Abstracts,* March 28, 2007, *www.hrcompliance. ceridian.com.*

5. "Diffusing the Equity Issue: How BC-BS Instituted a Gender-Balanced Pay Plan," *Pay for Performance Report,* July 2003, 1–2.

6. "Nearly 40% of Workers Have Had Workplace Romance," *Newsline,* January 31, 2007, *www.spherion.com.*

7. Alexandra Kalev, Erin Kelly, and Frank Dobbin, "Best Practices of Best Guesses: Assessing the Efficacy of Corporate Affirmative Action and Diversity Policies," *American Sociological Review,* 71 (2006), 589–618.

8. M. R. Carrell, E. E. Mann, and T. H. Sigler, "Defining Workforce Diversity Programs and Practices in Organizations: A Longitudinal Study," *Labor Law Journal,* Spring 2006, 5–12.

INTERNET RESOURCES

Equal Employment Opportunity Commission—For information on the Equal Employment Opportunity Commission's purpose, employment discrimination facts, enforcement statistics, and details on technical assistance programs, link to their site at: *http://eeoc.gov*

American Institute for Managing Diversity—To learn about the nation's leading nonprofit think tank dedicated to promoting and furthering the field of diversity management, link to their site at: *www.aimd.org.*

SUGGESTED READINGS

F. D. Blau et al., *The Economics of Women, Men, and Work* (Upper Saddle River, NJ: Pearson, 2006), 348–369.

D. Bennett-Alexander and L. Hartman, *Employment Law for Business* (McGraw Hill, Irwin, 2007).

J. Buckley, *EEO Compliance Guide* (Aspen Publishers, 2007).

R. Seymour and John Aslin, *EEO Law Update* (BNA Books 2007).

Staffing

HR—MEETING MANAGEMENT CHALLENGES

Finding and correctly choosing the right people for jobs in any company is a major HR issue. Staffing is seen by many as the most critical part of HR. Consideration needed includes:

- The qualities that are necessary for a person to be able to do a particular job
- The need to find people with those qualities
- The need to hire the best person in the applicant pool

Nature of Job Analysis

Effective staffing is vital in HR Management. Hiring the right people for the right job makes it more likely that the organization will perform effectively. The staffing processes are comprised of three major activities: job analysis, recruiting, and selection. Each of these components are discussed in this chapter.

The focus of job analysis centers on using a formal system to gather data about what people actually do in their jobs. These data are used to generate job descriptions and job specifications.

The most basic building block of HR management, job analysis, is a systematic way of gathering and analyzing information about the content, context, and human requirements of jobs. Using job analysis to document what employees do is important because the legal defensibility of an employer's recruiting and selection procedures, performance appraisal system, employee disciplinary actions, and pay practices rests in part on the foundation of job analysis.

Various methods and sources of data can be used to conduct job analyses. The real value of job analysis begins as the information is compiled into job descriptions and job specifications.

Job analysis involves collecting information on the characteristics of a job that differentiate it from other jobs. The information generated by job analysis may be useful in redesigning jobs, but its primary purpose is to capture a clear understanding of what is done on a job and what capabilities are needed to do it

FIGURE 4-1 Job Analysis in Perspective

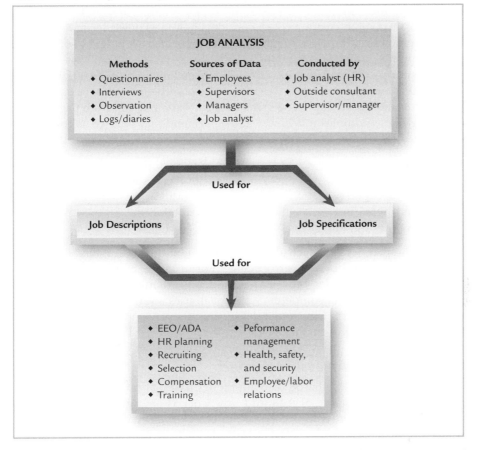

as designed. There are two approaches to job analysis; one focuses on tasks performed in the job, the other on competencies needed for job performance. An overview of job analysis is shown in Figure 4-1.

Task-Based Job Analysis

Task-based job analysis is the most common form and focuses on the tasks, duties, and responsibilities performed in a job. A **task** is a distinct, identifiable work activity composed of motions, whereas a **duty** is a larger work segment composed of several tasks that are performed by an individual. Because both tasks and duties describe activities, it is not always easy or necessary to distinguish between the two. For example, if one of the employment supervisor's duties is to interview applicants, one task associated with that duty would be asking questions. **Responsibilities** are obligations to perform certain tasks and duties.

Competency-Based Job Analysis.   Unlike the traditional approach to analyzing jobs, which identifies the tasks, duties, knowledge, and skills associated with a job, the competency approach considers how the knowledge and skills are used. Competencies are individual capabilities that can be linked to enhanced performance by individuals or teams.

The concept of competencies varies widely from organization to organization. **Technical competencies** often refer to specific knowledge and skills employees have. For example, skills for using specialized software to design Web pages or for operating highly complex machinery and equipment may be cited as competencies. Some of the following have been identified as *behavioral competencies*:

- Customer focus
- Team orientation
- Technical expertise
- Results orientation
- Communication effectiveness
- Leadership
- Conflict resolution
- Innovation
- Adaptability
- Decisiveness

The competency approach also attempts to identify the hidden factors that are often critical to superior performance. For instance, many supervisors talk about employees' attitudes, but they have difficulty identifying exactly what they mean by "attitude." The competency approach uses a variety of methodologies to help supervisors articulate examples of what they mean by attitude and how those factors affect performance.

Choosing a Job Analysis Approach

Whether to use the task-based or competency-based approach to job analysis is affected by the nature of jobs and how work is changing. In some high-technology industries, employees work in cross-functional project teams and shift from project to project. Organizations in these industries focus less on performing specific tasks and duties and more on competencies needed to attain results.

However, in many industries, traditional jobs will continue to exist. Traditional task-based job analysis can provide a defensible basis for such activities as compensation, selection, and training, all of which may be the subject of legal action by employees if they believe they are being wronged in some way. The traditional job analysis approach has been used successfully to substantiate employment decisions. Currently, there is little legal precedent regarding competency analysis, which leaves it open to legal challenge as not being documented as well as the traditional approach. For that reason, task-based job analysis is more widely used.

Stages in the Job Analysis Process

The process of job analysis must be conducted in a logical manner, following appropriate management and professional psychometric practices. Therefore, analysts usually follow a multi-stage process, regardless of the specific job analysis methods used.

Planning the Job Analysis.   A crucial aspect of the job analysis process is the planning done before gathering data from managers and employees. Probably the most important consideration is to identify the objectives of the job analysis, from just updating job descriptions to revising the compensation programs in the organization. Whatever the purpose identified, it is vital to obtain the support of top management.

Preparing for and Introducing the Job Analysis.   Preparation for job analysis begins with identification of the jobs under review. For example, are the jobs to be analyzed hourly jobs, clerical jobs, all jobs in one division, or all jobs in the entire organization? Reviewing existing job descriptions, organization charts, previous job analysis information, and other industry-related resources is part of the planning. This phase identifies those who will be involved in conducting the job analysis and the methods to be used. A crucial step is communicating and explaining the process to managers, affected employees, and other people.

Conducting the Job Analysis.   If questionnaires are used, it is often helpful to have employees return them to supervisors or managers for review before giving them back to those conducting the job analysis. Questionnaires should be accompanied by a letter explaining the process and instructions for completing and returning them. Once data from job analyses are compiled, the information should be sorted by job, organizational unit, and job family.

Developing Job Descriptions and Job Specifications.   Generally, organizations find that having managers and employees write job descriptions is not recommended for several reasons. First, it reduces consistency in format and details, both of which are important given the legal consequences of job descriptions. Second, managers and employees vary in their writing skills. Also, they may write the job descriptions and job specifications to reflect what they do and what their personal qualifications are, not what the job requires. However, completed drafts should be reviewed with managers and supervisors.

Maintaining and Updating Job Descriptions and Job Specifications.   Once job descriptions and specifications have been completed and reviewed by all appropriate individuals, a system must be developed for keeping them current. One effective way to ensure that appropriate reviews occur is to use job descriptions and job specifications in other HR activities. For example, each time a vacancy occurs, the job description and specifications should be reviewed and revised as necessary *before* recruiting and selection efforts begin. Similarly, in some organizations, managers and employees review their job descriptions during each performance appraisal interview.

Job Analysis and the Americans with Disabilities Act (ADA)

HR managers and their organizations must identify job activities and then document the steps taken to identify job responsibilities. One result of the ADA is increased emphasis by employers on conducting job analyses, as well as developing and maintaining current and accurate job descriptions and job specifications.

The ADA requires that organizations identify the **essential job functions**, which are the fundamental duties of a job. These do not include the marginal functions of the positions. Marginal job functions are duties that are part of a job but are incidental or ancillary to the purpose and nature of the job.

Job Analysis and Wage/Hour Regulations

Typically, job analysis identifies the percentage of time spent on each duty in a job. This information helps determine whether someone should be classified as exempt or non-exempt under the wage/hour laws.

The federal Fair Labor Standards Act (FLSA) and most state wage/hour laws indicate that the percentage of time employees spend on manual, routine, or clerical duties affects whether they must be paid overtime for hours worked in excess of 40 hours a week. To be exempt from overtime, the employees must perform their *primary duties* as executive, administrative, professional, or outside sales employees. *Primary* has been interpreted to mean occurring at least 50% of the time.

· ·

Job Descriptions and Job Specifications

The output from analysis of a job is used to develop a job description and the job specifications. Together, these two documents summarize job analysis information in a readable format and provide the basis for defensible job-related actions. They also identify individual jobs for employees by providing documentation from management.[1] Figure 4-2 shows a representative job description that illustrates the necessary components.

In most cases, the job description and job specifications are combined into one document that contains several sections. A **job description** identifies the tasks, duties, and responsibilities of a job. It describes what is done, why it is done, where it is done, and, briefly, how it is done.

While the job description describes activities to be done, the job specifications list the knowledge, skills, and abilities (KSAs) an individual needs to perform a job satisfactorily. KSAs include education, experience, work skill requirements, personal abilities, and mental and physical requirements. It is important to note that accurate **job specifications** identify what KSAs a person needs to do the job, not necessarily the current employee's qualifications.

There are many reasons why a company might succeed; however, unless managers can hire the right people for the right jobs, a company might not be able to fully satisfy its mission, vision, and overarching long-term objectives. **Selection** is the process of choosing individuals with qualifications needed to fill jobs in an organization. The following discussion considers recruiting and then selection.

FIGURE 4-2 Sample Job Description

Identification Section:	
Position Title: Human Resource Manager	
Department: Human Resources	EEOC Class: O/M
Reports to: President	FLSA Status: Exempt

General Summary: Directs HR activities of the firm to ensure compliance with laws and policies, and assists President with overall HR planning

Essential Job Functions:

1. Manages compensation and benefits programs for all employees, resolves compensation and benefits questions from employees, and negotiates with benefits carriers (20%)
2. Ensures compliance with both internal policies and applicable state and federal regulations and laws, including EEO, OSHA, and FLSA (20%)
3. Identifies HR planning issues and suggested approaches to President and other senior managers (15%)
4. Assists managers and supervisors to create, plan, and conduct training and various development programs for new and existing employees (15%)
5. Recruits candidates for employment over telephone and in person. Interviews and selects internal and external candidates for open positions (10%)
6. Reviews and updates job descriptions, assisted by department supervisors, and coordinates performance appraisal process to ensure timely reviews are completed for all employees (10%)
7. Administers various HR policies and procedures and helps managers resolve employee performance and policy issues (10%)
8. Performs other duties as needed and directed by President

Knowledge, Skills, and Abilities:

- Knowledge of HR policies, HR practices, and HR-related laws and regulations
- Knowledge of company products and services and policies and procedures
- Knowledge of management principles and practices
- Skill in operating equipment, such as personal computer, software, and IT systems
- Skill in oral and written communication
- Ability to communicate with employees and various business contacts in a professional and courteous manner
- Ability to organize multiple work assignments and establish priorities
- Ability to negotiate with others and resolve conflicts, particularly in sensitive situations
- Ability to pay close attention to detail and to ensure accuracy of reports and data
- Ability to make sound decisions using available information while maintaining confidentiality
- Ability to create a team environment and sustain employee commitment

Education and Experience: Bachelor's degree in HR management or equivalent, plus 3–5 years' experience

Physical Requirements:	**Percentage of Work Time Spent on Activity**			
	0%–24%	**25%–49%**	**50%–74%**	**75%–100%**
Seeing: Must be able to read computer screen and various reports				X
Hearing: Must be able to hear well enough to communicate with employees and others				X
Standing/walking	X			
Climbing/stooping/kneeling	X			
Lifting/pulling/pushing	X			
Fingering/grasping/feeling: Must be able to write, type, and use phone system				X

Working Conditions: Good working conditions with the absence of disagreeable conditions

Note: The statements herein are intended to describe the general nature and level of work performed by employees, but are not a complete list of responsibilities, duties, and skills required of personnel so classified. Furthermore, they do not establish a contract for employment and are subject to change at the discretion of the employer.

Recruiting

The staffing process matches people with jobs through recruiting and selection. **Recruiting** is the process of generating a pool of qualified applicants for organizational jobs. If the number of available candidates equals the number of people to be hired, no real selection is required—the choice has already been made. The organization must either leave some openings unfilled or take all the candidates.

Recruiting is about finding *qualified* applicants. For example, simply acquiring the human resources necessary to replace normal workforce attrition and provide for growth probably will require an employer to:

- Know the industry to successfully recruit qualified employees
- Identify keys to success in the labor market, including competitors' recruiting efforts
- Cultivate networks and relationships with sources of prospective employees
- Promote the company brand so that the organization is known as a good place to work
- Create recruiting metrics in order to measure the effectiveness of recruiting efforts

Strategic recruiting becomes more important as labor markets shift and become more competitive. HR planning helps to align HR strategies with organizational goals and plans. It is important that recruiting be viewed as a part of strategic HR planning because recruiting is the mechanism that makes the plans work. For example, Walgreens, the drugstore chain, at times has had to cut back its strategy to expand and open new stores because of a shortage of trained pharmacists. Extensive recruiting and more lead time are now a key part of Walgreens' strategic expansion efforts.

Strategy is a general framework that provides guidance for actions. If a company is driven by technology, recruiting must determine how to bring in the best technologists. If the strategy of a company is based on marketing, the focus should be on where the company will look to find the best marketing candidates.

Recruiting can be expensive. But an offsetting concept that must be considered is the *cost of unfilled jobs*. For example, consider a company in which three important related jobs are vacant. These three vacancies cost the company $300 for each business day the jobs remain vacant. If the jobs are not filled for four months, the cost is about $26,000 for the failure to recruit for those jobs in a timely fashion.

Labor Markets

Because staffing takes place in different labor markets that can vary a great deal, learning some basics about labor markets aids in understanding recruiting.[2] Labor markets are the external supply pool from which employers attract employees.

The supply of workers in various labor markets differs substantially and affects staffing. An organization recruits in a number of different labor markets, including geographic, industry, occupational, educational, and technical. The labor markets can be viewed in several ways to provide information that is useful for recruiting. Looking at projections for the labor force by age, participation rates, annual rates of labor force growth, and growth in employment in certain occupations will help alert recruiters to trends in the labor markets.

Geographic Labor Markets.   One common way to classify labor markets is based on geographic location. Some markets are local, some area or regional, some national, and others international. Local and area labor markets vary significantly in terms of workforce availability and quality.

Changes in a geographic labor market may force shifts in recruiting efforts. If a new major employer locates in a regional labor market, then other employers may see a decline in their numbers of applicants. For instance, following the opening of large automobile manufacturing plants in South Carolina, Tennessee, Kentucky, and Alabama, some nearby employers, particularly smaller manufacturing firms, had to raise their wages to prevent turnover of the existing workers.

Attempting to recruit locally for a job market that is really a nationally competitive market will likely result in disappointing applicant rates. For example, a catalog retailer will likely not be able to recruit a senior merchandising manager from only the small town where the firm is located. Conversely, it may not need to recruit nationally for workers to fill administrative support jobs.

Industry and Occupational Labor Markets.   Labor markets also can be classified by industry and occupation. The demand for truck drivers, hotel workers, nurses, teachers, and others has been strong, creating tight labor markets in the industries served by those occupations.

Labor markets are based on the KSAs required for the jobs. These markets include physical therapists, HR managers, engineers, accountants, welders, and bank tellers. One occupational area of extreme volatility in the past several years has been the *information technology* (IT) labor market, which has fluctuated from being extremely tight several years ago, to rather soft after many dot. coms failed, and again is becoming more limited as IT jobs are expanding. Another example is that currently welders are in very tight supply, with pay over $50,000/year and sign-on bonuses and good benefits available.

Another way to look at labor markets is by considering educational and technical qualifications to define the people being recruited. Employers may need individuals with specific licenses, certifications, or educational backgrounds. For instance, a shortage of business professors with PhDs is forecasted to affect many colleges and universities in the next few years due to the retirement of many baby boomers from faculty positions. Other examples include shortages of certified auto mechanics, heating and air-conditioning technicians, and network-certified computer specialists.

Recruiting Presence, Image, and Training

Recruiting efforts may be viewed as either continuous or intensive. *Continuous* efforts to recruit offer the advantage of keeping the employer in the recruiting market. For example, with college recruiting, some organizations may find it advantageous to have a recruiter on a given campus each year. Employers that visit a campus only occasionally are less likely to build a following at that school over time.

Intensive recruiting may take the form of a vigorous recruiting campaign aimed at hiring a given number of employees, usually within a short period of time. Such efforts may be the result of failure in the HR planning system to identify needs in advance or to recognize drastic changes in workforce needs due to unexpected workloads.

Employment "Branding" and Image. A factor impacting recruiting is portraying a positive image of the employer. The way the "employment brand" of the organization is viewed by both employees and outsiders is crucial to attracting applicants and retaining employees, who also may describe the organization in positive or negative terms to others.

Organizations seen as desirable employers are better able to attract more qualified applicants than are organizations with poor reputations. For example, one firm had good pay and benefits, but its work demands were seen as excessive, and frequent downsizings had resulted in some terminations and transfers. The result was high turnover and a low rate of applicants interested in applying for employment at the company.

Training of Recruiters. Another important strategic issue is how much training will be given to recruiters. In addition to being trained on interviewing techniques, communications skills, and knowledge of the jobs being filled, it is crucial that recruiters learn the types of actions that violate EEO regulations and how to be sensitive to diversity issues with applicants. Training in those areas often includes interview do's and don'ts and appropriate language to use with applicants. Racist, sexist, and other inappropriate remarks hurt the image of the employer and may result in legal complaints.

Employment Advertising

The Equal Employment Opportunity Commission (EEOC) guidelines state that no direct or indirect references implying gender or age are permitted. Some examples of impermissible terminology are "young and enthusiastic," "recent college graduate," "Christian values," and "journeyman lineman."

Additionally, employment advertisements should indicate that the employer has a policy of complying with equal employment regulations. Advertisements should contain a general phrase, such as Equal Opportunity Employer, or more specific designations, such as EEO/M-F/AA/ADA. Employers demonstrate inclusive recruiting by having diverse individuals represented in company materials, in advertisements, and as recruiters. Microsoft, Prudential Insurance, Bristol-Myers Squibb, and other firms have found that making diversity visible in recruiting efforts has helped them recruit more individuals with more varied backgrounds.[3]

Recruiting Nontraditional Workers

The growing difficulty that many employers have had in attracting and retaining workers has led them to recruit workers from what, for some, are nontraditional labor pools. Nontraditional sources may include:

- Older workers
- Stay-at-home moms
- Single parents
- Welfare-to-work workers
- Homeless/substance-abuse workers
- Workers with disabilities

Older workers may include retirees who have become bored (or need money), those who have been involuntarily laid off, or career changers wanting to try a new field in mid-career. Single parents may be attracted to a family-friendly employer that offers flexibility because it is frequently difficult to balance job and

FIGURE 4-3 Advantages and Disadvantages of Internal and External Recruiting Sources

Recruiting Source	Advantages	Disadvantages
Internal	• The morale of the promotee is usually high. • The firm can better assess a candidate's abilities. • Recruiting costs are lower for some jobs. • The process is a motivator for good performance. • The process causes a succession of promotions. • The firm has to hire only at entry level.	• "Inbreeding" results. • Those not promoted may experience morale problems. • Employees may engage in "political" infighting for promotions. • A management development program is needed.
External	• New "blood" brings new perspectives. • Training new hires is cheaper and faster because of prior external experience. • The new hire has no group of "political supporters" in the organization. • The new hire may bring new industry insights.	• The firm may not select someone who will fit the job or the organization. • The process may cause morale problems for internal candidates not selected. • The new employee may require a longer adjustment or orientation time.

family life. Stay-at-home moms may consider part-time work that is available during times when the children are at school. Welfare-to-work applicants often need training in basic work skills such as reporting to work on time and doing what they are told—putting a premium on an employer's training program. Employees with disabilities present a variety of challenges depending on the nature of the disability, but if an employer can be flexible, such workers can be a good source of employees. Homeless and substance-abuse workers also come with a variety of problems. Some cities have non-profit groups interested in seeing these people succeed at work that provide support and some training to them.

Recruiting Source Choices: Internal vs. External

Recruiting strategy and policy decisions entail identifying where to recruit, whom to recruit, and how to recruit. One of the first decisions determines the extent to which internal or external sources and methods will be used. Both promoting from within the organization (internal recruitment) and hiring from outside the organization (external recruitment) come with advantages and disadvantages. Figure 4-3 shows some of the major pluses and minuses of each.

· ·

Internal Recruiting Methods

The most common internal recruiting methods include: organizational databases, job postings, promotions and transfers, current-employee referrals, and re-recruiting of former employees and applicants.

Internal Recruiting Processes

Within the organization, tapping into employee databases, job postings, promotions, and transfers provides ways for current employees to move to other jobs. Filling openings internally may add motivation for employees to stay and grow in the organization rather than pursuing career opportunities elsewhere.

Employee Databases.   The increased use of HR management systems allows HR staff members to maintain background and KSA information on existing employees. As openings arise, HR can access databases by entering job requirements and then get a listing of current employees meeting those requirements. Various types of employment software sort employee data by occupational fields, education, areas of career interests, previous work histories, and other variables.

Job Posting.   The major means for recruiting current employees for other jobs within the organization is job posting, a system in which the employer provides notices of job openings and employees respond by applying for specific openings. Without some sort of job posting system, it is difficult for many employees to find out what jobs are open elsewhere in the organization. The organization can notify employees of job vacancies in a number of ways, including posting notices on the company intranet and Internet Web site, using employee newsletters, and sending out e-mails to managers and employees. In a unionized organization, job posting and bidding can be quite formal because the procedures are often spelled out in labor agreements.

Promotions and Transfers. Many organizations choose to fill vacancies through promotions or transfers from within whenever possible. As employees transfer or are promoted to other jobs, individuals must be recruited to fill their vacated jobs. Planning on how to fill those openings should occur before the job transfers or promotions, not afterward. It is clear that people in organizations with fewer levels may have less frequent chances for promotion.

Current-Employee Referrals. A reliable source of people to fill vacancies is composed of acquaintances, friends, and family members of employees. The current employees can acquaint potential applicants with the advantages of a job with the company, furnish letters of introduction, and encourage candidates to apply. However, using only word-of-mouth or current-employee referrals can violate equal employment regulations if protected-class individuals are under-represented in the current organizational workforce. Therefore, some external recruiting might be necessary to avoid legal problems in this area.

Re-Recruiting of Former Employees and Applicants. Former employees and former applicants represent another source for recruitment. Both groups offer a time-saving advantage because something is already known about them. Seeking them out as candidates is known as *re-recruiting* because they were successfully recruited previously. Former employees are considered an internal source in the sense that they have ties to the employer, and may be called "boomerangers" because they left and came back.

. . . .

External Recruiting Sources

What makes an external applicant consider a specific employer? What attracts the right kind of applicants? Characteristics of the job and organization, how the recruiting is conducted, and whether the applicant sees a fit are important elements in successfully recruiting external candidates according to recent research.[4] These attractions apply regardless of the source of the applicants. Many external sources are available for recruiting. In some tight labor markets, multiple sources and methods will be used to attract candidates for the variety of jobs available in organizations. Some of the more prominent methods are highlighted next.

College and University Recruiting

College or university students are a significant source for entry-level professional and technical employees. Most universities maintain career placement offices in which employers and applicants can meet. A number of considerations affect an employer's selection of colleges and universities at which to conduct interviews. The major determinants are:

- Current and anticipated job openings
- Reputations of the colleges and universities
- Experiences with placement offices and previous graduates
- Organizational budget constraints
- Market competition for graduates
- Cost of available talent and typical salaries

School Recruiting

High schools or vocational/technical schools may be valuable sources of new employees for some organizations. Many schools have a centralized guidance or placement office. Promotional brochures that acquaint students with starting jobs and career opportunities can be distributed to counselors, librarians, or others. Participating in career days and giving company tours to school groups are other ways of maintaining good contact with school sources. Cooperative programs in which students work part-time and receive some school credits also may be useful in generating qualified future applicants for full-time positions.

Labor Unions

Labor unions are a good source of certain types of workers. In such industries as electric and construction, unions have traditionally supplied workers to employers. A labor pool is generally available through a union, and workers can be dispatched from it to particular jobs to meet the needs of the employers.

In some instances, the union can control or influence recruiting and staffing needs. An organization with a strong union may have less flexibility than a non-union company in deciding who will be hired and where that person will be placed. Unions can also benefit employers through apprenticeship and cooperative staffing programs, as they do in the building and printing industries.

Employment Agencies

Every state in the United States has its own state-sponsored employment agency. These agencies operate branch offices in many cities throughout the states and do not charge fees to applicants or employers.

Private employment agencies also operate in most cities. For a fee collected from either the employee or the employer, these agencies do some preliminary screening and put the organization in touch with applicants. Private employment agencies differ considerably in the levels of service, costs, policies, and types of applicants they provide. Employers can reduce the range of possible problems from these sources by giving complete descriptions and specifications for jobs to be filled.

Media Sources

Media sources such as newspapers, magazines, television, radio, and billboards are widely used.[5] Some firms have used direct mail with purchased lists of individuals in certain fields or industries. Whatever medium is used, it should be tied to the relevant labor market and should provide sufficient information on the company and the job.

Job Fairs and Special Events

Employers in tight labor markets or who are needing to fill a large number of jobs quickly have used job fairs and special recruiting events. Job fairs also have been held by economic development entities, employer and HR associations, and other community groups to help bring employers and potential job candidates together. For instance, to fill jobs in one metropolitan area, the local SHRM chapter annually sponsors a job fair at which 75–125 employers can meet applicants. Publicity in the city draws more than 1,000 potential recruits. One cautionary note: Some employers at this and other job fairs may see current employees "shopping" for jobs at other employers.

....

Internet Recruiting

The Internet has become the primary means for many employers to search for job candidates and for applicants to look for jobs. The explosive growth in general Internet use is a key reason. Internet users tap the Internet to search for jobs almost as frequently as they read classified ads in newspapers. Many of them also post or submit résumés on the Internet.

E-Recruiting Places

Several sites are used for Internet recruiting. The most common ones are Internet job boards, professional/career Web sites, and employer Web sites.

Internet Job Boards.   Numerous Internet job boards, such as Monster, Yahoo!, and Hot Jobs, provide places for employers to post jobs or search for candidates. Job boards provide access to numerous candidates. However, many individuals accessing the sites are "job lookers" who are not serious about changing jobs, but are checking out compensation levels and job availability in their areas of interest. Also, a recruiter for a firm can pretend to be an applicant in order to check out what other employers are looking for in similar job candidates and offering as compensation, in order to maintain recruiting competitiveness. Despite these concerns, HR recruiters find general job boards useful for generating applicant responses.

Professional/Career Web sites.   Many professional associations have employment sections on their Web sites. As illustration, for HR jobs see the Society for Human Resource Management site, *www.shrm.org*, or the American Society for Training and Development site, *www.astd.org*. A number of private corporations maintain specialized career or industry Web sites to focus on IT, telecommunications, engineering, medicine, or other areas. Use of these more targeted Web sites reduces somewhat the recruiters' search time and efforts. Also, posting jobs on such Web sites is likely to target applicants specifically interested in the job field and may reduce the number of less-qualified applicants who actually apply.

Employer Web sites.   Despite the popularity of job boards and association job sites, many employers have found their own Web sites to be more effective and efficient when recruiting candidates. Numerous employers have included employment and career information on their sites. Many company Web sites have a tab labeled "Employment" or "Careers." This is the place where recruiting (internal and external) is often conducted. On many of these sites, job seekers are encouraged to e-mail résumés or complete on-line applications. According to one survey, about 16% of hires come through a company's Web site—a much higher proportion than come from on-line job boards.[5]

Advantages and Disadvantages of Internet Recruiting

Employers have found a number of advantages to using Internet recruiting. A primary one is that many employers have saved money using Internet recruiting versus other recruiting methods such as newspaper advertising, employment agencies, and search firms.

The positives associated with Internet recruiting come with a number of disadvantages. In getting broader exposure, employers also may get more unqualified applicants. HR recruiters find that Internet recruiting creates additional work for HR staff members. More résumés must be reviewed, more e-mails need to be dealt with, and expensive specialized software may be needed to track the increased number of applicants resulting from many Internet recruiting efforts. A primary concern is that many individuals who access job sites are just browsers who may submit résumés just to see what happens, but they are not seriously looking for new jobs.

· ·

Increasing Recruiting Effectiveness

Efforts to evaluate recruiting may be used to make recruiting activities more effective. Use of the data to target different applicant pools, tap broader labor markets, use different recruiting methods, improve internal handling and interviewing of applicants, and train recruiters and managers can increase recruiting effectiveness. The following technology-aided approaches to recruiting have made recruiting more effective for big employers:

- *Résumé mining*—a software approach to getting the best résumés for a fit from a big database
- *Applicant tracking*—an approach that takes an applicant all the way from a job listing to performance appraisal results

- *Employer career websites*—a convenient recruiting place on an employer's Web site where applicants can see what jobs are available and apply
- *Internal mobility*—a system that tracks prospects in the company and matches them with jobs as they come open

The non-technical issues make a big difference in recruiting too. For example:

- Personable recruiters who communicate well with applicants
- Emphasizing positives about the job and employer within a realistic job preview
- Fair and considerate treatment of applicants in the recruiting process
- Enhancing applicants' perceived fit with the organization

When the unemployment rate is low and good employees are difficult to hire, the preceding suggestions can help. These approaches and others are part of effective recruiting to set the basis for selection.

....

Selection and Placement

Selection is about choosing the best person for the job. Placement is fitting a person to the right job. Placement of human resources should be seen primarily as a matching process that can affect many different employment outcomes. How well an employee is matched to a job can affect the amount and quality of an employee's work, as well as the training and operating costs required to prepare the individual for work life. Finally, employee morale can also be an issue because good fit encourages individuals to be positive about what they accomplish on the job.

Criteria, Predictors, and Job Performance

Effective selection of employees involves using criteria and predictors of job performance. At the heart of an effective selection system must be knowledge of what constitutes appropriate job performance, as well as what employee characteristics are associated with that performance. First, an employer needs to identify the criteria associated with successful employee performance. Using these criteria as a generalized definition, an employer must then determine the KSAs required for individuals to be successful on the job. A selection criterion is a characteristic that a person must possess to successfully perform work. Figure 4-4 shows that ability, motivation, intelligence, conscientiousness, appropriate risk, and permanence might be good selection criteria for many jobs. Factors that might be more specific to managerial jobs include "leading and deciding," "supporting and cooperating," "organizing and executing," and "enterprising and performing."[6]

Predictors can take many forms such as application forms, tests, interviews, education requirements, or years of experience, but these factors should be used only if they are found to be valid predictors of specific job performance. Using

FIGURE 4-4 Job Perfomance, Selection Criteria, and Predictions

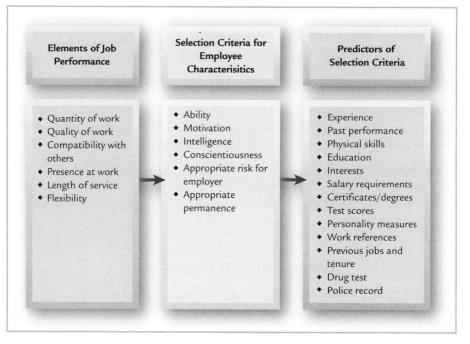

invalid predictors can result in selecting the "wrong" candidate and rejecting the "right" one, affecting the ability to accomplish operational objectives.

Combining Predictors

If an employer chooses to use only one predictor such as a pencil-and-paper test to select the individuals to be hired, the decision becomes straightforward. If the test is valid and encompasses a major dimension of a job, and the applicant does well on the test, he or she should be given a job offer. When an employer uses predictors such as "three years of experience," "possesses a college degree," and "acceptable aptitude test score," job applicants are evaluated on all of these requirements to identify the best-qualified candidates. In other words, multiple predictors are usually combined in some way. Two approaches for combining different predictors are:

- *Multiple hurdles:* A minimum cutoff is set on each predictor, and each minimum level must be "passed." For example, a candidate for a sales representative job must achieve a minimum education level, a certain score on a sales aptitude test, and a minimum score on a structured interview to be hired.
- *Compensatory approach:* Scores from individual predictors are added and combined into an overall score, thereby allowing a higher score on one predictor to offset, or compensate for, a lower score on another. The combined index takes into consideration performance on all predictors.

The Selection Process

A series of consistant steps leading to a hiring decision is a good basis for a successful selection process. Such a process may contain applicant job-interest record, pre-employment screening, tests, interviews, and background investigation.

Applicant Job Interest

Individuals wanting employment can indicate interest in a number of ways. Traditionally, individuals submitted résumés by mail or fax, or applied in person at an employer's location. But with the growth in Internet recruiting, many individuals complete applications on-line or submit résumés electronically.

Regardless of how individuals express interest in employment, the selection process has an important public relations dimension. Discriminatory hiring practices, impolite interviewers, unnecessarily long waits, unreturned telephone inquiries, inappropriate testing procedures, and lack of follow-up responses can produce unfavorable impressions of an employer. Job applicants' perceptions of the organization will be influenced by how they are treated.

Application Forms.   Application forms are universally used and can take on different formats. Properly prepared, the application form serves four purposes:

- It is a record of the applicant's desire to obtain a position.
- It provides the interviewer with a profile of the applicant that can be used during the interview.
- It is a basic employee record for applicants who are hired.
- It can be used for research on the effectiveness of the selection process.

An organization should retain all applications and hiring-related documents and records for *three years*. Guidelines from the EEOC and court decisions require that the data requested on application forms must be job related. Illegal questions frequently found on application forms ask for the following information:

- Marital status
- Height/weight
- Number and ages of dependents
- Information on spouse
- Date of high school graduation
- Contact in case of emergency

Immigration Forms.   The Immigration Reform and Control Act of 1986, as revised in 1990, requires that within 72 hours of hiring, an employer must determine whether a job applicant is a U.S. citizen, registered alien, or illegal alien. Applicants who are not eligible to work in this country are not supposed to be hired.

Employers use the Federal I-9 form to identify the status of potential employees. Employers are responsible for ensuring the legitimacy of documents submitted by new employees, such as U.S. passports, birth certificates, original Social Security cards, and driver's licenses. Also, employers who hire employees on special visas must maintain appropriate documentation and records. However, many employers are not performing these immigration status background checks for different reasons, even though they can be performed quickly online and with limited cost the employer. That is why legislation to restrict hiring illegal immigrants has become such a controversial political issue.

Pre-Employment Screening

Many employers conduct pre-employment screening to determine if applicants meet the minimum qualifications for open jobs. Other employers have every interested individual complete an application first. While these completed application forms become the basis for pre-screening information, collecting, storing, and tracking the forms can create significant work for HR staff members.

The use of electronic pre-employment screening has grown. Much of this screening utilizes computer software to review the many résumés and application forms received during the recruiting and selection process. Many large companies use different types of software to receive, evaluate, and track the applications of many potential employees.

Selection Testing

Many different kinds of tests can be used to help select qualified employees. Literacy tests, skill-based tests, psychological measurement tests, and honesty tests are often utilized to assess various individual factors that are deemed important for the work to be performed. These useful employment tests allow companies to predict which applicants will be the most successful after being hired.

Ability Tests.   Tests that assess an individual's ability to perform in a specific manner are grouped as ability tests. These are sometimes further differentiated into *aptitude tests* and *achievement tests.* Cognitive ability tests measure an individual's thinking, memory, reasoning, verbal, and mathematical abilities. Tests such as these can be used to determine applicants' basic knowledge of terminology and concepts, word fluency, spatial orientation, comprehension and retention span, general and mental ability, and conceptual reasoning. The Wonderlic Personnel Test and the General Aptitude Test Battery (GATB) are two widely used tests of this type. Managers need to ensure that these tests assess cognitive abilities that are job related.

Personality Tests.   Personality is a unique blend of individual characteristics that can affect how a person interacts with his or her work environment. As such, many organizations utilize various personality tests that assess the degree to which candidates' attributes match specific job criteria. Many types of personality tests are available, including the Minnesota Multiphasic Personality Inventory (MMPI) and the Myers-Briggs test.

Although many different personality characteristics exist, some experts believe that there is a relatively small number of underlying *major* traits. The most widely accepted approach to studying these underlying personality traits (although not the only one) is the "Big Five" personality framework. The Big Five traits are generally considered to be useful predictors of various types of job performance in different occupations.[7] The factors are shown in Figure 4-5.

FIGURE 4-5 Big Five Personality Characteristics

Several of the Big Five traits are related to various dimensions of burnout and accident involvement in both non-work and work contexts.

Honesty/Integrity Tests. Companies are utilizing different tests to assess the honesty and integrity of applicants and employees. Employers use these tests as a screening mechanism to prevent the hiring of unethical employees, to reduce the frequency of lying and theft on the job, and to communicate to applicants and employees alike that dishonesty will not be tolerated. In other words, honesty/integrity tests may be valid as broad screening devices for organizations if used properly.

Selection Interviewing

Selection interviewing of job applicants is done both to obtain additional information and to clarify information gathered throughout the selection process. Interviews are commonly conducted at two levels: first, as an initial screening interview to determine if the person has met minimum qualifications, and then later, as an in-depth interview with HR staff members and/or operating managers to determine if the person will fit into the designated work area.

Before the in-depth interview, information from all available sources is pooled so that the interviewers can reconcile conflicting information that may have emerged from tests, application forms, and references. Also, interviewers must obtain as much pertinent information as possible about the applicants given the limited time of the interview itself, and evaluate this information against job standards.

Structured Interviews. A structured interview uses a set of standardized questions asked of all applicants so that comparisons can more easily be made. This type of interview allows an interviewer to prepare job-related questions in advance and then complete a standardized interviewee evaluation form that provides documentation indicating why one applicant was selected over another. The structured interview is useful in the initial screening process because many applicants can be effectively evaluated and compared. However, the structured interview does not have to be rigid. The predetermined questions should be asked in a logical manner but do not have to be read word for word down the list. Also, the applicants should be allowed adequate opportunity to explain their answers, and each interviewer should probe with additional questions until she or he fully understands the responses. Because of this process, the structured interview can be more reliable and valid than other interview approaches.

Effective Interviewing. Many people think that the ability to interview is an innate talent, but this contention is difficult to support. Just being personable and liking to talk is no guarantee that someone will be an effective interviewer.

Interviewing skills are developed through training. A number of suggestions for making interviewing more effective are as follows:

- *Plan the interview.* Interviewers should review all information before the interview, and then identify specific areas for questioning. Preparation is critical because many interviewers have not done their research.
- *Control the interview.* This includes knowing in advance what information must be collected, systematically collecting it during the interview, and stopping when that information has been collected. An interviewer should not monopolize the conversation.
- *Use effective questioning techniques.* Utilize questions that will produce full and complete answers that can be evaluated based on job relatedness.

Background Investigation

Background investigation may take place either before or after the in-depth interview. Although the process requires time and money, it generally proves beneficial when making selection decisions. The value of background investigation is evident when the investigation reveals that applicants have misrepresented their qualifications and backgrounds. Some of the more common types of false information given during the application process are the dates of employment and academic study, past jobs, and academic credentials.

Background information can be obtained from a number of sources. Some of these sources include criteria such as past job records, credit history, testing, and educational and certification records.

Criminal background checks are also common because there has been an increase in claims that companies are staffing irresponsibly.[8] A majority of large U.S. firms including the very largest conduct such checks to avoid negligent staffing lawsuits, corporate theft, and terrorism. In fact, many organizations use outside vendors that specialize in conducting background checks because these outside firms can provide such services much more efficiently and effectively.

Various federal and state laws protect the rights of individuals whose backgrounds may be investigated during pre-employment screening. An employer's most important action when conducting a background investigation is to obtain from the applicant a signed release giving the employer permission to conduct the investigation.

Risks of Negligent Hiring and Negligent Retention

As indicated previously, failing to check references and candidate backgrounds can cost a company greatly. Some organizations have become targets of lawsuits that charge them with negligence in hiring workers who have committed violent acts on the job. Lawyers say that an employer's liability hinges on how well it investigates an applicant's background. Consequently, details provided on the application form should be investigated extensively, and these efforts should be documented.

Negligent hiring occurs when an employer fails to check an employee's background, and the employee later injures someone on the job. There is a potential negligent hiring problem when: the employer hired an unfit employee, the background check was insufficient, or the employer did not research potential risk factors that would have prevented the positive hire decision.[9] Similarly, **negligent retention** occurs when an employer becomes aware that an employee may be unfit for employment, but continues to employ the person, and the person injures someone.

Applicant Flow Documentation

Employers must collect applicant data on race, sex, and other demographics to fulfill EEO reporting requirements. Many employers ask applicants to provide EEOC reporting data in a flow form that may be attached to the application form. It is important that employers review this flow form separately and not use it in any other selection efforts to avoid claims of impropriety. Because completing the form is voluntary, employers can demonstrate that they tried to obtain the data.

NOTES

1. "Can You Provide Guidance on Writing Job Descriptions?," *HR Comply/Newsletter Abstracts,* July 7, 2004, *www.hrcomply.com/newsletter.*
2. Grace Lee, "Epidemics, Labour Markets and Unemployment," *International Journal of Human Resource Management,* 16, (2005), 752–771.
3. William H. Burgess III, "Dibs on Diversity Recruiting," *Network Journal,* June 2003, 12–13.
4. D. S. Chapman et al., "Applicant Attraction to Organization and Job Choice: A Meta-Analytic Review of the Correlates of Recruiting Outcomes," *Journal of Applied Psychology,* 90 (2005), 928–944.
5. Mo Edjlali, "The 2 Keys to Killer Job Ads," *Electronic Recruiting Exchange,* July 27, 2006, 1–3.
6. Dave Bartram, "The Great Eight Competencies: A Criterion-Centric Approach to Validation," *Journal of Applied Psychology,* 90 (2005), 1185–1203.
7. Mitchell G. Rothstein and Richard D. Goffin, "The Use of Personality Measures in Personnel Selection: What Does Current Research Support?" *Human Resource Management Review,* 16 (2006), 155–180.
8. Gregory M. Davis, "Criminal Background Checks for Employment Purposes," *SHRM Legal Report,* July/August 2006, 1, 5–8.
9. Fay Hansen, "Taking 'Reasonable' Action to Avoid Negligent Hiring Claims," *Workforce Management,* December 11, 2006, 31.

INTERNET RESOURCES

Uniform Guidelines-This Web site is a free site on the use of selection procedures and tests to ensure compliance with federal laws. Visit their Web site at: *www.uniformguidlelines.com*

Business.Com-This Web site provides resources and links to companies that provide employee background checks, criminal history checks, and pre-employment screening. Visit their site at: *www.business.com*

SUGGESTED READINGS

M.P. Brannick, et. al. *Job and Work Analysis,* 2nd ed. (Sage Pub. Inc., 2007).

Christopher W. Pritchard, *101 Strategies for Recruiting Success,* (AMACOM, 2006).

S. Rogers, *High Performance Recruiting* (Universe, 2007).

C. Stewart and W. Cash, *Interviewing: Principle and Practice* 11th ed. (McGraw Hill, 2005).

CHAPTER 5

Training
and Talent
Management

HR—MEETING MANAGEMENT CHALLENGES

Improving the performance of employees in an organization frequently means training and managing the talent. Various challenges make talent management one of the most vital HR topics. Current issues include:

- Designing effective and efficient training programs
- Identifying and developing the talent in the organization
- Dealing with careers from the standpoint of both the organization and the individual

The competitive pressures facing organizations today require that staff members' knowledge and ideas be current and that they have skills and abilities that can deliver results. As organizations compete and change, training of employees and managers becomes even more critical than before. Employees must adapt to the many changes facing organizations and be trained continually to maintain and update their capabilities.

Talent management is concerned with enhancing the attraction, development, and retention of key human resources. Many organizations recently have established talent management initiatives, including expanded training efforts.

Nature of Training

Training is the process whereby people acquire capabilities to perform jobs. Training provides employees with specific, identifiable knowledge and skills for use in their present jobs. Organizational usage of training may include "hard" skills such as teaching sales representatives how to use intranet resources, a branch manager how to review an income statement, or a machinist apprentice how to set up a drill press. "Soft" skills are critical in many instances and can be taught as well. They may include communicating, mentoring, managing a meeting, and working as part of a team.

Training represents a significant HR expenditure for most employers. But it is too often viewed tactically rather than strategically, which means that training is seen as a short-term activity rather than one that has longer-term effects on organizational success. Fortunately, more and more employers have recognized that training must be increased.

Strategic Training

Strategic training is linked to how the organization will accomplish its goals. It can have numerous organizational benefits. First, strategic training enables HR and training professionals to get intimately involved with the business, partner with operating managers to help solve their problems, and make significant contributions to organizational results. Additionally, a strategic training mind-set reduces the likelihood of thinking that training alone can solve most employee or organizational problems. It is not uncommon for operating managers and trainers to react to most important performance problems by saying "I need a training program on X." With a strategic training focus, the organization is more likely to assess such requests to determine what training and/or non-training approaches might address the most important performance goals.

Organizational Competitiveness and Training

Currently, U.S. employers spend at least $60 billion annually on training. For the typical employer, training expenditures are almost 2% of payroll expenses, and run over $800 per eligible employee, according to a study by the American Society for Training and Development (ASTD). Organizations that see training as especially crucial to business competitiveness average $1,400 in training expenditures per eligible employee.[1]

The nature of technological innovation and change is such that if employees are not trained all the time, they may fall behind and the company could become less competitive. For example, consider the telecommunications industry today compared with five years ago, with all the new technologies (wireless, Internet, and Web-based services, etc.) and the accompanying competitive shifts. Without continual training, organizations may not have staff members with the knowledge, skills, and abilities (KSAs) needed to compete effectively.

Training also can affect organizational competitiveness by aiding in the retention of employees. One reason why many individuals stay or leave organizations is career training and development opportunities. Employers that invest in training and developing their employees may well enhance retention efforts.

Figure 5-1 shows how training may help accomplish certain organizational strategies. Ideally, the upper management group sees the training function as providing valuable intelligence about the necessary core skills.

Integration of Performance and Training

Job performance, training, and employee learning must be integrated to be effective, and HR plays a crucial role in this integration. Organizations are seeking more authentic (and hence more effective) training experiences for their

FIGURE 5-1 Linking Organizational Strategies and Training

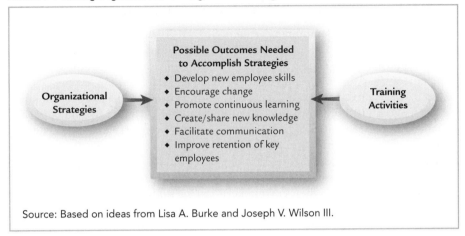

**Possible Outcomes Needed
to Accomplish Strategies**
- Develop new employee skills
- Encourage change
- Promote continuous learning
- Create/share new knowledge
- Facilitate communication
- Improve retention of key
  employees

Organizational
Strategies

Training
Activities

Source: Based on ideas from Lisa A. Burke and Joseph V. Wilson III.

employees by using real business problems to advance employee learning. Rather than separating the training experience from the context of actual job performance, trainers incorporate everyday business issues as learning examples, thus increasing the realism of training exercises and scenarios. As part of management training at GE, managers are given actual business problems to solve, and they must present their solutions to the firm's business leaders. Using real situations for practice is yet another way of merging the lines between training, learning, and job performance.

Training Components

Training plans allow organizations to identify what is needed for employee performance *before* training begins. It is at this stage that fit with strategic issues is ensured. Effective training efforts consider the following questions:

- Is there really a need for the training?
- Who needs to be trained?
- Who will do the training?
- What form will the training take?
- How will knowledge be transferred to the job?
- How will the training be evaluated?

Training Process.   The way firms organize and structure their training affects the way employees experience the training, which in turn influences the effectiveness of the training. Effective training requires the use of a systematic training process, which includes assessment, design, delivery, and evaluation. Using such a process reduces the likelihood that unplanned, uncoordinated, and haphazard training efforts will occur. A discussion of each phase of the training process follows.

···

Training Needs Assessment

Assessing organizational training needs represents the diagnostic phase of a training plan. This assessment considers issues of employee and organizational performance to determine if training can help. Needs assessment measures the competencies of a company, a group, or an individual as they relate to what is required in the strategic plan. It is necessary to find out what is happening and what should be happening before deciding if training will help, and if it will help, what kind is needed. For instance, suppose that in looking at the performance of clerks in a billing department, a manager identifies problems that employees have with their data-entry and keyboarding abilities, and she decides that they would benefit from instruction in these areas. As part of assessing the training needs, the manager has the clerks take a data-entry test to measure their current keyboarding skills. Then the manager establishes an objective of increasing the clerks' keyboarding speed to 60 words per minute without errors. The number of words per minute without errors is the criterion against which training success can be measured, and it represents the way in which the objective is made specific.

The three sources of information used to analyze training needs are organizational, job, and individual. Each is discussed next.

Organizational Analyses

Training needs can be diagnosed by analyzing organizational outcomes and looking at future organizational needs. A part of planning for training is the identification of the KSAs that will be needed now and in the future as both jobs and the organization change. Both internal and external forces will influence training and must be considered when doing organizational analyses. For instance, the problems posed by the technical obsolescence of current employees and an insufficiently educated labor pool from which to draw new workers should be confronted before those issues become critical.

Organizational analyses comes from various operational measures of organizational performance. On a continuing basis, detailed analyses of HR data reveal training weaknesses. Departments or areas with high turnover, high absenteeism, low performance, or other deficiencies can be pinpointed. Following an analysis of such problems, training objectives then can be developed.

Job/Task Analyses

The second way of doing training needs analysis is to review the jobs involved and the tasks performed in those jobs. By comparing the requirements of jobs with the KSAs of employees, training needs can be identified. Current job specifications can be a source for such an analysis. For example, at a manufacturing firm, analyses identified the tasks performed by engineers who served as technical instructors for other employees. By listing the tasks required of a technical instructor, management established a program to teach specific instructional skills; thus, the engineers were able to become more successful instructors.

Individual Analyses

The third means of diagnosing training needs focuses on individuals and how they perform their jobs. The following sources are examples that are useful for individual analyses:

- Performance appraisals
- Skill tests
- Individual assessment tests
- Records of critical incidents
- Assessment center exercises
- Questionnaires and surveys
- Job knowledge tools
- Internet input

. . . .

Training Design

Once training objectives have been determined, training design can start. Whether job specific or broader in nature, training must be designed to address the assessed specific needs. Effective training design considers learning concepts and a wide range of different approaches to training.

Working in organizations should be a continual learning process, and learning is the focus of all training activities. Different approaches are necessary because learning is a complex psychological process. There are three primary considerations when designing training: (1) determining learner readiness, (2) understanding different learning styles, and (3) designing training for transfer. Each of these elements must be considered for the training design to mesh and produce effective learning.

Learner Readiness

For training to be successful, learners must be ready to learn. Learner readiness means individuals having the ability to learn, which many people have. However, if effective learning is to occur, individuals must also have the motivation to learn and self-efficacy.

Ability to Learn.   Learners must possess basic skills, such as fundamental reading and math proficiency, and sufficient cognitive abilities. Companies may discover that some workers lack the requisite skills to comprehend their training effectively. Various firms have found that a significant number of job applicants and current employees lack the reading, writing, and math skills needed to do the jobs. Employers might deal with the lack of basic employee skills in several ways:

- Offer remedial training to people in their current workforce who need it.
- Hire workers who are deficient and then implement specific workplace training.
- Work with local schools to help better educate potential hires for jobs.

Motivation to Learn.   A person's desire to learn training content is referred to as "motivation to learn" and is influenced by multiple factors. For example, differences in gender and ethnicity and the resulting experiences may affect the motivation of adult learners. The student's motivation level may also be influenced by the instructor's motivation and ability, friends' encouragement to do well, classmates' motivation levels, the physical classroom environment, and the training methods used. Regardless of what the motivation is, without it, the student will not learn the material.

Self-Efficacy.   Learners must also possess **self-efficacy**, which refers to a person's belief that he or she *can* successfully learn the training program content. For learners to be ready for and receptive to the training content, they must feel that it is possible for them to learn it.

Learning Styles

In designing training interventions, trainers also should consider individual learning styles. For example, *auditory* learners learn best by listening to someone else tell them about the training content. *Tactile* learners must "get their hands on" the training resources and use them. *Visual* learners think in pictures and figures and need to see the purpose and process of the training. Trainers who address all these styles by using multiple training methods can design more effective training.

Training many different people from diverse backgrounds poses a significant challenge in today's work organizations. In addition to considering cultural, gender, and race/ethnicity diversity, training design sometimes must address some special issues presented by adult learning. Certainly, the training design must consider that all the trainees are adults, but they come with widely varying learning styles, experiences, and personal goals.

Adult Learning.   Malcolm Knowles's classic work on adult learning suggests five principles for designing training for adults. That and subsequent work by others suggests that adults:

- Have the need to know why they are learning something.
- Have a need to be self-directed.
- Bring more work-related experiences into the learning process.
- Enter into a learning experience with a problem-centered approach to learning.
- Are motivated to learn by both extrinsic and intrinsic factors.

Behavior Modeling.   The most elementary way in which people learn—and one of the best—is through behavior modeling, or copying someone else's behavior. The use of behavior modeling is particularly appropriate for skill training in which the trainees must use both knowledge and practice. It can aid in the transfer and usage of those skills by those trained.[2] For example, a new supervisor can receive training and mentoring on how to handle disciplinary discussions with employees by observing as the HR director or department manager deals with such problems.

Behavior modeling is used extensively as the primary means for training supervisors and managers in interpersonal skills. Fortunately or unfortunately, many supervisors and managers end up modeling the behavior they see their bosses use. For that reason, effective training should include good examples of how to handle interpersonal and other issues and problems.

Reinforcement and Immediate Confirmation.   The concept of reinforcement is based on the **law of effect**, which states that people tend to repeat responses that give them some type of positive reward and to avoid actions associated with negative consequences. Closely related is a learning concept called immediate confirmation, which is based on the idea that people learn best if reinforcement and feedback are given as soon as possible after training. Immediate confirmation corrects errors that, if made throughout the training, might establish an undesirable pattern that would need to be unlearned. It also aids with the transfer of training to the actual work done.

Transfer of Training

Finally, trainers should design training for the highest possible transfer from the class to the job. Transfer occurs when trainees actually use on the job what knowledge and information they learned in training. How much training effectively gets transferred to the job is estimated to be relatively low, given all of the time and money spent, because many employees do not apply training to their jobs within the first year. Employees may use the training immediately, but then decrease its use over time.

Certain variables affect the continuation of training transfer, depending on the nature and type of training. Verifying the effectiveness of training transfer is part of training evaluation. Effective transfer of training meets two conditions. First, the trainees can take the material learned in training and apply it to the job context in which they work. Second, employees maintain their use of the learned material over time.

. . . .

Training Delivery

Once training has been designed, then the actual delivery of training can begin. Regardless of the type of training done, a number of approaches and methods can be used to deliver it. The growth of training technology continues to expand the available choices, as Figure 5-2 shows.

Whatever the approach used, a variety of considerations must be balanced when selecting training delivery methods. The common variables considered are:

- Nature of training
- Subject matter
- Number of trainees
- Individual vs. team
- Self-paced vs. guided

- Training resources/costs
- E-learning vs. traditional learning
- Geographic locations
- Time allotted
- Completion timeline

FIGURE 5-2 Methods Companies Use to Deliver Training

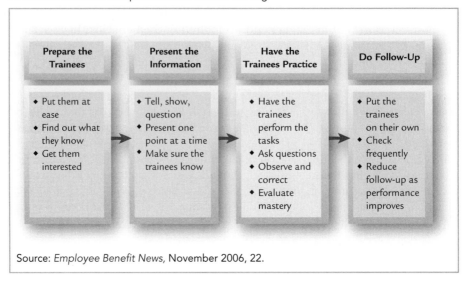

Source: *Employee Benefit News*, November 2006, 22.

Internal Training

Internal training generally applies very specifically to the organization and its jobs. It is popular because it saves the cost of sending employees away for training and often avoids the cost of outside trainers. Skills-based technical training is conducted inside organizations. Due to rapid changes in technology, the building and updating of technical skills may become crucial training needs. Basic technical skills training is also being mandated by federal regulations in areas where the Occupational Safety and Health Administration (OSHA), the Environmental Protection Agency (EPA), and other agencies have jurisdiction.

Informal Training.   One internal source of training is informal training, which occurs through interactions and feedback among employees. Much of what the employees know about their jobs they learn informally from asking questions and getting advice from other employees and their supervisors, rather than from formal training programs.

On-the-Job Training.   The most common type of training at all levels in an organization is *on-the-job training (OJT)* because it is flexible and relevant to what employees do. In contrast with informal training, which often occurs spontaneously, OJT should be planned. The supervisor or manager conducting the training must be able to both teach and show the employees what to do, as figure 5-2 shows.

However, OJT has some problems. Often, those doing the training may have no experience in training, no time to do it, and no desire to participate in it. Under such conditions, learners essentially are on their own, and training likely will not be effective. Another problem is that OJT can disrupt regular work. Unfortunately, OJT can amount to no training at all in some circumstances, especially if the trainers simply abandon the trainees to learn the job alone. Also, bad habits or incorrect information from the supervisor or manager can be transferred to the trainees.

Cross Training.   A variety of on-the-job training is cross training, which occurs when people are trained to do more than one job—theirs and someone else's. For the employer, the advantages of cross training are flexibility and development. However, although cross training is attractive to the employer, it is not always appreciated by employees, who often feel that it requires them to do more work for the same pay. To counteract such responses, learning "bonuses" can be awarded for successfully completing cross training to make it more appealing to employees.

External Training

External training, or training that takes place outside the employing organization, is used extensively by organizations of all sizes. Large organizations use external training if they lack the capability to train people internally or when many people need to be trained quickly. External training may be the best option for training in smaller firms due to limitations in the size of their HR staffs and in the number of employees who need various types of specialized training. Whatever the size of the organization, external training occurs for several reasons:

- It may be less expensive for an employer to have an outside trainer conduct training in areas where internal training resources are limited.
- The organization may have insufficient time to develop internal training materials.
- The HR staff may not have the necessary level of expertise for the subject matter in which training is needed.
- There are advantages to having employees interact with managers and peers in other companies in training programs held externally.

Outsourcing of Training.   Many employers of all sizes outsource training to external training firms, consultants, and other entities. According to data from ASTD, approximately 25% to 30% of training expenditures go to outside training sources. Interestingly, over a recent three-year period, the outsourcing of training has not increased dramatically.[3] The reasons may be cost concerns, a greater emphasis on internal linking of training to organizational strategies, and other issues.

Educational Assistance Programs.   Some employers pay for additional education for their employees. Typically, the employee pays for courses that apply to a college degree and is reimbursed upon successful completion of a course. The amounts paid by the employer are considered non-taxable income for the employee up to amounts set by federal laws. But one concern is that traditional forms of employee educational programs pose risks for the employer. Upon completion of the degree, the employee may choose to take the new skills and go elsewhere. Employers must plan to use these skills upon employee graduation to improve the retention of those employees.

Orientation: On-Boarding for New Employees

The most important and widely conducted type of regular training is done for *new* employees. Orientation is the planned introduction of new employees to their jobs, co-workers, and the organization, and is offered by most employers. It requires cooperation between individuals in the HR unit and operating managers and supervisors. In a small organization without an HR department, the new employee's supervisor or manager usually assumes most of the responsibility for orientation. In large organizations, managers and supervisors, as well as the HR department, generally work as a team to orient new employees. Unfortunately, many new employee orientation sessions still come across as boring, irrelevant, and a waste of time to both new employees and their department supervisors and managers.

The term *on-boarding* is sometimes being used to describe orientation. This usage reflects that getting new employees, including executives, to immediately begin performing successfully is important. Effective orientation helps to achieve several key purposes:

- Establishes a favorable employee impression of the organization and the job.
- Provides organization and job information.
- Enhances interpersonal acceptance by co-workers.
- Accelerates socialization and integration of the new employee into the organization.
- Ensures that employee performance and productivity begin more quickly.

E-Learning: On-Line Training

E-learning is use of the Internet or an organizational intranet to conduct training on-line. E-learning is growing in popularity with employers. The major advantages are cost savings and access to more employees. Estimates are that corporate training conducted through learning technology today will be doubled in the next few years. Almost 30% of learning hours are totally technology based, according to an ASTD report. Also, e-learning is seen as more highly preferred by workers under the age of 30 years.[4]

Advantages and Disadvantages of E-Learning. The rapid growth of e-learning makes the Internet or an intranet a viable means for delivering training content. But e-learning has both advantages and disadvantages that must be considered. In addition to being concerned about employee access to e-learning and desire to use it, some employers worry that trainees will use e-learning to complete courses quickly but will not retain and use much of what they learned. Taking existing training materials, putting them on the Internet, and cutting the training budget is not the way to succeed with e-learning. An important question is: Can this material be learned just as well on-line as through conventional methods?

In sum, e-learning is the latest development in training delivery. Some of the biggest obstacles to using it will continue to be keeping up with the rapid change in technological innovation, knowing when and how much to invest, and designing e-courses appropriately. Undoubtedly, e-learning will have a major impact on HR and training, but there are no "ten easy steps" to making e-learning successful.

. . . .

Training Evaluation

Evaluation of training compares the post-training results to the pre-training objectives of managers, trainers, and trainees. Too often, training is conducted with little thought of measuring and evaluating it later to see how well it worked. Because training is both time consuming and costly, it should be evaluated.

Training Evaluation Metrics

Training is expensive, and it is an HR function that requires measurement and monitoring. Cost-benefit analysis and return on investment (ROI) analysis are commonly used to do so, as are various benchmarking approaches.

Cost-Benefit Analysis. Training results can be examined through cost-benefit analysis, which is comparison of costs and benefits associated with training. There are four stages in calculating training costs and benefits[8]:

1. *Determine training costs.* Consider direct costs such as design, trainer fees, materials, facilities, and other administration activities.

2. *Identify potential savings results.* Consider employee retention, better customer service, fewer work errors, quicker equipment production, and other productivity factors.

3. *Compute potential savings.* Gather data on the performance results and assign dollar costs to each of them.

4. *Conduct costs and savings benefits comparisons.* Evaluate the costs per participant, the savings per participant, and how the cost-benefits relate to business performance numbers.

Return on Investment Analysis. In organizations, training is often expected to produce an ROI. Still, in too many circumstances, training is justified because someone liked it, rather than on the basis of accountability for resources. According to one study, firms that measure ROI on training spend 1% to 3% of payroll on training. But higher performing firms spend even more. The ROI of these companies has been determined to be 137% over five years, which is much more than the ROI at organizations spending less on training.[5] This study suggests that training can produce significant financial results for employers.

Benchmarking.   In addition to evaluating training internally, some organizations use benchmark measures to compare it with training done in other organizations. To do benchmarking, HR professionals gather data on training in their organization and compare them with data on training at other organizations in the same industry and of a similar size. Comparison data are available through the American Society for Training and Development and its Benchmarking Service. This service has training-related data from more than 1,000 participating employers who complete detailed questionnaires annually. Training also can be benchmarked against data from the American Productivity & Quality Center and the Saratoga Institute.

Training Evaluation Designs

With or without benchmarking data, internal evaluations of training programs can be designed in a number of ways. The rigor of the three designs discussed next increases with each level.

Post-Measure.   The most obvious way to evaluate training effectiveness is to determine after the training whether the individuals can perform the way management wants them to perform. Assume that a customer service manager has 20 representatives who need to improve their data-entry speeds. After a one-day training session, they take a test to measure their speeds. If the representatives can all type the required speed after training, was the training beneficial? It is difficult to say; perhaps most of them could have done as well before training. Tests after training do not always clearly indicate whether a performance is a result of the training or could have been achieved without the training.

Pre-/Post-Measure.   By differently designing the evaluation just discussed, the issue of pre-test skill levels can be considered. If the manager had measured the data-entry speed before and after training, she could have known whether the training made any difference. However, a question would have remained: Was any increase in speed a response to the training, or did these employees simply work faster because they knew they were being tested? People often perform better when they know their efforts are being evaluated.

Pre-/Post-Measure with a Control Group.   Another evaluation design can address the preceding problem. In addition to testing the 20 representatives who will be trained, the manager can test another group of representatives who will not be trained, to see if they do as well as those who are to be trained. This second group is called a control group. After training, if the trained representatives work significantly faster than those who were not trained, the manager can be reasonably sure that the training was effective.

· ·

Talent Management

Talent management can be seen as a bridge. As illustrated in Figure 5-3, talent management activities provide the means to ensure that individuals who have been recruited and selected are retained as sucessful employees. Talent management activities include training, individual career planning, and HR development efforts. Additionally, succession planning involves identifying future workforce needs and what candidates will be available to fill them.

A part of talent management is the implementation and use of electronic, Web-based, computer software. Vendors have developed software for various parts of talent management, such as tracking training, providing succession planning replacement charts, or online performance appraisal systems. But these systems must be integrated, rather than run as separate programs. The need for such integration is seen in a survey that concluded that 40% of all talent management systems have little or no integration of the various elements.[6]

As talent management has evolved, some design issues have been identified. Each of these issues reflects differences in how talent management is viewed and the organizational priorities that exist.

Targeting Jobs

The first issue is to identify the types of jobs that will be the focus of talent management. In some organizations talent management focuses on the CEO and other executive jobs, rather than more broadly. Other organizations target primarily senior-management jobs, mid-level managers, and other key jobs. The groups and individuals seen as "talent" are senior leaders, mid-managers, and key technical and other contributors. However, those three groups only represent about one-third of the total workforces of many employers.

FIGURE 5-3 Talent Management Bridge

Targeting High-Potential Individuals

Another issue associated with talent management is how it is used with individuals in organizations. One problem identified with fulfilling effective talent management needs is that not all managers at different levels are committed to the time and effort required, which can limit successful activities.

Some organizations focus talent management efforts primarily on "high-potential" individuals, often referred to as "high-pos." Attracting, retaining, and developing high-pos have become emphases of senior managers and HR efforts. Some firms classify individuals as being in the top 10% and then set limits on the number of people who can participate in intensive talent management efforts. For instance, participation in leadership development programs might be limited to only those who are likely to become executives within 18 months.

. . . .

Careers and Career Planning

A career is the series of work-related positions a person occupies throughout life. People pursue careers to satisfy individual needs. Managing careers is an important part of talent managment, but individuals and organizations view careers in distinctly different ways.

Changing Nature of Careers

The old model of a career in which a person worked his or her way up the ladder in one organization is becoming rarer. Indeed, in a few industries, changing jobs and companies every year or two is becoming more common. U.S. workers in high-demand jobs, such as information technologists and pharmacists, often dictate their own circumstances to some extent. For instance, the average 30- to 35-year-old in the United States typically may have already worked for up to seven different firms. However, physicians, teachers, economists, and electricians do not change jobs as frequently. As would be expected, valuable employees even in some of these professions who are deluged with job offers switch jobs at a higher rate than in the past.

Careers and Work–Life Balance.   Various signs indicate that the patterns of individuals' work lives are changing in many areas: more freelancing, more working at home, more frequent job changes, more job opportunities, but less security. Rather than letting jobs define their lives, more people set goals for the type of lives they want and then use jobs to meet those goals. However, for dual-career couples and working women, balancing work demands with personal and family responsibilities is difficult to do.

For employers, career issues have changed too. The best people will not go to workplaces viewed as undesirable, because they do not have to do so. Employers must focus on retaining and developing talented workers by providing coaching, mentoring, and appropriate assignments.

Organization-Centered Career Planning

Careers are different from before, and their evolution puts a premium on career development by both the employers and the employees. Effective career planning considers both organization-centered and individual-centered perspectives. Figure 5-4 summarizes the perspectives and interaction between the organizational and individual approaches to career planning.

Organization-centered career planning focuses on identifying career paths that provide for the logical progression of people between jobs in an organization. Individuals follow these paths as they advance in organizational units. For example, a person might enter the sales department as a sales representative, then be promoted to account director, to sales manager, and finally to vice president of sales.

Career Paths.   Employees need to know their strengths and weakness, and they often discover those through company-sponsored assessments. Then, career paths to develop the weak areas and fine-tune the strengths are developed. Career paths represent employees' movements through opportunities over time. Although most career paths are thought of as leading upward, good opportunities also exist in cross-functional or horizontal directions.

Working with employees to develop career paths has aided employers in retaining key employees. At EchoStar Communications, use of a career path program has led to greater retention of entry-level call center employees. Career progression opportunities are identified to employees who perform well and who see EchoStar as a place to stay and grow career-wise.

Employer Websites and Career Planning.   Many employers have careers sections on their Websites. Such sections can be used to list open jobs for current employees looking to change jobs. An employer's Website is a link to the

FIGURE 5-4 Organizational and Individual Career Planning Perspectives

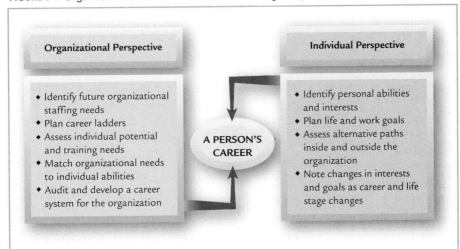

external world, but should also be seen as a link to existing employee development. Sites also can be used for career assessment, information, and instruction. When designing Websites, firms should consider the usefulness of the careers section for development as well as recruitment.

Individual-Centered Career Planning

Organizational changes have altered career plans for many people. Individuals have had to face "career transitions"—in other words, they have had to find new jobs. These transitions have identified the importance of individual-centered career planning, which focuses on an individual's responsibility for a career rather than on organizational needs. It is done by the employees themselves when they analyze their individual goals and capabilities. Such efforts might consider situations both inside and outside the organization that could expand a person's career. Individuals are the only ones who can know for certain what they consider to be successful careers, but they do not always act to that end. For example, few college students enrolled in business programs know exactly what they want to do upon graduation; many can eliminate some types of jobs but might be interested in any of several others.

Individual Career Planning Components.   For individuals to successfully manage their own careers, they should perform several activities. The three key ones are as follows:

- *Self-assessment:* Individuals need to think about what interests them, what they do not like, what they do well, and their strengths and weaknesses. Career advisors use a number of tools to help people understand themselves. Common professional tests include the Strong Interest Inventory to determine preferences among vocational occupations, and the Allport-Vernon-Lindzey Study of Values to identify a person's dominant values.
- *Feedback on reality:* Employees need feedback on how well they are doing, how their bosses see their capabilities, and where they fit in organizational plans for the future. One source of this information is through performance appraisal feedback and career development discussions.
- *Setting of career goals:* Deciding on a desired path, setting some timetables, and writing down these items all set the stage for a person to pursue the career of choice. These career goals are supported by short-term plans for the individual to get the experience or training necessary to move forward toward the goals.

Career Progression

Theorists in adult development describe the first half of life as the young adult's quest for competence and for a way to make a mark in the world. According to this view, a person attains happiness during this time primarily through achievement and the acquisition of capabilities.

The second half of life is different. Once the adult starts to measure time from the expected end of life rather than from the beginning, the need for competence and acquisition changes to the need for integrity, values, and well-being. For many people, internal values take precedence over external scorecards or accomplishments such as wealth and job-title status. In addition, mature adults already possess certain skills, so their focus may shift to interests other than skills acquisition. Career-ending concerns, such as life after retirement, reflect additional shifts.

Late-Career/Retirement Issues. Whether retirement comes at age 50 or age 70, it can require a major adjustment for many people. Some areas of emotional adjustment faced by many retirees include self-direction, a need to belong, sources of achievement, personal space, and goals. To help address concerns over these issues, as well as anxieties about finances, some employers offer pre-retirement planning seminars for employees.

U.S. companies will face a severe shortage of badly needed skills in the coming decade unless they act now to convince top-performing older employees to delay or phase in their retirement. Career development for people toward the ends of their careers may be managed in a number of ways. Phased-in retirement, consulting arrangements, and callback of some retirees as needed all act as means for gradual disengagement between the organization and the individual. However, phased-in retirement (which is widely seen as a good situation for all involved) faces major obstacles in current pension laws. Under many pension plans, employees who are working may not receive pension benefits until they reach a normal retirement age.

Forced early retirement often occurs as a result of downsizings and organizational restructurings. These events have required thousands of individuals, including many managers and professionals, to determine what is important to them while still active and healthy. As a result, some of these people begin second careers rather than focusing primarily on leisure activities or travel. To be successful with early retirement, management must avoid several legal issues, such as forced early retirement and pressuring older workers to resign.

Career Plateaus. Those who do not change jobs may face another problem: career plateaus. Many workers define career success in terms of upward mobility. As the opportunities to move up decrease, some employers try to convince employees they can find job satisfaction in lateral movement. Such moves can be reasonable if employees learn new skills that increase individual marketability in case of future layoffs, termination, or organizational re-structurings.

One strategy for individuals to get off career plateaus is to take seminars and university courses. This approach may reveal new opportunities for plateaued employees. Rotating workers to other departments is another way to deal with career plateaus. A computer chip manufacturer instituted a formal "poaching" program that encouraged managers to recruit employees from other departments, thereby giving employees greater opportunities to experience new challenges without having to leave the employer. Some plateaued individuals change careers and go into other lines of work altogether.

Career Transitions and HR

Career transitions can be stressful for individuals who change employers and jobs. Three career transitions are of special interests to HR: organizational entry and socialization, transfers and promotions, and job loss.

Starting as a new employee can be overwhelming. "Entry shock" is especially difficult for younger new hires who find the work world very different from school. Entry shock following graduation includes the following concerns:

- *Supervisors:* The boss/employee relationship is different from the student/teacher relationship.
- *Feedback:* In school, feedback is frequent and measurable, but that is not true of most jobs.
- *Time:* School has short (quarter/semester) time cycles, whereas time horizons are longer at work.
- *The work:* Problems are more tightly defined at school; at work, the logistical and political aspects of solving problems are less certain.

Transfers and promotions offer opportunities for employees to develop. However, unlike new hires, employees who have moved to new positions are often expected to perform well immediately, though that may not be realistic. International transfers cause even more difficulties than in-country transfers for many.

Job loss as a career transition has been most associated with downsizing, mergers, and acquisitions. Losing a job is a stressful event in one's career, frequently causing depression, anxiety, and nervousness. The financial implications and the effects on family can be extreme as well. Yet the potential for job loss continues to increase for many individuals, and effectively describing their concerns should be considered in career transition decision making.[7]

··

Special Individual Career Issues

The goals and perspectives in career planning may differ for organizations and individuals, but three issues can be problematic. Those issues are highlighted next.

Technical and Professional Workers

Technical and professional workers, such as engineers, scientists, physical therapists, and IT systems experts, present a special challenge for organizations. Many of these individuals want to stay in their technical areas rather than enter management; yet advancement in many organizations frequently requires a move into management. Most of these people like the idea of the responsibility and opportunity associated with professional advancement, but they do not want to leave the professional and technical puzzles and problems at which they excel.

An attempt to solve this problem, a dual-career ladder, is a system that allows a person to advance up either a management or a technical/professional ladder.

Dual-career ladders are now used at many firms, most commonly in technology-driven industries such as pharmaceuticals, chemicals, computers, and electronics. For instance, a telecommunications firm created a dual-career ladder in its IT department to reward talented technical people who do not want to move into management.

Women and Careers

According to the U.S. Bureau of Labor Statistics, the percentage of women in the workforce has more than doubled since 1970, and will reach almost 50% by 2010. Women are found in all occupations and jobs, but their careers may have a different element than those of men. Women give birth to children, and in most societies they are also primarily responsible for taking care of their children. The effect of this biology and sociology is that women's careers are often interrupted for childbirth and child rearing.

Work, Family, and Careers.   The career approach for women frequently is to work hard before children arrive, plateau or step off the career track when children are younger, and go back to career-focused jobs that allow flexibility when they are older. This approach is referred to as **sequencing**. But some women who sequence are concerned that the job market will not welcome them when they return, or that the time away will hurt their advancement chances, and some women's careers are stifled due to their career interruptions.

The interaction and conflicts among home, family, and a career affect the average woman differently than they do men. By the time men and women have been out of school for six years, many women may have worked on average 30% less time than men. These and other career differences provide different circumstances for many females. Employers can tap into the female labor market to a greater extent with child-care assistance, flexible work policies, and a general willingness to be accommodating.

Dual-Career Couples

As the number of women in the workforce continues to increase, particularly in professional careers, so does the number of dual-career couples. The U.S. Bureau of Labor Statistics estimates that over 80% of all couples are dual-career couples. Marriages in which both mates are managers, professionals, or technicians have doubled over the past two decades. Problem areas for dual-career couples include family issues and job transfers that require relocations.

Family-Career Issues.   For dual-career couples with children, family issues may conflict with career progression. Thus, one partner's flexibility may depend on what is "best" for the family. Additionally, it is important that the career development problems of dual-career couples be recognized as early as possible. Whenever possible, having both partners involved in planning, even when one is not employed by the company, may enhance the success of such efforts.

Relocation of Dual-Career Couples. Traditionally, employees accepted transfers as part of upward mobility in organizations. However, for some dual-career couples, the mobility required because of one partner's transfer often interferes with the other's career. In addition to having two careers, dual-career couples often have established support networks of co-workers, friends, and business contacts to cope with both their careers and their personal lives. Relocating one partner in a dual-career couple may mean upsetting this carefully constructed network for the other person or creating a "commuting" relationship.

Developing Human Resources

Development represents efforts to improve employees' abilities to handle a variety of assignments and to cultivate employees' capabilities beyond those required by the current job. Development benefits both organizations and individuals. Employees and managers with appropriate experiences and abilities may enhance organizational competitiveness and the ability to adapt to a changing environment. In the development process, individuals' careers also may evolve and gain new or different focuses.

Because development differs from training, in many organizations greater focus is being placed on development rather than simply on training. It is possible to train many people to answer customer service questions, drive a truck, enter data in a computer system, or assemble a television. However, development in areas such as judgment, responsibility, decision making, and communication presents a bigger challenge. These areas may or may not develop through life experiences of individuals. As a key part of talent management, a planned system of development experiences for all employees, not just managers, can help expand the overall level of capabilities in an organization.

Lifelong Learning

Learning and development are closely linked. For most people, lifelong learning and development are likely and desirable. For many professionals, lifelong learning may mean meeting continuing education requirements to retain certificates. For example, lawyers, CPAs, teachers, dentists, and nurses must complete continuing education requirements in most states to keep their licenses to practice. For other employees, learning and development may involve training to expand existing skills and to prepare for different jobs, for promotions, or even for new jobs after retirement.

Re-Development

Whether due to a desire for career change or because the employer needs different capabilities, people may shift jobs in mid-life or mid-career. Re-developing people in the capabilities they need is logical and important. In the last decade, the number of college enrollees over the age of 35 has increased dramatically. But helping employees go back to college is only one way of re-developing them. Some companies offer re-development programs to recruit experienced workers from other fields. For example, different firms needing truck drivers, reporters, and IT workers have sponsored second-career programs. Public-sector employers have been using re-development opportunities as a recruiting tool as well.

HR Development Approaches

The most common development approaches can be categorized under three major headings, as Figure 5-5 depicts. Investing in human intellectual capital, whether on or off the job or in learning organizations, becomes imperative as "knowledge work," such as research skills and specialized technology expertise, increases for almost all employers. But identifying the right mix and approaches for development needs for different individuals requires analyses and planning.

Management Development

Although development is important for all employees, it is essential for managers. Without appropriate development, managers may lack the capabilities to best deploy and manage resources (including employees) throughout the organization.

Experience plays a central role in management development. Indeed, experience often contributes more to the development of senior managers than does classroom training, because much of it occurs in varying circumstances on the job over time. Yet, in many organizations it is difficult to find managers for middle-level jobs. Some individuals refuse to take middle-management jobs, feeling that they are caught between upper management and supervisors. Similarly, not all companies take the time to develop their own senior-level managers. Instead, senior managers and executives often are hired from the outside.

At the beginning level for managerial development is the first-line supervisory job. It is often difficult to go from being a member of the work group to being the boss. Therefore, the new supervisors who are used to functioning as individual contributors often require new skills and mindsets to be successful supervisors.

FIGURE 5-5 HR Development Approaches

A number of employers conduct *pre-supervisor training*. This effort is done to provide realistic job previews of what supervisors will face and to convey to individuals that they cannot just rely on their current job skills and experience in their new positions.

Executive Education.   Executives in an organization often face difficult jobs due to changing and unknown circumstances. "Churning" at the top of organizations and the stresses of executive jobs contribute to increased turnover in these positions. In an effort to decrease turnover and increase management development capabilities, organizations are using specialized education for executives. This type of training includes executive education traditionally offered by university business schools and adds strategy formulation, financial models, logistics, alliances, and global issues. Enrollment in Executive Masters of Business Administration (EMBA) degree programs is popular also.

Problems with Management Development Efforts

Development efforts are subject to certain common mistakes and problems. Many of the management development problems in firms have resulted from inadequate HR planning and a lack of coordination of HR development efforts. Common problems include the following:

- Failing to conduct adequate needs analysis
- Trying out fad programs or training methods
- Substituting training instead of selecting qualified individuals

Another common management problem is **encapsulated development**, which occurs when an individual learns new methods and ideas, but returns to a work unit that is still bound by old attitudes and methods. The development was "encapsulated" in the classroom and is essentially not used on the job. Consequently, it is common for individuals who participate in development programs paid for by their employers to become discouraged and move to new employers that allow them to use their newly developed capabilities more effectively.

· ·

Succession Planning

Planning for the succession of key executives, managers, and other employees is an important part of talent management. Succession planning is the process of identifying a long-term plan for the orderly replacement of key employees. In many industries succession planning is increasingly seen as a major concern. The primary cause is the huge workforce changes and shortages that are expected to occur as the baby-boomer generation continues to retire. The U.S. Census Bureau has estimated that over 75 million baby boomers will retire or be planning retirement transitions by 2010.[8]

Often the employees in the firms tapped to take the boomers' jobs are currently in their 30s and 40s and have 10 to 15 years of work experience. But these employees often have work–family issues that impact their careers. For instance, with women composing almost half of the U.S. workforce, some women in this group may have small children and may want to work part-time or shorter weeks. However, their jobs may not be compatible with such flexibility, which may affect succession planning and leadership development opportunities for them.

Succession Planning Process

Whether in small or large firms, succession planning is linked to strategic HR planning. In that process, both the quantity and the capabilities of potential successors must be linked to organizational strategies and plans.

Two coordinated activities begin the actual process of succession planning. First, the development of preliminary replacement charts ensures that the right individuals with sufficient capabilities and experience to perform the targeted jobs are available at the right time. Replacement charts (similar to depth charts used by football teams) both show the backup "players" at each position and identify positions without current qualified backup players. The charts identify who could take over key jobs if someone leaves, retires, dies unexpectedly, or otherwise creates a vacancy. Second, assessment of the capabilities and interests of current employees provides information that can be placed into the preliminary replacement charts.

Succession in Small and Closely Held Organizations. Succession planning can be especially important in small and medium-sized firms, but studies show that few of these firms formalize succession plans.[5] In fact, more than half of the respondents in one study named lack of succession planning as the biggest threat facing small businesses. In closely held family firms (those that are not publicly traded on stock exchanges), multiple family members often are involved. But in others, the third- and fourth-generation family members are not employees and many do not want to be involved, other than as owners or as members of the Board of Directors.

"Make or Buy" Talent? To some extent, employers face a "make-or-buy" choice: develop ("make") competitive human resources, or hire ("buy") them already developed from somewhere else. Many organizations show an apparent preference for buying rather than making scarce employees in today's labor market. Current trends indicate that technical and professional people usually are "bought" because of the amount of skill development already achieved, rather than internal individuals being picked because of their ability to learn or their behavioral traits. However, hiring rather than developing internal human resource capabilities may not fit certain industry competitive environments.

Value of Succession Planning

Many employers are doing succession planning formally or informally. But to justify these efforts, it is important that determinations be made to identify the benefits and value of succession planning. Key benefits include:

- Having an adequate supply of employees to fill future key openings
- Providing career paths and plans for employees, which aids in employee retention and performance motivation

- Continually reviewing the need for individuals as organizational changes occur more frequently
- Enhancing the organizational "brand" and reputation as a desirable place to work

Common Succession Planning Mistakes

The greatest succession focus of Boards of Directors is on CEO succession. The reasons why boards have increased the priority of CEO succession have become more complex due to regulatory and other changes. Specifically, Sarbanes-Oxley Act provisions have added more demands on boards to do CEO succession planning. However, one survey found that about half of board members of firms felt their CEO succession planning efforts were less effective than needed.

Focusing only on CEO and top management succession is one of the most common mistakes made. Other mistakes include:

- Starting too late, when openings are already occurring
- Not linking well to strategic plans
- Allowing the CEO to direct the planning and make all succession decisions
- Looking only internally for succession candidates

Longer-term succession planning should include mid-level and lower-level managers, as well as other key non-management employees. Some firms target key technical, professional, and sales employees as part of succession planning. Others include customer service representatives, warehouse specialists, and additional hourly paid employees who may be able to move up into other jobs or departments.

Succession planning is an important part of employers seeing talent management strategically. Actions such as career planning, HR development efforts, and succession planning are aiding in fulfilling the expectations and goals important for future workforce needs.

NOTES

1. *ASTD State of the Industry Report*, 2006, *www.astd.org.*
2. P. J. Taylor, D. F. Russ-Eft, and D. W. L. Chan, "A Meta-Analytic Review of Behavior Modeling," *Journal of Applied Psychology*, 90 (2005), 692–709.
3. Mark E. Van Buren, *ASTD State of the Industry Report, 2003* (Alexandria, VA: American Society of Training and Development, 2005), 11–12, *www.astd.org.*
4. American Society of Training and Development, *www.astd.org.*
5. Tom Casey and Carey Guggenheim, *Buch Consultants,* June 6, 2005, *www.workforce.com.*
6. "Talent Management Software Is Bundling Up," *Workforce Management,* October 9, 2006, 35.
7. Herminica Ibarra and Kent Lineback, "What's Your Story?" *Harvard Business Review,* January 2005, 64–71.
8. *www.census.gov,* 2006.

INTERNET RESOURCES

American Society for Training and Development-This Website on training and development contains information on research, education seminars, and conferences. Link to the ASTD Website at: *www.astd.org.*

Career Builder-This Website provides links to on-line career resources. Visit their Website at: *www.careerbuilder.com*

SUGGESTED READINGS

Malcolm S. Knowles, Elwood F. Holton III, and Richard A. Swanson, *The Adult Learner,* 6th ed. (New York: Elsevier, 2005).

Mel Siberman, *Active Training* (New York: Pfeffer, 2006).

Talent Management: The State of the Art (New York: Towers Perrin, 2005).

J. Barbazette, *Successful New Employer Orientation,* 3rd ed. Pfeiffer, 2007.

Performance Management and Appraisal

HR—MEETING MANAGEMENT CHALLENGES

An effective performance management system focuses on identifying, measuring, and dealing with employees performance evaluations. These issues are discussed in this chapter so that effective performance-management systems can contribute to organizational results. Key aspects include:

- Why organizational strategies are linked to a performance management system.
- Establishing a legally defensible and effective performance appraisal system.
- How to address performance problems and concerns with individuals.

Employers want employees who perform their jobs well. Performance management is used to identify, communicate, measure, and reward employees who do just that. Performance management system design is one of the key methods HR management uses to contribute to organizational performance.

The Nature of Performance Management

Performance management should originate with what the organization needs to accomplish to meet its strategic objectives. Each employee has some contribution to make to those greater objectives through his or her job. In a sense, the sum of all performances in all jobs in the organization should equal the strategic plan for the organization.

In some situations performance management is confused with one of its component parts—performance appraisal. **Performance management** is a series of activities designed to ensure that the organization gets the performance it needs from its employees. **Performance appraisal** is the process of determining how well employees do their job relative to a standard and communicating that information to the employee.

Effective Performance Management

An effective performance management system should do the following:

- Make clear what the organization expects.
- Provide performance information to employees.
- Identify areas of success and needed development.
- Document performance for personnel records.

Figure 6-1 shows how performance management facilitates turning an organization's strategy into results. However, just having a strategic plan does not

FIGURE 6-1 Performance Management Linkage

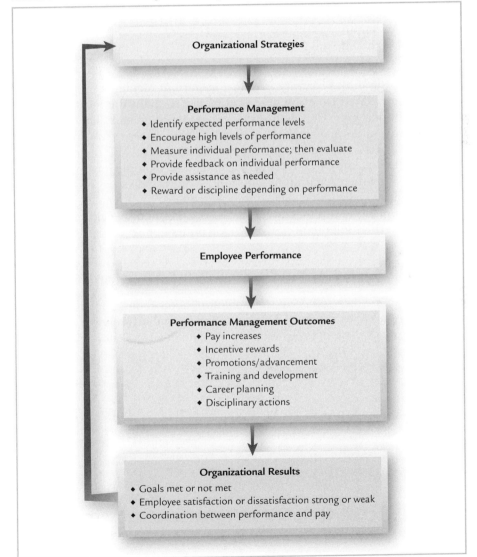

guarantee that any action will occur on the plan. When organizational strategies have been defined, they must be translated to department or unit level actions. Then those actions must be assigned to individuals who must be held responsible for their performance measured.

Identifying and Measuring Employee Performance

The most critical performance criteria vary from job to job, but the employee performance measures common to *most* jobs include the following:

- Quantity of output
- Quality of output
- Timeliness of output
- Presence at work

Specific **job duties** identify the most important elements in a given job. Duties are identified from job descriptions that contain the most important parts of individual jobs. They define what the organization pays employees to do. Therefore, the performance of individuals on those important job duties should be measured and compared against appropriate standards and the results communicated to the employee. To complicate matters, multiple job duties are the rule rather than the exception in most jobs. A given individual might demonstrate better performance on some duties than others. Additionally, some duties might be more important than others to the organization. Weights can be used to show the relative importance of several job duties in one job.

Types of Performance Information

Managers can use three different types of information about how employees are performing their jobs, as Figure 6-2 shows. **Trait-based information** identifies a character trait of the employee—such as attitude, initiative, or creativity—and

FIGURE 6-2 Types of Performance Information

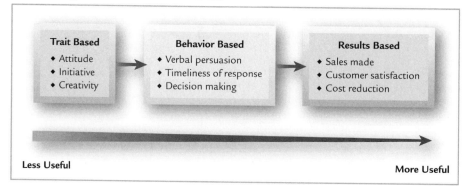

Trait Based	Behavior Based	Results Based
◆ Attitude	◆ Verbal persuasion	◆ Sales made
◆ Initiative	◆ Timeliness of response	◆ Customer satisfaction
◆ Creativity	◆ Decision making	◆ Cost reduction

Less Useful   More Useful may or may not be job related. Because traits tend to be ambiguous, court decisions have generally held that trait-based performance appraisals are too vague to use when making performance-based HR decisions such as promotions or terminations.

Behavior-based information focuses on specific behaviors that lead to job success. For a salesperson, the behavior "verbal persuasion" can be observed and used as information on performance. Behavioral information clearly specifies the behaviors management wants to see. However, identifying successful use of verbal persuasion for a salesperson might be difficult because an approach that is successful when used by one salesperson may not be successful when used by another.

Results-based information considers employee accomplishments. For jobs in which measurement is easy and obvious, a results-based approach works well. However, that which is measured tends to be emphasized, and that emphasis may leave out equally important but unmeasurable parts of the job. For example, a car sales representative who gets paid *only* for sales may be unwilling to do paperwork or other work not directly related to selling cars.

Performance measures can also be viewed as objective or subjective. The **objective measures** can be observed—for example, the number of cars sold or the number of invoices processed can be counted. **Subjective measures** require judgment on the part of the evaluator and are more difficult to determine. One example of a subjective measure is a supervisor's ratings of an employee's "attitude," which cannot be seen directly. Consequently, both objective and subjective measures should be used carefully.

Performance Standards

Performance standards define the expected levels of performance, and are labeled *benchmarks* or *goals* or *targets*—depending on the approach taken. Realistic, measurable, clearly understood performance standards benefit both organizations and employees. Well-defined standards ensure that everyone involved knows the levels of accomplishment expected.

Both numerical and non-numerical standards can be established. Sales quotas and production output standards are familiar numerical performance standards. A standard of performance can also be based on non-numerical criteria. Assessing whether someone has met a performance standard, especially a non-numerical one, can be difficult, but usually can be done. Establishing performance standards makes assessing a person's performance level, even non-numerical performance, much more useful.

Measuring performance in many businesses is difficult. Yet the performance of people is commonly a basic productivity measure. On an individual level, cost per employee, incidents per employee per day, number of calls per product, cost per call, sources of demand for services, and service calls per day are common measures. Once managers have determined appropriate measures of the variance in their company, they can deal with waste and service delivery. *Performance that is measured can be managed.*[2]

. . . .

Performance Appraisals

Performance appraisals are used to assess an employee's performance and to communicate that performance to the employee. Performance appraisal is variously called *employee rating, employee evaluation, performance review, performance evaluation,* or *results appraisal.*

Performance appraisals are widely used for administering wages and salaries, giving performance feedback, and identifying individual employee strengths and weaknesses. Most U.S. employers use performance appraisal systems for office, professional, technical, supervisory, middle management, and non-union production workers.

Uses of Performance Appraisals

Organizations generally use performance appraisals in two potentially conflicting ways. One use is to provide a measure of performance for consideration in making pay or other administrative decisions about employees. This *administrative* role often creates stress for managers doing the appraisals. The other use focuses on the *development* of individuals. In this role, the manager acts more as counselor and coach than as a judge, which may change the tone of the appraisal. The developmental performance appraisal emphasizes identifying current training and development needs, as well as planning employees' future opportunities and career directions. Figure 6-3 shows both uses for performance appraisal.

Administrative Uses of Appraisals. Three administrative uses of appraisal impact managers and employees the most: (1) determining pay adjustments; (2) making job placement decisions on promotions, transfers, and demotions; and (3) choosing employee disciplinary actions up to and including termination of employment.

FIGURE 6-3 Conflicting Uses for Performance Appraisal

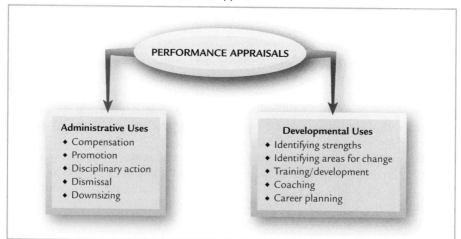

A performance appraisal system is often the link between additional pay and rewards that employees receive and their job performance. Performance-based compensation affirms the idea that pay raises are given for performance accomplishments rather than based on length of service (seniority) or granted automatically to all employees at the same percentage levels. To improve the administrative processes of performance appraisals, many employers have implemented software so that managers can prepare appraisals electronically.

Many U.S. workers say that they see little connection between their performance and the size of their pay increases due to flaws in the performance appraisal processes.[3] However, the use of performance appraisals to determine pay is common. Consequently, many people argue that performance appraisals and pay discussions should be separated.

Employers are interested in the other administrative uses of performance appraisal as well, such as decisions about promotions, terminations, layoffs, and transfer assignments. Promotions and demotions based on performance must be documented through performance appraisals; otherwise, legal problems can result.

Developmental Uses of Appraisals.   For employees, the performance appraisal can be a primary source of information and feedback, which are often key to their future development. In the process of identifying employee strengths, weaknesses, potentials, and training needs through performance appraisal feedback, supervisors can inform employees about their progress, discuss areas where additional training may be beneficial, and outline future development plans.

The purpose of such feedback is both to reinforce satisfactory employee performance and to address performance deficiencies. Positive reinforcement for desired behaviors contributes to both individual and organizational development. The development function of performance appraisal also can identify areas in which the employee might wish to grow.

A number of decisions must be made when designing performance appraisal systems. Some important ones are identifying the appraisal responsibilities of the HR unit and of the operating managers, the type of appraisal system to use, the timing of appraisals, and who conducts appraisals.

Informal vs. Systematic Appraisal Processes.   Performance appraisals can occur in two ways: informally and/or systematically. A supervisor conducts an **informal appraisal** whenever necessary. A manager communicates this evaluation through conversation on the job, over coffee, or by on-the-spot discussion of a specific occurrence. Although informal appraisal is useful and necessary, it should not take the place of systematic formal appraisal.

A **systematic appraisal** is used when the contact between a manager and employee is formal, and a system is in place to report managerial impressions and observations on employee performance. Systematic appraisals feature a regular time interval, which distinguishes them from informal appraisals. Both employees and managers know that performance will be reviewed on a regular basis, and they can plan for performance discussions.

Timing of Appraisals. Most companies require managers to conduct appraisals once or twice a year, most often annually. Employees commonly receive an appraisal 60 to 90 days after hiring, again at six months, and annually thereafter.

To separate the administrative and developmental uses of appraisals, some employers implement the following appraisal schedule: First there is a performance review and discussion. Some time after that a separate training, development, and objective-setting session is held. Within two weeks, a compensation adjustment discussion takes place. Having three separate discussions provides both the employee and the employee's manager with opportunities to focus on the administrative, developmental, and compensation issues. Using this framework is generally better than addressing all three areas in one discussion of an hour or less, once a year.

Legal Concerns and Performance Appraisals

Because appraisals are supposed to measure how well employees are doing their jobs, it may seem unnecessary to emphasize that performance appraisals must be job related. Courts have ruled in some cases that performance appraisals were discriminatory and not job related. Legal concerns have also arisen with the use of forced-distribution rating systems. In these systems, managers are forced to rate a certain percentage of employees as "outstanding," another percentage as "satisfactory," and still another percentage as "needing improvement."

A number of court decisions over 30 years have focused attention on performance appraisals, particularly on equal employment opportunity (EEO) concerns. The uniform guidelines issued by the Equal Employment Opportunity Commission (EEOC) and various court decisions make it clear that performance appraisals must be job related, non-discriminatory, and documented.

. . . .

Who Conducts Appraisals?

Performance appraisals can be conducted by anyone familiar with the performance of individual employees. Possible combinations include the following:

- Supervisors rating their employees
- Employees rating their superiors
- Team members rating each other
- Employees rating themselves
- Outside sources rating employees
- A variety of parties providing multisource, or 360°, feedback

Supervisory Rating of Subordinates

The most widely used means of rating employees is based on the assumption that the immediate supervisor is the person most qualified to evaluate an employee's performance realistically and fairly. To help themselves provide accurate evaluations, some supervisors keep performance logs noting their employees' accomplishments. These logs provide specific examples to use when rating performance. Figure 6-4 shows the traditional review process by which supervisors conduct performance appraisals on employees.

Employee Rating of Managers

A number of organizations today ask employees or group members to rate the performance of supervisors and managers. Having employees rate managers provides several advantages. First, in critical manager/employee relationships, employee ratings can be quite useful for identifying competent managers. Second, this type of rating program can help make a manager more responsive to employees. This advantage can quickly become a disadvantage if the manager focuses on being "nice" rather than on managing. Finally, employee appraisals can contribute to career development efforts for managers by identifying areas for growth.

FIGURE 6-4 Traditional Performance Appraisal Process

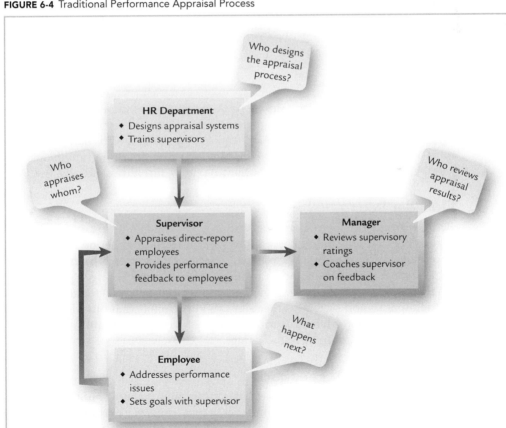

A major disadvantage of having employees rate managers is the negative reaction many superiors have to being evaluated by employees. Also, the fear of reprisals may prompt workers to rate their managers only on the way the managers treat them, not on critical job requirements. The problems associated with this appraisal approach limit its usefulness to certain situations, including managerial development and improvement efforts.[4]

Team/Peer Rating

Having employees and team members rate each other is another type of appraisal. Peer and team ratings are especially useful when supervisors do not have the opportunity to observe each employee's performance but other work group members do. One challenge of this approach is how to obtain ratings with virtual or global teams, in which the individuals work primarily through technology, not in person. Another challenge is how to obtain ratings from and for individuals who are on different special project teams throughout the year.

Some contend that any performance appraisal, including team/peer ratings, can negatively affect teamwork and participative management efforts. Although team members have positive or negative information on one another's performance, they may not choose to share it. Despite the problems, team/peer performance ratings are probably inevitable, especially where work teams are used extensively.

Self-Rating

Self-appraisal works in certain situations. As a self-development tool, it forces employees to think about their strengths and weaknesses and set goals for improvement. Employees working in isolation or possessing unique skills may be the only ones qualified to rate themselves. However, employees may not rate themselves as supervisors would rate them; they may use quite different standards.

Outsider Rating

People outside the immediate work group may be called in to conduct performance reviews. This field review approach can include someone from the HR department as a reviewer, or completely independent reviewers from outside the organization. Examples include a review team evaluating a college president or a panel of division managers evaluating a supervisor's potential for advancement in the organization. A disadvantage of this approach is that outsiders may not know the important demands within the work group or organization. Use of such input has led to multisource ratings.

Multisource/360° Feedback

Multisource rating, or 360° feedback, has grown in popularity. Multisource feedback recognizes that for a growing number of jobs, employee performance is multidimensional and crosses departmental, organizational, and even global boundaries. The major purpose of 360° feedback is *not* to increase uniformity by soliciting like-minded views. Instead, it is designed to capture evaluations of the individual employee's different roles. Significant administrative time and paperwork are required to request, obtain, and summarize feedback from multiple raters. Use of Web-based systems can significantly reduce the administrative demands of multisource ratings.

One concern is whether 360° appraisals improve the process or simply multiply the number of problems by the total number of raters. Also, some wonder whether multisource appraisals really create better decisions that offset the additional time and investment required. These issues appear to be less threatening when the 360° feedback is used *only for development*. But they may effectively reduce the use of multisource appraisals as an administrative tool in many situations.

Methods for Appraising Performance

Performance can be appraised by a number of methods. Some employers use one method for all jobs and employees, some use different methods for different groups of employees, and others use a combination of methods. The following discussion highlights different tools that can be used and some of the pluses and minuses of each.

Category Scaling Methods

The simplest methods for appraising performance are category scaling methods, which require a manager to mark an employee's level of performance on a specific form divided into categories of performance. A *checklist* uses a list of statements or words from which raters check statements most representative of the characteristics and performance of employees. Often, a scale indicating perceived level of accomplishment on each statement is included, which becomes a type of graphic rating scale.

Graphic Rating Scales. The **graphic rating scale** allows the rater to mark an employee's performance on a continuum. Because of its simplicity, this method is used frequently. Three dimensions of graphic rating scales are: *descriptive categories* (such as quantity of work, attendance, and dependability), *job duties* (taken from the job description), and *behavioral dimensions* (such as decision making, employee development, and communication effectiveness). As Figure 6-5 shows, standards must be defined for consistency.

Graphic rating scales in many forms are widely used because they are easy to develop; however, they encourage errors on the part of the raters, who may depend too heavily on the form to define performance. Also, graphic rating scales tend to emphasize the rating instrument itself and its limitations. If they fit the person and the job, the scales work well. However, if they fit poorly, managers and employees who must use them frequently complain about "the rating form."

FIGURE 6-5 Sample Terms for Defining Standards

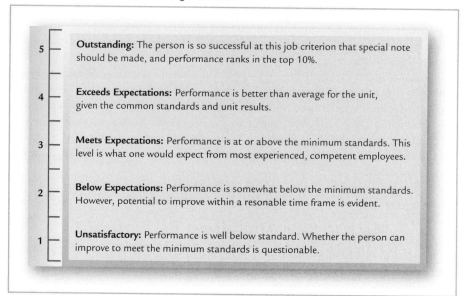

A key point must be emphasized. Regardless of the scales used, the focus should be on the job duties and responsibilities identified in job descriptions. The closer the link between the scales and what people actually do, as identified in current and complete job descriptions, the stronger the relationship between the ratings and the job, as viewed by employees and managers. Also, should the performance appraisal results be challenged by legal actions, the more performance appraisals are tied to what people actually do, the more likely employers are to prevail in those legal situations.

Behavioral Rating Scales. In an attempt to overcome some of the concerns with graphic rating scales, employers may use behavioral rating scales, which are designed to assess an employee's *behaviors* instead of other characteristics. Different approaches are used, but all describe specific examples of employee job behaviors. In a behaviorally anchored rating scale (BARS), these examples are "anchored" or measured against a scale of performance levels.

Several problems are associated with the behavioral approaches. First, developing and maintaining behaviorally anchored rating scales require extensive time and effort. In addition, various appraisal forms are needed to accommodate different types of jobs in an organization. For instance, because nurses, dietitians, and admissions clerks in a hospital all have distinct job descriptions, a separate BARS form needs to be developed for each.

Comparative Methods

Comparative methods require that managers directly compare the performance levels of their employees against one another. For example, a supervisor would compare the performance of one employee with that of others. Comparative techniques include ranking and forced distribution.

Ranking.   The **ranking method** lists all employees from highest to lowest in performance. The primary drawback of the ranking method is that the sizes of the differences between individuals are not well defined. For example, the performances of individuals ranked second and third may differ little, while the performances of those ranked third and fourth differ a great deal. This drawback can be overcome to some extent by assigning points to indicate the sizes of the gaps. Ranking also means someone must be last, which ignores the possibility that the last-ranked individual in one group might be equal to the top-ranked employee in a different group. Further, the ranking task becomes unwieldy if the group to be ranked is large.

Forced Distribution.   This technique is used for distributing ratings that are generated with any of the other appraisal methods and comparing the ratings of people in a work group. With the **forced distribution** method, the ratings of employees' performance are distributed along a bell-shaped curve.

Forced distribution is used in some form by an estimated 30% of all firms with performance appraisal systems. At General Electric, in the "20/70/10" program, managers identify the top 20% and reward them richly so that few will leave. The bottom 10% are given a chance to improve or leave. The forced distribution system is controversial because of both its advantages and its disadvantages, which are discussed next.[5]

One reason why firms have mandated the use of forced distributions for appraisal ratings is to deal with "rater inflation." The use of a forced distribution system makes managers identify each of the high, average, and low performers. Thus, high performers can be rewarded and developed, while low performers can be "encouraged" to improve or leave.

A number of actions are recommended to address if a forced distribution system is to be used. They include many that are similar to those for making other methods of appraisals more legal and effective[6]:

- Use specific, objective criteria and standards.
- Involve employees in planning and designing the programs.
- Ensure that sufficient numbers of people are rated, so that statistical rankings are relevant.
- Train managers, and review their ratings to ensure that they are job related, not based on favoritism.

The forced distribution method suffers from several drawbacks. One problem is that a supervisor may resist placing any individual in the lowest (or the highest) group. Difficulties also arise when the rater must explain to an employee why she or he was placed in one group and others were placed in higher groups. Further, with small groups, the assumption that a bell-shaped or other distribution of performance occurs may be faulty. As a result of such drawbacks, forced distribution systems have been challenged legally, and a number of firms have settled lawsuits and agreed to modify their performance appraisal processes.

Narrative Methods

Managers and HR specialists may be required to provide complete written appraisal information. In the **critical incident method**, the manager keeps a written record of both highly favorable and unfavorable actions performed by an employee during the entire rating period. When a "critical incident" involving an employee occurs, the manager writes it down. The critical incident method can be used with other methods to document the reasons why an employee was given a certain rating.

The **essay method** requires a manager to write a short essay describing each employee's performance during the rating period. The essay method allows the rater more flexibility than other methods do. As a result, appraisers often combine the essay with other methods.

Management by Objectives

Management by objectives (MBO) specifies the performance goals that an individual and manager mutually identify. Each manager sets objectives derived from the overall goals and objectives of the organization; however, MBO should not be a disguised means for a superior to dictate the objectives of individual managers or employees. Other names for MBO include *appraisal by results, target coaching, work planning and review, performance objective setting,* and *mutual goal setting.*

Implementing a guided self-appraisal system using an MBO is a four-stage process. The stages are as follows:

1. *Job review and agreement*
2. *Development of performance standards*
3. *Setting of objectives*
4. *Continuing performance discussions*

The MBO process seems to be most useful with managerial personnel and employees who have a fairly wide range of flexibility and control over their jobs. When imposed on a rigid and autocratic management system, MBO often has failed. Emphasizing penalties for not meeting objectives defeats the developmental and participative nature of MBO.

Combinations of Methods

No single appraisal method is best for all situations. Therefore, a performance measurement system that uses a combination of methods may be sensible in certain circumstances. Using combinations may offset some of the advantages and disadvantages of individual methods.

When managers can articulate what they want a performance appraisal system to accomplish, they can choose and mix methods to realize those advantages. For example, one combination might include a graphic rating scale of performance on major job criteria, a narrative of developmental needs, and an overall ranking of employees in a department. Different categories of employees (e.g., salaried exempt, salaried non-exempt, and maintenance) might require different combinations of methods.

. . . .

Performance Appraisal Training
for Managers and Employees

Court decisions on the legality of performance appraisals and research on appraisal effectiveness both stress the importance of training managers and employees on performance management and conducting performance appraisals. Managers with positive views of the performance appraisal system are more likely to use the system effectively. Unfortunately, such training occurs only sporadically or not at all in many organizations.

For employees, performance appraisal training focuses on the purposes of appraisal, the appraisal process and timing, and how performance criteria and standards are linked to job duties and responsibilities. Some training also discusses how employees should rate their own performance and use that information in discussions with their supervisors and managers.

Most systems can be improved by training supervisors in how to do performance appraisals. Some topics covered in appraisal training include:

- Appraisal process and timing
- Performance criteria and job standards that should be considered
- How to communicate positive and negative feedback
- When and how to discuss training and development goals
- Conducting and discussing the compensation review
- How to avoid common rating errors

Rater Errors

There are many possible sources of error in the performance appraisal process. One of the major sources is mistakes made by raters. Although completely eliminating these errors is impossible, making raters aware of them through training is helpful.

A common rater is *varying standards*. When appraising employees, a manager should avoid applying different standards and expectations for employees performing similar jobs.

Another common error is the **recency effect**, when a rater gives greater weight to recent events when appraising an individual's performance. The opposite is the **primacy effect**, which occurs when a rater gives greater weight to information received first.

Rating Patterns and Biases.   Rating patterns may exhibit leniency or strictness. The leniency error occurs when ratings of all employees fall at the high end of the scale. The strictness error occurs when a manager uses only the lower part of the scale to rate employees. To avoid conflict, managers often rate employees higher than they should. This "ratings boost" is especially likely when no manager or HR representative reviews the completed appraisals.

Rater bias occurs when a rater's values or prejudices distort the rating. Such bias may be unconscious or quite intentional. For example, a manager's dislike of certain ethnic groups may cause distortion in appraisal information for some people. Use of age, religion, seniority, sex, appearance, or other "classifications" also may skew appraisal ratings if the appraisal process is not properly designed.

Performance Criteria Errors.   The **halo effect** occurs when a rater scores an employee high on all job criteria because of performance in one area. For example, if a worker has few absences, her supervisor might give her a high rating in all other areas of work, including quantity and quality of output, without really thinking about the employee's other characteristics separately. The opposite is the *horns effect*, which occurs when a low rating on one characteristic leads to an overall low rating.

Another problem is the **contrast error**, which is the tendency to rate people relative to others rather than against performance standards. Although it may be appropriate to compare people at times, the performance rating usually should reflect comparison against performance standards, not against other people.

Appraisal Feedback

After completing appraisals, managers need to communicate results in order to give employees a clear understanding of how they stand in the eyes of their immediate superiors and the organization. Organizations commonly require managers to discuss appraisals with employees. The appraisal feedback interview provides an opportunity to clear up any misunderstandings on both sides. In this interview, the manager should focus on coaching and development, and not just tell the employee, "Here is how you rate and why." Emphasizing development gives both parties an opportunity to consider the employee's performance as part of appraisal feedback.

Appraisal Interview

The appraisal interview presents both an opportunity and a danger. It can be an emotional experience for the manager and the employee because the manager must communicate both praise and constructive criticism. A major concern for managers is how to emphasize the positive aspects of the employee's performance while still discussing ways to make needed improvements. If the interview is handled poorly, the employee may feel resentment, which could lead to conflict in future working relationships.

Employees usually approach an appraisal interview with some concern. They may feel that discussions about performance are both personal and important to their continued job success. At the same time, they want to know how their managers feel about their performance. Figure 6-6 summarizes hints for an effective appraisal interview for supervisors and managers.

Feedback as a System

The three commonly recognized components of a feedback system are data, evaluation of that data, and some action based on the evaluation. *Data* are factual pieces of information regarding observed actions or consequences. Most often,

FIGURE 6-6 Appraisal Interview Hints for Supervisors and Managers

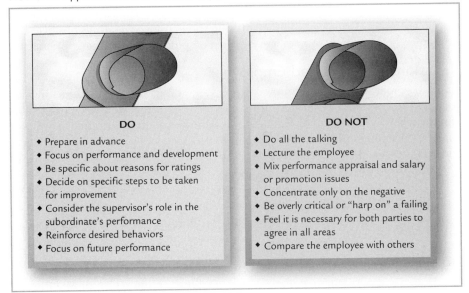

DO	DO NOT
◆ Prepare in advance	◆ Do all the talking
◆ Focus on performance and development	◆ Lecture the employee
◆ Be specific about reasons for ratings	◆ Mix performance appraisal and salary or promotion issues
◆ Decide on specific steps to be taken for improvement	◆ Concentrate only on the negative
◆ Consider the supervisor's role in the subordinate's performance	◆ Be overly critical or "harp on" a failing
◆ Reinforce desired behaviors	◆ Feel it is necessary for both parties to agree in all areas
◆ Focus on future performance	◆ Compare the employee with others

data are facts that report what happened, but data alone rarely tell the whole story. Someone must evaluate the meaning or value of the data.

Evaluation is the way the feedback system reacts to the facts, and it requires performance standards. Managers might evaluate the same factual information differently than would customers (for example, regarding merchandise exchange or credit decisions) or co-workers. Evaluation can be done by the person supplying the data, by a supervisor, or by a group.

For feedback to cause change, some decisions must be made regarding subsequent *action*. In traditional appraisal systems, the manager makes specific suggestions regarding future actions the employee might take. Employee input often is encouraged as well. In 360° feedback situations, it may be necessary to involve those providing information if the subsequent actions are highly interdependent and require coordination with the information providers.[7] Regardless of the process used, the feedback components (data, evaluation, and action) are necessary parts of a successful performance appraisal feedback system.

Reactions of Managers

Managers and supervisors who must complete appraisals of their employees often resist the appraisal process. Many managers feel that their role calls on them to assist, encourage, coach, and counsel employees to improve their performance. However, being a judge on the one hand and a coach and a counselor on the other hand may cause internal conflict and confusion for managers.

Knowing that appraisals may affect employees' future careers also may cause altered or biased ratings. This problem is even more likely when managers know that they will have to communicate and defend their ratings to the employees, their bosses, or HR specialists. Managers can easily avoid providing negative feedback to an employee in an appraisal interview and thus avoid unpleasantness in an interpersonal situation by making the employee's ratings positive. But avoidance helps no one. A manager owes an employee a well-done appraisal.

Reactions of Appraised Employees

Employees may well see the appraisal process as a threat and feel that the only way for them to get a higher rating is for someone else to receive a low rating. This win/lose perception is encouraged by comparative methods of rating. Emphasis on the self-improvement and developmental aspects of appraisal is an effective means to reduce these reactions from those participating in the appraisal process.

Effective Performance Management

Regardless of the approach used, managers must understand the intended outcome of performance management. When performance management is used to develop employees as resources, it usually works. When one key part of performance management, a performance appraisal, is used to punish employees, performance management is less effective.

Done well, performance management can lead to higher employee motivation and satisfaction. To be effective, a performance management system, including the performance appraisal processes, should be:

- Consistent with the strategic mission of the organization
- Beneficial as a development tool
- Useful as an administrative tool
- Legal and job related
- Viewed as generally fair by employees
- Effective in documenting employee performance

NOTES

1. "Survey: Failure to Deal with Poor Performers May Decrease Engagement of Other Employees," *Newsline,* June 22, 2006.
2. Eric Harmon, Scott Hensel, and T. E. Lukes, "Measuring Performance in Services," *The McKinsey Quarterly,* 2006, 2–7.
3. "Communicating Beyond Ratings Can Be Difficult," *Workforce Management,* April 24, 2006, 35.
4. Clinton Longnecker, "Managerial Performance Appraisals: The Good, The Bad, and The Ugly," *HR Advisor,* May/June 2005, 19–26.
5. Jena McGregor, "The Struggle to Measure Performance," *Business Week,* January 9, 2006, 26–28.
6. Steve Scullen, Paul Bergey, and Lynda Aiman-Smith, "Forced Distribution Rating Systems and the Improvement of Workforce Potential," *Personnel Psychology,* 58 (2005), 1–31.
7. D. Van Fleet, T. Peterson, and E. Van Fleet, "Closing the Performance Feedback Gap with Expert Systems," *The Academy of Management Executive,* August 2005, 38–53.

INTERNET RESOURCES

Office of Personnel Management— Performance Management Technical Assistance. This Web site contains information on managing performance, including a Performance Measurement Handbook, and is available at its Web site: *http://www.opm.gov/perform*

International Society for Performance Improvement (ISPI)—Improving human resource performance in workplaces is the focus of this association. Links to numerous resources are available at its Web site: *http://www.ispi.org*

SUGGESTED READINGS

Herman Aguinis, *Performance Management,* (Prentice-Hall, 2007.)

David A.J. Axon, ed. *Best Practices in Planning and Performance Management,* 2nd ed., (Wiley, 2007.)

T.V. Rao, *Performance Management & Appraisal Systems,* (Sage Publications, 2004.)

Dean R. Spitzer, *Transforming Performance Management,* (AMACOM, 2007.)

Compensation Strategies and Practices

HR—MEETING MANAGEMENT CHALLENGES

Pay is always an issue with both management and employees. How can you have a "fair" pay system? The following points are at the heart of compensation.

- Understand what it is the organization wants to do with its pay
- Design a rational pay system
- Understand executive compensation

Total rewards are the monetary and non-monetary rewards provided to employees in order to attract, motivate, and retain them. Critical to an effective rewards approach is the need to balance the interests and costs of the employers with the needs and expectations of employees. In some industries, such as financial services, health care, education, and hospitality, employee payroll and benefits comprise more than 60% of all operating costs. Although actual costs can be easily calculated, the value derived by employers and employees may prove more difficult to identify.

Nature of Total Rewards and Compensaton

Because so many organizational funds are spent on employees, it is critical for top management and HR executives to match total rewards systems and practices with what the organization is trying to accomplish. Employers must balance their costs at a level that rewards employees sufficiently for their knowledge, skills, abilities, and performance accomplishments. A number of important decisions must be made to achieve the following objectives:

- Legal compliance with all appropriate laws and regulations
- Cost effectiveness for the organization
- Internal, external, and individual equity for employees

- Performance enhancement for the organization
- Performance recognition and talent management for employees

Types of Compensation

Rewards can be both intrinsic and extrinsic. *Intrinsic rewards* may include praise for completing a project or meeting performance objectives. Other psychological and social forms of compensation also reflect intrinsic type of rewards. The *Extrinsic rewards* are tangible and take both monetary and non-monetary forms. One tangible component of a compensation program is *direct compensation,* whereby the employer exchanges monetary rewards for work done and performance results achieved. **Base pay** and **variable pay** are the most common forms of direct compensation. Indirect compensation commonly consists of employee **benefits**.

Base Pay.   The basic compensation that an employee receives, usually as a wage or a salary, is called base pay. Many organizations use two base pay categories, *hourly* and *salaried,* which are identified according to the way pay is distributed and the nature of the jobs. Hourly pay is the most common means and is based on time. Employees paid hourly receive wages, which are payments directly calculated on the amount of time worked. In contrast, people paid salaries receive consistent payments each period regardless of the hours worked. Being paid a salary has typically carried higher status for employees than has being paid a wage. However, overtime may have to be paid to certain salaried employees as defined by federal and state laws.

Variable Pay.   Another type of direct pay is variable pay, which is compensation linked directly to individual, team, or organizational performance. The most common types of variable pay for most employees are bonuses and incentive program payments. Executives often receive longer-term rewards such as stock options.

Benefits.   Many organizations provide numerous extrinsic rewards in an indirect manner. With indirect compensation, employees receive the tangible value of the rewards without receiving actual cash. A **benefit** is an indirect reward—for instance, health insurance, vacation pay, or a retirement pension—given to an employee or a group of employees for organizational membership, regardless of performance. Often employees do not directly pay for all of the benefits they receive.

Compensation Philosophies

Two basic compensation philosophies lie on opposite ends of a continuum, as shown in Figure 7-1. At one end of the continuum is the **entitlement philosophy;** at the other end is the **performance philosophy**. Most compensation systems fall somewhere in between.

Entitlement Philosophy.   The **entitlement philosophy** assumes that individuals who have worked another year are entitled to pay increases, with little regard for performance differences. Many traditional organizations that give automatic

FIGURE 7-1 Continuum of Compensation Philosophies

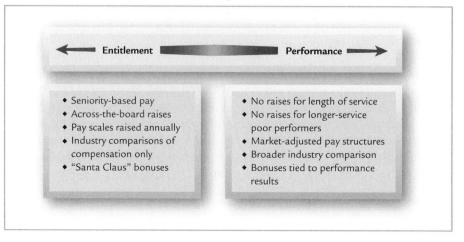

increases to their employees every year are practicing the entitlement philosophy. These automatic increases may be referred to as *cost-of-living raises,* even if they are not tied specifically to economic indicators. Further, most of those employees receive the same or nearly the same percentage increase each year. Bonuses in many entitlement-oriented organizations are determined in a manner that often fails to reflect operating results. Therefore, employees "expect" the bonuses, which become another form of entitlement.

Performance Philosophy.   The pay-for-**performance philosophy** requires that compensation changes reflect performance differences. Organizations operating under this philosophy do not guarantee additional or increased compensation simply for completing another year of organizational service. Instead, they structure pay and incentives to reflect performance differences among employees. Thus, employees who perform satisfactorily maintain or advance their compensation levels more than marginal performers. Also, the bonuses and incentives are based on individual, group, and/or organizational performance.

Few organizations totally follow performance-oriented compensation practices, but the overall trend is toward greater use of pay-for-performance systems. A survey of *Fortune 1000* firms found that over 80% of the firms use some types of performance-based compensation plans. The study found that recent growth had been greater in individual incentive plans and team/group reward systems than organization-wide gainsharing, profit sharing, and stock option plans.[1] Such plans may help reduce employee turnover and increase employee commitment and retention.

The total rewards approach reflects a more performance-oriented philosophy because it tries to place more value on individuals and their performance rather than just on paying for having a job. When determining compensation, managers factor in elements such as how much an employee knows or how competent an employee is. Some organizations use compensation and variable pay programs as part of a total rewards approach for all levels of employees. Widespread use of various incentive plans, team bonuses, organizational gain-sharing programs, and other designs links growth in compensation and variable pay to results. Regularly communicating to employees and managers the compensation philosophy helps reinforce the organizational commitment to it.

HR Metrics and Compensation

Employers spend huge amounts of money for employee compensation, and just like any other area of expenditures, compensation expenditures should be evaluated to determine their effectiveness. Many measures can be used for this evaluation. Employee turnover/retention is one widely used factor. This usage assumes that how well compensation systems operate affects employees' decisions about staying or leaving the organization.

The numbers for calculating these measures are readily available to most HR professionals and Chief Financial Officers, but such calculations are not made in many firms. Often the importance of using these numbers is not a priority for managers or CFOs. Ideally, compensation metrics should be computed each year, and then compared with metrics from past years to show how the rate of compensation changes compares with the rate of changes in the organization overall (revenues, expenses, etc.).

....

Compensation System
Design Issues

Depending on the compensation philosophies, strategies, and approaches identified for an organization, a number of decisions are made that affect the design of the compensation system. Some important ones are highlighted next.

Compensation Fairness and Equity

Most people in organizations work in order to gain rewards for their efforts. Whether employees are considering base pay or variable pay, the extent to which they perceive their compensation to be fair often affects their performance, how they view their jobs, and their employers. This factor may lead to lower or higher turnover rates. Also, pay satisfaction has been found to be linked to organizational-level performance outcomes.

Equity.   Equity is the perceived fairness between what a person does (inputs) and what the person receives (outcomes). Individuals judge equity in compensation by comparing their input (effort and performance) against the effort and performance of others and against the outcomes (the rewards received).

These comparisons are personal and are based on individual perceptions, not just facts. A study by Salary.com found that almost 60% of the workers surveyed believed they were underpaid. But according to reviews of compensation databases, less than 20% were actually underpaid.[2] These findings illustrate how the perceptions of individuals are critical in how equity is viewed.

External Equity.   If an employer does not provide compensation that employees view as equitable in relation to the compensation provided to other employees performing similar jobs in other organizations, that employer is likely to experience higher turnover. Other drawbacks include greater difficulty in recruiting qualified and high-demand individuals. Also, by not being competitive, the employer is more likely to attract and retain individuals with less knowledge and fewer skills and abilities, resulting in lower overall organizational performance. Organizations track external equity by using pay surveys, which are discussed later in this chapter, and by looking at the compensation policies of competing employers.

Internal Equity in Compensation.   Equity internally means that employees receive compensation in relation to the knowledge, skills, and abilities (KSAs) they use in their jobs, as well as their responsibilities and accomplishments. Two key issues—procedural justice and distributive justice—relate to internal equity.

   Procedural justice is the perceived fairness of the process and procedures used to make decisions about employees, including their pay. As it applies to compensation, the entire process of determining base pay for jobs, allocating pay increases, and measuring performance must be perceived as fair.

   A related issue that must be considered is **distributive justice**, which is the perceived fairness in the distribution of outcomes. As one example, if a hardworking employee whose performance is outstanding receives the same across-the-board raise as an employee with attendance problems and mediocre performance, then inequity may be perceived. Likewise, if two employees have similar performance records but one receives a significantly greater pay raise, the other may perceive an inequity due to supervisory favoritism or other factors not related to the job.

Market Competitiveness and Compensation

The market competitiveness of compensation has a significant impact on how equitably employees view compensation. Providing competitive compensation to employees, whether globally, domestically, or locally, is a concern for all employers. Some organizations establish specific policies about where they wish to be positioned in the labor market. These policies use a *quartile strategy*. Data in pay surveys reveal that the dollar differential between quartiles is generally 15% to 20%.

"Meet the Market" Strategy.   Most employers choose to position themselves in the *second quartile* (median), in the middle of the market, as identified by pay data from surveys of other employers' compensation plans. Choosing this level attempts to balance employer cost-pressures and the need to attract and retain employees, by providing mid-level compensation scales that "meet the market" for the employer's jobs.

"Lag the Market" Strategy.   An employer using a *first-quartile* strategy may choose to "lag the market" by paying below market levels, for several reasons. If the employer is experiencing a shortage of funds, it may be unable to pay more. Also, when an abundance of workers is available, particularly those with lower skills, a below-market approach can be used to attract sufficient workers at a lesser cost. Some employers hire illegal immigrants at below-market rates because of the large numbers of those individuals who want to work in the United States. The downside of this strategy is that it increases the likelihood of higher worker turnover. If the labor market supply tightens, then attracting and retaining workers becomes more difficult.

"Lead the Market" Strategy.   The *third-quartile* strategy uses an aggressive approach to "lead the market." This strategy may enable a company to attract and retain sufficient workers with the required capabilities and to be more selective when hiring. Because it is a higher-cost approach, organizations often look for ways to increase the productivity of employees receiving above-market wages.

Selecting a Quartile.   The pay levels and pay structures used can affect organizational performance. Individual employee pay levels will vary around the quartile level, depending on experience, performance, and other individual factors. Deciding in which quartile to position pay structures is a function of a number of considerations. The financial resources available, competitiveness pressures, and the market availability of employees with different capabilities are external factors. For instance, some employers with extensive benefits programs or broad-based incentive programs may choose a first-quartile strategy so that their overall compensation costs and levels are competitive.

· ·

Legal Constraints on Pay Systems

Compensation systems must comply with many government constraints. The important areas addressed by the laws include minimum-wage standards and hours of work. The following discussion examines the laws and regulations affecting base compensation; laws and regulations affecting incentives and benefits are examined in later chapters.

Fair Labor Standards Act (FLSA)

The major federal law affecting compensation is the Fair Labor Standards Act (FLSA), which was originally passed in 1938. Compliance with FLSA provisions is enforced by the Wage and Hour Division of the U.S. Department of Labor. To meet FLSA requirements, employers must keep accurate time records and maintain those records for three years. Penalties for wage and hour violations often include awards of up to two years of back pay for affected current and former employees.

To update and modernize the provisions of the FLSA, the U.S. Department of Labor made some changes in 2004. The provisions of both the original act and subsequent revisions focus on the following major areas:

- Establish a minimum wage.
- Discourage oppressive use of child labor.
- Encourage limits on the number of hours employees work per week, through overtime provisions (exempt and non-exempt statuses).

Minimum Wage.   The FLSA sets a minimum wage to be paid to the broad spectrum of covered employees. The actual minimum wage can be changed only by congressional action. A lower minimum wage is set for "tipped" employees, such as restaurant workers, but their compensation must equal or exceed the minimum wage when average tips are included. Minimum wage levels have sparked significant political discussions and legislative maneuvering at both the federal and state levels for the past decade. Consequently, a three-stage increase in the federal minimum wage occurred beginning in 2007. Note that if a state's minimum wage is higher, employers must meet the state level rather than the federal level.

Debate also surrounds the payment of a living wage versus the minimum wage. A living wage is one that is supposed to meet the basic needs of a worker's family. In the United States, the living wage typically aligns with the amount needed for a family of four to be supported by one worker so that family income is above the officially identified "poverty" level. Without waiting for U.S. federal laws to change, over 80 cities have passed local living-wage laws. Ethical, economic, and employment implications affect both sides of this issue.[3]

Child Labor Provisions.   The child labor provisions of the FLSA set the minimum age for employment with unlimited hours at 16 years. For hazardous occupations (see Chapter 9), the minimum is 18 years of age. Individuals 14 to 15 years old may work outside school hours with certain limitations. Many employers require age certificates for employees because the FLSA makes the employer responsible for determining an individual's age. A representative of a state labor department, a state education department, or a local school district generally issues such certificates.

Exempt and Non-Exempt Statuses.   Under the FLSA, employees are classified as exempt or non-exempt. Exempt employees hold positions for which employers are not required to pay overtime. Non-exempt employees must be paid overtime. The current FLSA regulations used to identify whether or not a job qualifies for exempt status identifies five categories of exempt jobs:

- Executive
- Administrative
- Professional (learned or creative)
- Computer employees
- Outside sales

As Figure 7-2 indicates, the regulations identify factors related to salaried pay levels per week, duties and responsibilities, and other criteria that must exist for jobs to be categorized as exempt. To review the details for each exemption, go to the U.S. Department of Labor's Website at *www.dol.gov.*

In base pay programs, employers often categorize jobs into groupings that tie the FLSA status and the method of payment together. Employers are required to pay overtime for *hourly* jobs in order to comply with the FLSA. Employees in positions classified as *salaried non-exempt* are covered by the overtime provisions of the FLSA and therefore must be paid overtime. Salaried

FIGURE 7-2 Determining Exempt Status Under the FLSA

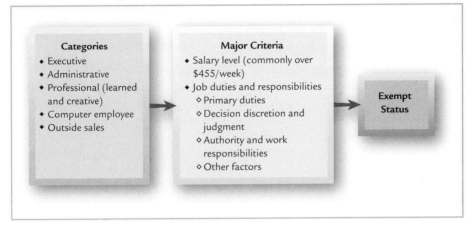

non-exempt positions sometimes include secretarial, clerical, and salaried blue-collar positions. A common mistake made by employers is to avoid paying overtime to any salaried employees, even though some do not qualify for exempt status. Misclassifying certain assistant managers is one example.

The FLSA does not require employers to pay overtime for *salaried exempt* jobs, although some organizations have implemented policies to pay a straight rate for extensive hours of overtime. For instance, some electric utilities pay first-line supervisors extra using a special rate for hours worked over 50 a week during storm emergencies. A number of salaried exempt professionals in various information technology jobs also receive additional compensation for working extensively more than 40 hours per week.

Overtime. The FLSA establishes overtime pay requirements. Its provisions set overtime pay at one and one-half times the regular pay rate for all hours over 40 a week, except for employees who are not covered by the FLSA. Overtime provisions do not apply to farm workers, who also have a lower minimum-wage schedule.

The workweek is defined as a consecutive period of 168 hours (24 hours × 7 days) and does not have to be a calendar week. If they wish to do so, hospitals and nursing homes are allowed to use a 14-day period instead of a 7-day week, as long as overtime is paid for hours worked beyond 8 in a day or 80 in a 14-day period. No daily number of hours requiring overtime is set, except for special provisions relating to hospitals and other specially designated organizations. Thus, if a manufacturing firm operates on a 4-day/10-hour schedule, no overtime pay is required by the act.

The most difficult part is distinguishing who is and is not exempt. Some recent costly settlements have prompted more white-collar workers to sue to receive overtime pay. Retail managers, reporters, sales reps, personal bankers, engineers, computer programmers, and claims adjusters have won in some cases as being non-exempt workers.

Common Overtime Issues.   For individuals who are non-exempt, there are a number of issues that employers must consider. A few of them include the following:

- *Compensatory time off:* "Comp" hours are given to an employee in lieu of payment for extra time worked. Unless it is given to non-exempt employees at the rate of one and one-half times the number of hours over 40 that are worked in a week, comp-time is illegal in the private sector. Also, comp-time cannot be carried over from one pay period to another. The only major exception to these provisions is for public-sector employees, such as fire and police officers, and a limited number of other workers.
- *Incentives for non-exempt employees:* Employers must add the amount of direct work-related incentives to a person's base pay. Then overtime pay should be calculated as one and one-half times the higher (adjusted) rate of pay.
- *Training time:* Must be counted as time worked by non-exempt employees unless it is outside regular work hours, not directly job related, and other aspects. College degree programs may not be affected by these provisions.
- *Travel time:* Must be counted as work time if it occurs during normal work hours, even on non-working days, unless the non-exempt person is a passenger in a car, bus, train, airplane, etc. Other complex clarifications regarding travel regulations affecting overtime should be reviewed by HR specialists to ensure compliance.

The complexity of overtime determination regulations can be confusing for managers, employees, and HR professionals. To review the above areas and additional ones, examine Sections 541, 775, 785, and others listed on the following U.S. Department of Labor Website: *www.dol.gov/dol/allcfr/ESA/Title_29/Chapter_V.htm.*

Acts Affecting Government Contractors

Several compensation-related acts apply to firms having contracts with the U.S. government. The Davis-Bacon Act of 1931 affects compensation paid by firms engaged in federal construction projects valued at over $2,000. It deals only with federal construction projects and requires that the "prevailing" wage be paid on all federal construction projects. The *prevailing wage* is determined by a formula that considers the rate paid for a job by a majority of the employers in the appropriate geographic area.

Two other acts require firms with federal supply or service contracts exceeding $10,000 to pay a prevailing wage. Both the Walsh-Healy Public Contracts Act and the McNamara-O'Hara Service Contract Act apply only to those who are working directly on a federal government contract or who substantially affect its performance.

Garnishment Laws

Garnishment occurs when a creditor obtains a court order that directs an employer to set aside a portion of an employee's wages to pay a debt owed a creditor. Regulations passed as a part of the Consumer Credit Protection Act established limitations on the amount of wages that can be garnished. Also, the act restricted the right of employers to discharge employees whose pay is subject to a single garnishment order. All 50 states have laws applying to wage garnishments.

Development of a Base Pay System

A base compensation system is developed using current job descriptions and job specifications. These information sources are used when *valuing jobs* and analyzing **pay surveys**. These activities are designed to ensure that the pay system is both internally equitable and externally competitive. The data compiled in these two activities are used to design *pay structures,* including **pay grades** and minimum-to-maximum *pay ranges.* After pay structures are established, individual jobs must be placed in the appropriate pay grades and employees' pay must be adjusted according to length of service and performance. Finally, the pay system must be monitored and updated.

Employers want their employees to perceive their pay levels as appropriate in relation to pay for jobs performed by others inside the organization. Frequently, employees and managers make comments such as "This job is more important than that job in another department, so why are the two jobs paid about the same?" Two general approaches for valuing jobs are available: job evaluation and market pricing. Both approaches are used to determine initial values of jobs in relation to other jobs in an organization, and they are discussed next.

Valuing Jobs with Job Evaluation Methods

Job evaluation is a formal, systematic means to identify the relative worth of jobs within an organization. Several job evaluation methods are available for use by employers of different sizes.

Point Method. The most widely used job evaluation method, the point method, breaks jobs down into various compensable factors and places weights, or *points,* on them. A compensable factor identifies a job value commonly present throughout a group of jobs. Compensable factors are derived from the job analysis and reflect the nature of different types of jobs.

A special type of point method, the *Hay system,* uses three factors and numerically measures the degree to which each of these factors is required in a job. The three factors are *know-how, problem-solving ability,* and *accountability.*

The point method is the most popular because it is relatively simple to use and it considers the components of a job rather than the total job. However, point systems have been criticized for reinforcing traditional organizational structures.

Legal Issues and Job Evaluation. Because job evaluation affects the employment relationship, specifically the pay of individuals, some legal issues are a concern. Critics have charged that traditional job evaluation programs place less weight on knowledge, skills, and working conditions for many female-dominated jobs in office and clerical areas than on the same factors for male-dominated jobs in craft and manufacturing areas. Employers counter that because they base their pay rates heavily on external equity comparisons in the labor market, they are simply reflecting rates the "market economy" sets for jobs and workers, rather than discriminating on the basis of gender.

Valuing Jobs Using Market Pricing

A growing number of employers have scaled back their use of "internal valuation" through traditional job evaluation methods. They have instead switched to market pricing, which uses market pay data to identify the relative value of jobs based on what other employers pay for similar jobs. Jobs are arranged in groups tied directly to similar survey data amounts.

Key to market pricing is identifying relevant market pay data for jobs that are good "matches" with the employer's jobs, geographic considerations, and company strategies and philosophies about desired market competitiveness levels. That is why some firms have used market pricing as part of strategic decisions in order to ensure market competitiveness of their compensation levels and practices.

Advantages of Market Pricing.   The primary advantage cited for the use of market pricing is that it closely ties organizational pay levels to what is actually occurring in the market, without being distorted by "internal" job evaluation. An additional advantage of market pricing is that it allows an employer to communicate to employees that the compensation system is truly "market linked," rather than sometimes being distorted by internal issues. Employees often see a compensation system that was developed using market pricing as having "face validity" and as being more objective than a compensation system that was developed using the traditional job evaluation methods.[4]

Disadvantages of Market Pricing.   The foremost disadvantage of market pricing is that for numerous jobs, pay survey data are limited or may not be gathered in methodologically sound ways. A closely related problem is that the responsibilities of a specific job in a company may be somewhat different from those of the "matching" job identified in the survey.

Finally, tying pay levels to market data can lead to wide fluctuations based on market conditions. For evidence of this, one has only to look back at the extremes of the information technology job market during the past decade, when pay levels varied significantly. For these and other types of jobs, the debate over the use of job evaluation versus market pricing is likely to continue because both approaches have pluses and minuses associated with them.

Pay Surveys

A pay survey is a collection of data on compensation rates for workers performing similar jobs in other organizations. Both job evaluation and market pricing are tied to surveys of the pay that other organizations provide for similar jobs.

Because jobs may vary widely in an organization, it is particularly important to identify benchmark jobs—ones that are found in many other organizations. Often these jobs are performed by individuals who have similar duties that require similar KSAs. For example, benchmark jobs commonly used in clerical/office situations are accounts payable processor, customer service representative, and receptionist. **Benchmark jobs** are used because they provide "anchors" against which individual jobs can be compared.

An employer may obtain surveys conducted by other organizations, access Internet data, or conduct its own survey. Many different surveys are available from a variety of sources.

Using Pay Surveys.   The proper use of pay surveys requires evaluating a number of factors to determine if the data are relevant and valid. The following questions should be answered for each survey:

- *Participants:* Does the survey cover a realistic sample of the employers with whom the organization competes for employees?
- *Broad-based:* Does the survey include data from employers of different sizes, industries, and locales?
- *Timeliness:* How current are the data (determined by the date the survey was conducted)?
- *Methodology:* How established is the survey, and how qualified are those who conducted it?
- *Job matches:* Does the survey contain job summaries so that appropriate matches to job descriptions can be made?

Pay Surveys and Legal Issues.   One reason for employers to use outside sources for pay surveys is to avoid charges that the employers are attempting "price fixing" on wages. One such case involved an HR group and nine hospitals in the Salt Lake City area. The consent decree that resulted prohibited healthcare facilities in Utah from cooperating when developing or conducting a wage survey. The hospitals can participate in surveys conducted by independent third-party firms only if privacy safeguards are met. Cases in several industries have alleged that by sharing wage data, the employers attempted to hold wages down artificially, in violation of the Sherman Antitrust Act.

··

Pay Structures

Once job valuations and pay survey data are gathered, pay structures can be developed using the process identified in Figure 7-3. Data from the valuation of jobs and the pay surveys may lead to the establishment of several different pay structures for different job families, rather than just one structure for all jobs. A job family is a group of jobs having common organizational characteristics. Organizations can have a number of different job families. Examples of some

FIGURE 7-3 Establishing Pay Structures

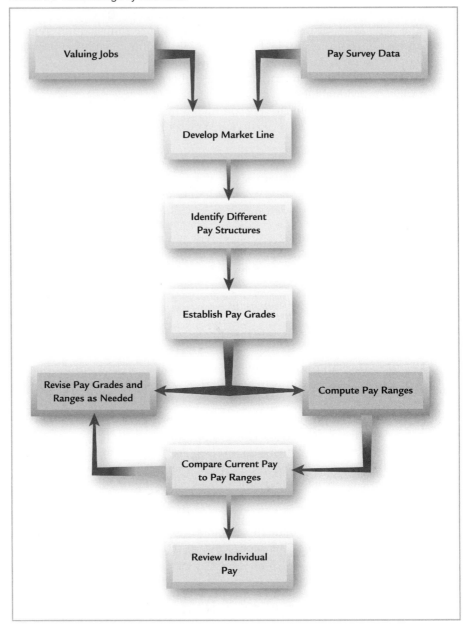

common pay structures based on different job families include: (1) hourly and salaried; (2) office, plant, technical, professional, and managerial; and (3) clerical, information technology, professional, supervisory, management, and executive. The nature, culture, and structure of the organization are considerations for determining how many and which pay structures to have.

Pay Grades

In the process of establishing a pay structure, organizations use pay grades to group individual jobs having approximately the same job worth. Although no set rules govern the establishment of pay grades, some overall suggestions can be useful. Generally, 11 to 17 grades are used in small and medium-sized companies, such as companies with fewer than 500 to 1,000 employees. Two methods are commonly used to establish pay grades: job evaluation data and use of job market banding.

Setting Pay Grades Using Job Evaluation Points.   The second approach to determining pay grades uses job evaluation points or other data generated from the traditional job evaluation methods discussed earlier in the chapter. This process ties pay survey information to job evaluation data by plotting a market line that shows the relationship between job value as determined by job evaluation points and job value as determined by pay survey rates. The statistical analysis done when determining market lines particularly focuses on the r^2 levels from the regression when the data are analyzed by different job families and groups. Generally, an r^2 of 0.85 or higher is desired. A market line uses data to group jobs having similar point values into pay grades. Pay ranges can then be computed for each pay grade.

Setting Pay Grades Using Market Banding.   Closely linked to the use of market pricing to value jobs, market banding groups jobs into pay grades based on similar market survey amounts. The midpoint of the survey average is used to develop pay range minimums and maximums. Market banding is becoming much more prevalant than job pointing in many firms.

Pay Ranges

The pay range for each pay grade also must be established. Using the market line as a starting point, the employer can determine minimum and maximum pay levels for each pay grade by making the market line the midpoint line of the new pay structure (see Figure 7-4). For example, in a particular pay grade, the maximum value may be 20% above the midpoint located on the market line, and the minimum value may be 20% below it. Once pay grades and ranges have been computed, then the current pay of employees must be compared with the draft ranges. A growing number of employers are reducing the number of pay grades and expanding pay ranges by broadbanding.

Broadbanding.   Broadbanding is the practice of using fewer pay grades with much broader ranges than in traditional compensation systems. Combining many grades into these broadbands is designed to encourage horizontal movement and therefore more skill acquisition. About one-quarter of all employers in one survey were using broadbanding.[5] The main advantage of broadbanding is that it is more consistent with the flattening of organizational levels and the growing use of jobs that are multi-dimensional. The primary reasons for using broadbanding are: (1) to create more flexible organizations, (2) to encourage competency development, and (3) to emphasize career development.

FIGURE 7-4 Example of Pay Grades and Pay Ranges

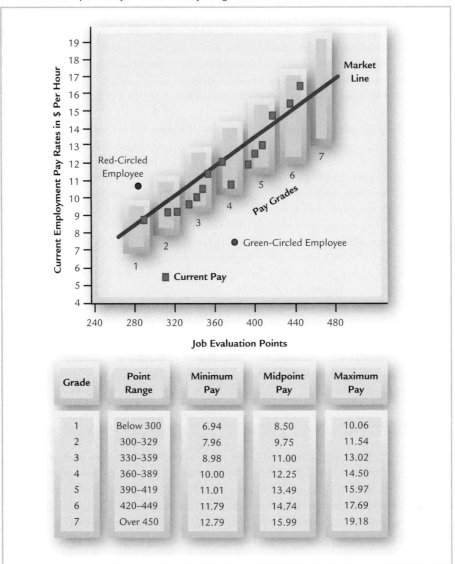

Grade	Point Range	Minimum Pay	Midpoint Pay	Maximum Pay
1	Below 300	6.94	8.50	10.06
2	300–329	7.96	9.75	11.54
3	330–359	8.98	11.00	13.02
4	360–389	10.00	12.25	14.50
5	390–419	11.01	13.49	15.97
6	420–449	11.79	14.74	17.69
7	Over 450	12.79	15.99	19.18

A problem with broadbanding is that many employees expect a promotion to be accompanied by a pay raise and movement to a new pay grade. As a result of removing this grade progression, the organization may be seen as offering fewer upward promotion opportunities. An additional concern identified by broadbanding of information technology (IT) jobs is that it can significantly impact salary levels and costs. Therefore, HR must closely monitor the effects of broadbanding. Despite these and other problems, it is likely that broadbanding will continue to grow in usage.

Individual Pay

Once managers have determined pay ranges, they can set the pay for specific individuals. Setting a range for each pay grade gives flexibility by allowing individuals to progress within a grade instead of having to move to a new grade each time they receive a raise. A pay range also allows managers to reward the better-performing employees while maintaining the integrity of the pay system. Regardless of how well a pay structure is constructed, there usually are a few individuals whose pay is lower than the minimum or higher than the maximum due to past pay practices and different levels of experience and performance. Two types are discussed next.

Red-Circled Employees.   A **red-circled employee** is an incumbent who is paid above the range set for the job. For example, assume that an employee's current pay is $10.92 an hour, but the pay range for that person's pay grade is $6.94 to $10.06 an hour. The person would be red circled. Management would try over a year or so to bring the employee's rate into grade.

Several approaches can be used to bring a red-circled person's pay into line. Although the fastest way would be to cut the employee's pay, that approach is not recommended and is seldom used. Instead, the employee's pay may be frozen until the pay range can be adjusted upward to get the employee's pay rate back into the grade. Another approach is to give the employee a small lump-sum payment but not adjust the pay rate when others are given raises.

Green-Circled Employees.   An individual whose pay is below the range is a **green-circled** employee. Promotion is a major contributor to this situation. Generally, it is recommended that the green-circled individual receive fairly rapid pay increases to reach the pay grade minimum. More frequent increases can be used if the minimum is a large amount above the incumbent's current pay.

Pay Compression.   One major problem many employers face is **pay compression**, which occurs when the pay differences among individuals with different levels of experience and performance become small. Pay compression occurs for a number of reasons, but the major one involves situations in which labor market pay levels increase more rapidly than current employees' pay adjustments.

In response to shortages of particular job skills in a highly competitive labor market, managers may occasionally have to pay higher amounts to hire people with those scarce skills. For example, suppose the job of specialized information systems analyst is identified as a $48,000 to $68,000 salary range in one company, but qualified individuals are in short supply and other employers are paying $70,000. To fill the job, the firm likely will have to pay the higher rate. Suppose also that several analysts who have been with the firm for several years started at $55,000 and have received 4% increases each year. These current employees may still be making less than the $70,000 paid to attract and retain new analysts from outside with less experience. One partial solution to pay compression is to have employees follow a step progression based on length of service, assuming performance is satisfactory or better. Other approaches are to provide better performers with higher raises, use project incentives, and adjust pay ranges more often. But addressing pay compression is crucial.

Determining Pay Increases

Decisions about pay increases are often critical ones in the relationships between employees, their managers, and the organization. Individuals express expectations about their pay and about how much of an increase is "fair," especially in comparison with the increases received by other employees. There are several ways to determine pay increases: performance, seniority, cost-of-living adjustments, across-the-board increases, and lump-sum increases. These methods can be used separately or in combination.

Performance-Based Increases

As mentioned earlier, a growing number of employers have shifted to more pay-for-performance philosophies and strategies. Consequently, they have adopted various means to provide employees with performance-based increases.

Targeting High Performers.   This approach focuses on providing the top performing employees with significantly higher pay raises. Some organizations target the top 10% of employees for significantly greater increases while providing more standard increases to the remaining satisfactory performers. According to a survey by Hewitt Associates in a recent year, average raises for the best performers were 9.9%, satisfactory performers got 3.6%, and low performers got 0% to 1.3%.[6]

The primary reason for having such significant differentials focuses on rewarding and retaining the critical high-performing individuals. Key to rewarding exceptional performers is identifying what their accomplishments have been above the normal work expectations. The more "standard" increases for the average performers are usually aligned with labor market pay adjustments, so that those individuals are kept competitive. The lower performers are given less because of their performance issues, which "encourages" them to leave their organizations.

Pay Adjustment Matrix.   Some system for integrating appraisals and pay changes must be developed and applied equally. Often, this integration is done through the development of a *pay adjustment matrix,* or *salary guide chart.* Use of pay adjustment matrices bases adjustments in part on a person's **compa-ratio,** which is the pay level divided by the midpoint of the pay range. To illustrate, the compa-ratio for an employee would be:

$$\text{Employee } J = \frac{\$13.35 \text{ (current pay)}}{\$15.00 \text{ (midpoint)}} \times 100 = 89 \text{ (Compa-ratio)}$$

Salary guide charts reflect a person's upward movement in an organization. That movement often depends on the person's performance, as rated in an appraisal, and on the person's position in the pay range, which has some relation to experience as well. A person's placement on the chart determines what pay raise the person should receive. According to the chart shown in Figure 7-5, if employee *J* is rated as exceeding expectations (3) with a compa-ratio of 89, that person is eligible for a raise of 7% to 9%.

Two interesting facets of the sample matrix illustrate the emphasis on paying for performance. First, individuals whose performance is below expectations receive small to no raises. This approach sends a strong signal that poor performers will not continue to receive increases just by completing another year of service.

Second, as employees move up the pay range, they must exhibit higher performance to obtain the same percentage raise as those lower in the range performing at the "Meets Performance Expectations" level (see Figure 7-5). This approach is taken because the firm is paying above the market midpoint but receiving only satisfactory performance rather than above-market performance.

FIGURE 7-5 Pay Adjustment Matrix

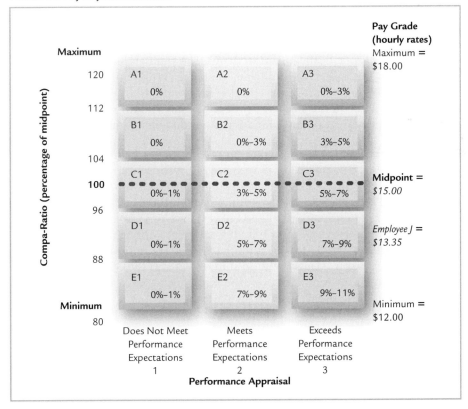

Charts can be constructed to reflect the specific pay-for-performance policies and philosophy in an organization.

Standardized Pay Adjustments

Several different methods are used to provide standardized pay increases to the employees which typically are not based on performance. The most common ones are discussed next.

Seniority.   Seniority, or time spent in the organization or on a particular job, can be used as the basis for pay increases. Many employers have policies that require a person to be employed for a certain length of time before being eligible for pay increases. Pay adjustments based on seniority often are set as automatic steps once a person has been employed the required length of time, although performance must be at least satisfactory in many non-union systems.

Cost-of-Living Adjustments.   A common pay-raise practice is the use of a *cost-of-living adjustment (COLA)*. Often, these adjustments are tied to changes in the Consumer Price Index (CPI) or some other general economic measure. However, numerous studies have revealed that the CPI overstates the actual cost of living.

Across-the-Board Increases.   Unfortunately, some employers give across-the-board raises and call them *merit raises,* which they are not. Usually the percentage raise is based on standard market percentage changes, or financial budgeting determinations not specifically linked to the COLA. If all employees get the same percentage pay increase, it is legitimately viewed as having little to do with merit or good performance. For this reason, employers should reserve the term *merit* for any amount above the standard raise, and they should state clearly which amount is for performance and which is the "automatic" amount.

Lump-Sum Increases.   Most employees who receive pay increases, either for merit or for seniority, first receive an increase in the amount of their regular monthly or weekly paycheck. For example, an employee who makes $12.00 an hour and then receives a 3% increase will move to $12.36 an hour.

In contrast, a lump-sum increase (LSI) is a one-time payment of all or part of a yearly pay increase. The pure LSI approach does not increase the base pay. Therefore, in the example of a person making $12.00 an hour, if an LSI of 3% is granted, the person receives a lump sum of $748.80 ($0.36 an hour × 2,080 working hours in the year). However, the base rate remains at $12.00 an hour, which slows down the progression of the base wages.

An LSI plan offers advantages and disadvantages. The major advantage of an LSI plan is that it heightens employees' awareness of what their performance levels "merited." Another advantage is that the firm can use LSIs to slow down the increase of base pay and thus reduce or avoid the compounding effect on succeeding raises. One disadvantage of LSI plans is that workers who take a lump-sum payment may become discouraged because their base pay has not changed.

Unions generally resist LSI programs because of their impact on pensions and benefits, unless the total amount used in those computations includes the LSI.

....

Executive Compensation

Many organizations, especially large ones, administer compensation for the executives differently from compensation for lower-level employees. At the heart of most executive compensation plans is the idea that executives should be rewarded if the organization grows in profitability and value over a period of years. Therefore, variable pay distributed through different types of incentives is a significant part of executive compensation.

Elements of Executive Compensation

Because high-salaried executives are in higher tax brackets, many executive compensation packages are designed to offer significant tax savings. These savings occur through use of deferred compensation methods whereby taxes are not due until after the executives leave the firm.

Executive Salaries and Benefits.   Salaries of executives vary by job type, size of employer, the industry, and other factors. In contrast, in large corporations, salaries may constitute a small part of the total package. Survey data on executive salaries are often reviewed by Boards of Directors to ensure that their organizations are competitive. Many executives are covered by *regular benefits plans* that are also available to non-executive employees, including traditional retirement, health insurance, and vacation plans. In addition, executives may receive *supplemental benefits* that other employees do not receive. For example, executive health plans with no co-payments and with no limitations on deductibles or physician choice are popular among small and middle-size businesses. Corporate-owned insurance on the life of the executive is also popular; this insurance pays both the executive's estate and the company in the event of death. One supplemental benefit that has grown in popularity is company-paid financial planning for executives. Trusts of various kinds may be designed by the company to help the executives deal with estate-planning and tax issues. Deferred compensation is another possible means of helping executives with tax liabilities caused by incentive compensation plans.

Executive Perquisites (Perks).   In addition to the regular benefits received by all employees, executives often receive benefits called perquisites. Perquisites (perks) are special benefits—usually non-cash items—for executives. Many executives value the status enhancement of these visible symbols, which allow them to be seen as "very important people" both inside and outside their organizations. Perks can also offer substantial tax savings because some of them are not taxed as income. Some commonly used executive perks are company cars, health club and country club memberships, first-class air travel, use of private jets, stress counseling, and chauffeur services.

Annual Executive Incentives and Bonuses.   Annual incentives and bonuses for executives can be determined in several ways. One way is to use a discretionary system whereby the CEO and the Board of Directors decide bonuses; the absence of formal, measurable targets detracts significantly from this approach. Another way is to tie bonuses to specific measures, such as return on investment, earnings per share, and net profits before taxes. More complex systems create bonus pools and thresholds above which bonuses are computed. Whatever method is used, it is important to describe it so that executives attempting to earn additional compensation understand the plan; otherwise, the incentive effect will be diminished.

Performance Incentives: Long Term vs. Short Term.   Use of executive performance-based incentives tries to tie executive compensation to the long-term growth and success of the organization. However, whether these incentives really emphasize the long term or merely represent a series of short-term rewards is controversial. Short-term rewards based on quarterly or annual performance may not result in the kind of long-run-oriented decisions necessary for the company to perform well over multiple years.

As would be expected, the total amount of pay-for-performance incentives varies by management level, with CEOs receiving significantly more than subsidiary or other senior managers. The typical CEO gets about half of all the total incentives paid to all senior managers and executives put together.

The most widely used long-term incentives are stock option plans. A *stock option* gives employees the right to buy stock in a company, usually at an advantageous price. Despite the prevalence of such plans, research has found little relationship between providing CEOs with stock options and subsequent firm performance.[7] Because of the numerous corporate scandals involving executives at Enron, WorldCom, Tyco, and elsewhere who received outrageously high compensation due to stock options and the backdating of those options, the use of stock options has been changing. Instead, more firms with publicly-traded stock are using means such as *restricted stock, phantom stock, performance shares*, and other specialized technical forms, which are beyond the scope of this discussion.

Another outcome of the recent corporate abuses by executives was passage of the Sarbanes-Oxley Act. This act has provisions that have affected the accounting and financial reporting requirements of different types of executive compensation. Also, the Financial Accounting Standards Board (FASB) has adopted rules regarding the expensing of stock options.

"Reasonableness" of Executive Compensation

The notion that monetary incentives tied to performance result in improved performance makes sense to most people. However, there is an ongoing debate about whether executive compensation in the United States is truly linked to performance. This is particularly of concern given the astronomical amounts of some executive compensation packages.

The reasonableness of executive compensation is often justified by comparison to compensation market surveys, but these surveys usually provide a range of compensation data that requires interpretation. Various questions have been suggested for determining if executive pay is "reasonable," including the following useful ones:

- Would another company hire this person as an executive?
- How does the executive's compensation compare with that for executives in similar companies in the industry?
- Is the executive's pay consistent with pay for other employees within the company?
- What would an investor pay for the level of performance of the executive?

A final question is tied to the customer loyalty dimension of CEO performance. Customers are asked "On a scale of 1 to 10 how likely is it that you would recommend us to your friends or colleagues?" The difference between the percentage of customers who give high responses and those who give low scores correlates highly with a company's revenue growth and can be used to measure one part of executive performance.[8]

Linkage Between Executive Compensation and Corporate Performance.
Of all the executive compensation issues that are debated, the one discussed most frequently is whether or not executive compensation levels are sufficiently linked to organizational performance. One key aspect of evaluating all the studies on this topic is the performance measures used. Numerous studies have examined different facets of this topic.[9] In many settings, financial measures such as return on equity, return to shareholders earnings per share, and net income before taxes are used to measure performance. However, a number of firms also incorporate non-financial organizational measures of performance when determining executive bonuses and incentives. Customer satisfaction, employee satisfaction, market share, productivity, and quality are other areas measured for executive performance rewards.

Measurement of executive performance varies from firm to firm. Some executive compensation packages use a short-term focus of one year, which may lead to large rewards for executive performance in a given year even though corporate performance over a multi-year period is mediocre. This difference is especially pronounced if the yearly measures are carefully chosen. Executives can even manipulate earnings per share by selling assets, liquidating inventories, or reducing research and development expenditures. All of these actions may make organizational performance look better, but they may also impair the long-term growth of the organization.

A number of other executive compensation issues and concerns exist. Figure 7-6 highlights the criticisms and counter-arguments of some common points of contention. One of the more controversial issues is that some executives seem to get large awards for negative actions. It seems contradictory from an employee's perspective to reward executives who often improve corporate results by cutting staff, laying off employees, changing pension plans, or increasing the deductible on the health insurance. But sometimes cost-cutting measures are necessary to keep a company afloat. However, a sense of reasonableness may be appropriate too; if rank-and-file employees suffer, giving bonuses and large payouts to executives appears counterproductive and even hypocritical.

FIGURE 7-6 Common Executive Compensation Criticisms

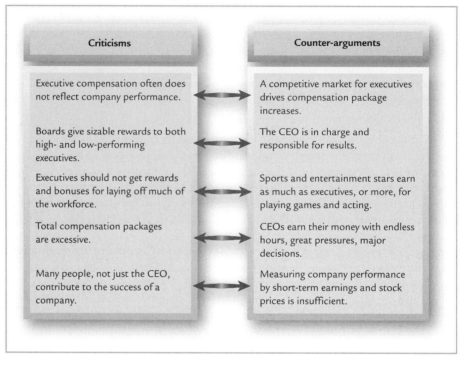

Criticisms	Counter-arguments
Executive compensation often does not reflect company performance.	A competitive market for executives drives compensation package increases.
Boards give sizable rewards to both high- and low-performing executives.	The CEO is in charge and responsible for results.
Executives should not get rewards and bonuses for laying off much of the workforce.	Sports and entertainment stars earn as much as executives, or more, for playing games and acting.
Total compensation packages are excessive.	CEOs earn their money with endless hours, great pressures, major decisions.
Many people, not just the CEO, contribute to the success of a company.	Measuring company performance by short-term earnings and stock prices is insufficient.

Executive Compensation and Boards of Directors.   In most organizations, the Board of Directors is the major policy-setting entity and must approve executive compensation packages. The compensation committee usually is a subgroup of the board, composed of directors who are not officers of the firm. Compensation committees generally make recommendations to the Board of Directors on overall pay policies, salaries for top officers, supplemental compensation such as stock options and bonuses, and additional perquisites for executives.

Increasingly, the independence of these committees has been criticized. One major concern voiced by many critics is that the base pay and bonuses of CEOs are often set by the members of board compensation committees, many of whom are CEOs of other companies with similar compensation packages. Also, the compensation advisors and consultants to the CEOs often collect large fees, and critics charge that those fees distort the objectivity of the advice given.

To counter criticism, some corporations have changed the composition of the compensation committees by taking actions such as prohibiting "insider" company officers from serving on them. Also, some firms have empowered the compensation committees to hire and pay compensation consultants without involving executive management. Finally, a tool called a "tally sheet" can provide the board with a fuller picture of a chief's entire compensation package.

NOTES

1. Edward E. Lawler III, "Pay Practice in *Fortune 1000* Corporations," *WorldatWork Journal,* Fourth Quarter 2003, 45–54.
2. For details of various compensation surveys and studies, go to *www.salary.com.*
3. David Neumark, "Detecting Effects of Living Wage Laws," *Industrial Relations,* 42(2003), 531–565.
4. Kimberly Merriman, "A Fairness Approach to Market-Based Pay," *Workspan,* March 2006, 48–50.
5. Mercer Human Resource Consulting, *2006 Compensation Planning Survey* (New York: Mercer Corporation, 2006).
6. Erin White, "The Best vs. the Rest." *The Wall Street Journal,* January 30, 2006, B1.
7. For example, see Scott Thurm, "Extra Pay: Many CEO's Receive Dividends on 'Phantom' Stock," *The Wall Street Journal,* May 4, 2006, 1; and Joann S. Lublin, "Boards Tie CEO Pay More Tightly to Performance." *The Wall Street Journal,* February 21, 2006, A1.
8. Jena McGregor, "Would You Recommend Us?" *Business Week,* January 30, 2006, 94–96.
9. For example, see James J. Corderio and Rajaram Viliyath, "Beyond Pay for Performance: A Panel Study of the Determinants of CEO Compensation." *American Business Review,* 21 (2003), 57–67; and Dan Dalton et al., "Meta-Analyses of Financial Performance and Equity: Fusion or Confusion?" *Academy of Management Journal,* 46(2003), 13–26.

INTERNET RESOURCES

Economic Research Institute—For resources on salary surveys, link to this site at: *www.trieri.com.*

The Riley Guide—For a directory of information resources and services on executive compensation, link to their Website at: *www.rileyguide.com/execpay.html*

SUGGESTED READINGS

Richard I. Henderson, *Compensation Management in a Knowledge-Based World,* 10th ed. (Prentice Hall, 2006).

Steve Balsam, *Executive Compensation.* (WorldatWork Press 2007).

G. Milkovich and J. Newman, *Compensation* 9th ed. (McGraw-Hill, Irwin, 2007).

The WorldatWork Handbook of Compensation, Benefits, and Total Rewards, (Wiley, 2007).

CHAPTER 8

Variable Pay and Benefits

HR—MEETING MANAGEMENT CHALLENGES

Variable pay and benefits offer employers opportunities to increase productivity and retention respectively. The opportunities presented by incentives and benefits will be present only if employers understand how they can work and their drawbacks. It is important to consider the following:

- Individual, group, and organization incentives can increase motivation
- Sales compensation provides opportunities to increase sales
- Benefits can be designed to fit the company's strategy

Tying pay to performance holds a promise that employers and employees both find attractive. For employees it can mean more pay and for employers it can mean more output per employee and therefore more productivity. However, it is much more difficult to design a successful incentive system than to simply pay employees hourly or with a set salary.

Pay for performance is being utilized by a growing number of employers. In today's competitive global economy, many employers believe that people become more productive if compensation varies directly according to their performance. Employers are adding to their traditional base pay programs by offering employees additional compensation tied to performance. The amount of payment varies based on the degree to which individual, group/team, and/or organizational performance goals are attained.

Benefits are given to workers for being part of the organization. A benefit is an indirect reward given to an employee or a group of employees for organizational membership. Benefits often include retirement plans, vacations with pay, health insurance, educational assistance, and many more programs.

In the United States, employers often fill the role of major provider of benefits for citizens. In many other nations, citizens and employers are taxed to pay for government-provided benefits, such as health-care and retirement programs. Although federal regulations require U.S. employers to provide certain benefits, U.S. employers voluntarily provide many others. First, variable pay will be considered.

Variable Pay: Incentives for Performance

Variable pay is compensation linked to individual, group/team, and/or organizational performance. Traditionally also known as *incentives,* variable pay plans attempt to provide tangible rewards to employees for performance beyond normal expectations. The philosophical foundation of variable pay rests on several basic assumptions:

- Some people perform better and are more productive than others.
- Employees who perform better should receive more compensation.
- Some of employees' total compensation should be tied directly to performance and results.
- Some jobs contribute more to organizational success than others.

Pay for performance has a different philosophical base than does the traditional compensation system, in which differences in job responsibilities are recognized through different amounts of base pay. In many organizations, length of service is a primary differentiating factor. However, giving additional rewards to some people and not others is seen as potentially divisive and as hampering employees' working together. These thoughts are part of the reason why many labor unions oppose pay-for-performance programs. In contrast, however, high-performing workers expect extra rewards for outstanding performance that increases organizational results.

Incentives can take many forms from simple praise, to "recognition and reward" programs that award trips and merchandise, to bonuses for performance accomplishments or for successful results for the company. Forty-nine percent of organizations have incentive programs for their employees.[1] The variety of possibilities, shown in Figure 8-1, are discussed later.

How well do incentive programs work? It varies from employer to employer, but one study found that a signifigant number of employees are unhappy with their company's incentive program. As a result employers change the programs by revising the measures, increasing goals, increasing awards, etc.

Developing Successful Pay-for-Performance Plans

Employers adopt variable pay or incentive plans for a number of reasons. Variable pay plans can be considered successful if they meet the objectives the organization had for them when they were initiated. The main ones include desires to do the following:

- Link strategic business goals and employee performance.
- Enhance organizational results and reward employees financially for their contributions.
- Reward employees and recognize different levels of employee performance.
- Achieve HR objectives, such as increasing retention, reducing turnover, recognizing training, or rewarding safety.

FIGURE 8-1 Examples of Incentives

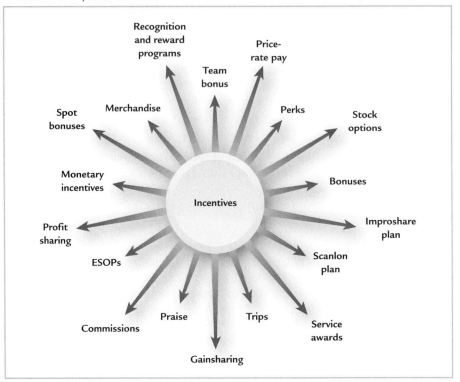

Metrics for Variable Pay Plans

The results of variable pay plans, like those in other areas of HR, should be measured to determine the success of the programs. Different measures of success can be used, depending on the nature of the plan and the goals set for it. An employer can start by deciding what it wants an incentive program to accomplish and then devise measures against which to check the outcomes.

A common metric for incentive plans is return on investment (ROI). For example, a company may consider a program that provides rewards in a lottery drawing each month for those employees who were not absent during that month will reduce absenteeism. An ROI metric would look at the dollar value of the improvement minus the cost of the program divided by the total cost. So if the reduction in absenteeism cost was $100,000 per year, but the program costs were $85,000, calculations would be $(100,000 - 85,000) \div 85,000$, or a bit more than a 17% return on the investment of $85,000 in the program.

Successes and Failures of Variable Pay Plans

Even though variable pay has grown in popularity, some attempts to implement it have succeeded and others have not. Incentives *do* work, but they are not a panacea because their success depends on multiple factors.

The positive view that many employers have of variable pay is not shared universally by all employees. If individuals see incentives as desirable, they are more likely to put forth the extra effort to attain the performance objectives that trigger the incentive payouts, but not all employees believe that they are rewarded when doing a good job. One problem is that some employees prefer that performance rewards increase their base pay, rather than be given as a one-time, lump-sum payment. Further, many employees prefer individual rewards to group/team or organizational incentives.

Given these underlying dynamics, providing variable pay plans that are successful can be complex and requires significant, continuing efforts. Figure 8-2 shows the three categories of variable pay plans. Some suggestions that appear to contribute to successful incentive plans are as follows:

- Develop clear, understandable plans that are continually communicated.
- Use realistic performance measures.
- Keep the plans current and linked to organizational objectives.
- Clearly link performance results to payouts that truly recognize performance differences.
- Identify variable pay incentives separately from base pay.

Individual Incentives

Individual incentive systems try to tie individual effort to additional rewards. Different types of individual incentive plans are discussed next.

Piece-Rate Systems.   The most basic individual incentive systems are piece-rate systems, whether straight or differential. Under a straight piece-rate system, wages are determined by multiplying the number of units produced (such as garments sewn or service calls handled) by the piece rate for one unit. Because the cost is the same for each unit, the wage for each employee is easy to figure, and labor costs can be accurately predicted.

FIGURE 8-2 Categories of Variable Pay Plans

A *differential piece-rate system* pays employees one piece-rate wage for units produced up to a standard output and a higher piece-rate wage for units produced over the standard. Managers often determine the quotas or standards by using time and motion studies. For example, assume that the standard quota for a worker is set at 300 units per day and the standard rate is 14 cents per unit. For all units over the standard, however, the employee receives 20 cents per unit. Under this system, the worker who produces 400 units in one day would get $62 in pay $(300 \times 14¢) + (100 \times 20¢)$. Many possible combinations of straight and differential piece-rate systems can be used, depending on situational factors.

Despite their incentive value, piece-rate systems are difficult to apply because determining standards is a complex and costly process for many types of jobs. In some instances, the cost of determining and maintaining the standards may be greater than the benefits derived. Also, jobs in which individuals have limited control over output or in which high standards of quality are necessary may be unsuited to piecework.

Bonuses.   Individual employees may receive additional compensation in the form of a **bonus**, which is a one-time payment that does not become part of the employee's base pay. Growing in popularity, individual bonuses are used at all levels in some firms.

A bonus can recognize performance by an employee, a team, or the organization as a whole. When performance results are good, bonuses go up. When performance results are not met, bonuses go down. Most employers base part of an employee's bonus on individual performance and part on company results, as appropriate.

Special Incentive Programs.   Numerous special incentive programs can be used to reward individuals, ranging from one-time contests for meeting performance targets to awards for performance over time. For instance, safe-driving awards are given to truck drivers with no accidents or violations on their records during a year. Although special programs can be developed for groups and for entire organizations, they often focus on rewarding high-performing individuals.

Group/Team Incentives

The use of groups/teams in organizations has implications for compensation. Although the use of groups/teams has increased substantially in the past few years, the question of how to compensate their members equitably remains a significant challenge. According to several studies, about 80% of large firms provide rewards for work groups or teams in some different ways.[2]

Team incentives can be cash bonuses for the team or they can take a form other than money, such as merchandise or trips. But group incentive situations may place social pressure on members of the group. Everyone in the group succeeds or fails. Therefore, individuals could argue that team incentives should be given to team members equally, although not everyone would agree.

Several decisions about how to distribute and allocate the group/team rewards must be made. The two primary ways for distributing those rewards are as follows:

1. *Same-size reward for each member:* With this approach, all members receive the same payout, regardless of job level, current pay, seniority, or individual performance differences.

2. *Different-size reward for each member:* With this approach, employers vary individual rewards depending on such factors as contribution to group/team results, current pay, years of experience, and skill levels of jobs performed.

Generally, managers view the concept of people working in groups/teams as beneficial. But to a large extent, many employees still expect to be paid according to individual performance. Until this individualism is recognized and compensation programs that are viewed as more equitable by more "team members" are developed, caution should be used when creating and implementing group/team incentives. The two most frequently used types of group/team incentives situations are work team results and gainsharing.

Group/Team Results.   Pay plans for groups/teams may reward all members equally on the basis of group output, cost savings, or quality improvement. The design of most group/team incentives is based on a "self-funding" principle, which means that the money to be used as incentive rewards is obtained through improvement of organizational results. A good example is gainsharing, which can be extended within a group or plantwide.

Gainsharing.   The system of sharing with employees greater-than-expected gains in profits and/or productivity is gainsharing. Also called *teamsharing* or *goalsharing*, the focus is to increase "discretionary efforts," that is, the difference between the maximum amount of effort a person can exert and the minimum amount of effort that person needs to exert to keep from being fired. Workers in many organizations are not paid for discretionary efforts, but are paid to meet the minimum acceptable level of effort required. When workers do demonstrate discretionary efforts, the organization can afford to pay them more than the going rate, because the extra efforts produce financial gains over and above the returns of minimal efforts. Some organizations have labeled their programs *goalsharing* to emphasize the attainment of results based on business strategy objectives.

To develop and implement a gainsharing or goalsharing plan, management must identify the ways in which increased productivity, quality, and financial performance can occur and decide how some of the resulting gains should be shared with employees. Often, measures such as labor costs, overtime hours, and quality benchmarks are used. Both organizational measures and departmental measures may be used, with the weights for gainsharing split between the two categories. Plans frequently require that an individual must exhibit satisfactory performance to receive the gainsharing payments.

Organizational Incentives

An organizational incentive system compensates all employees in the organization according to how well the organization as a whole performs during the year. The basic concept behind organizational incentive plans is that overall results may depend on organization-wide or plantwide cooperation. The purpose of these plans is to produce better results by rewarding cooperation throughout the organization. For example, conflict between marketing and production can be overcome if management uses an incentive system that emphasizes organization-wide profit and productivity. To be effective, an organizational incentive program should include everyone from non-exempt employees to managers and executives. Two common organizational incentive systems are profit sharing and employee stock plans.

Profit Sharing.   As the name implies, profit sharing distributes some portion of organizational profits to employees. The primary objectives of profit-sharing plans include the following:

- Increase productivity and organizational performance.
- Attract or retain employees.
- Improve product/service quality.
- Enhance employee morale.

Typically, the percentage of the profits distributed to employees is set by the end of the year before distribution. In some profit-sharing plans, employees receive portions of the profits at the end of the year; in others, the profits are deferred, placed in a fund, and made available to employees on retirement or on their departure from the organization.

When used throughout an organization, including with lower-echelon workers, profit-sharing plans can have some drawbacks. First, employees must trust that management will disclose accurate financial and profit information. As many people know, both the definition and level of profit can depend on the accounting system used and on decisions made. To be credible, management must be willing to disclose sufficient financial and profit information to alleviate the skepticism of employees, particularly if profit-sharing levels fall from those of previous years. Second, profits may vary a great deal from year to year, resulting in windfalls or losses beyond the employees' control. Third, payoffs are generally far removed by time from employees' efforts and, therefore, higher rewards may not be strongly linked to better performance.

Employee Stock Plans.   Two types of organizational incentive plans use employer stock ownership to reward employees. The goal of these plans is to get employees to think and act like "owners."[3]

A **stock option plan** gives employees the right to purchase a fixed number of shares of company stock at a specified exercise price for a limited period of time. If the market price of the stock exceeds the exercise price, employees can then exercise the option and buy the stock. The number of firms giving stock options to non-executives has declined some in recent years, primarily due to changing laws and accounting regulations.

An employee stock ownership plan (ESOP) is designed to give employees significant stock ownership in their employers. Establishing an ESOP creates several advantages. The major one is that the firm can receive favorable tax treatment on the earnings earmarked for use in the ESOP. Another is that an ESOP gives employees a "piece of the action" so that they can share in the growth and profitability of their firm. Employee ownership may motivate employees to be more productive and focused on organizational performance.

Many people approve of the concept of employee ownership as a kind of "people's capitalism." However, the sharing can also be a disadvantage for employees because it makes both their wages/salaries and their retirement benefits dependent on the performance of their employers.

··

Sales Compensation

The compensation paid to employees involved with sales and marketing is partly or entirely tied to individual sales performance. Salespeople who sell more can receive more total compensation than those who sell less. Sales incentives are perhaps the most widely used individual incentives. The intent is to stimulate more effort from salespeople to earn more money.

A number of legal experts and academics express concerns that some sales incentives programs encourage unethical behavior, particularly if compensation is based solely on commissions. For instance, there have been consistent reports that individuals in other countries buying major industrial equipment have received bribes or kickbacks from sales representatives. The bribes are paid from the incentives received by the sales representatives. This criticism applies especially with major transactions such as large industrial machines, aircraft contracts, and even large insurance policies.

Types of Sales Compensation Plans

Sales compensation plans can be of several general types, depending on the degree to which total compensation includes some variable pay tied to sales performance. A look at three general types of sales compensation and some challenges to sales compensation follows.

Salary Only.   Some companies pay salespeople only a salary. The **salary-only approach** is useful when an organization emphasizes serving and retaining existing accounts, over generating new sales and accounts. This approach is frequently used to protect the income of new sales representatives for a period of time while they are building up their sales clientele. Generally, the employer extends the salary-only approach for new sales representatives to no more than six months, at which point it implements a salary-plus-commission or salary-plus-bonuses system (discussed later in this section). Salespeople who want extrinsic rewards function less effectively in salary-only plans because they are less motivated to sell without additional performance-related compensation.

Straight Commission.   In the **straight commission system,** a sales representative receives a percentage of the value of the sales that are made. Consider a sales representative working for a consumer products company. She receives no compensation if she makes no sales, but she receives a percentage of the total amount of all sales revenues she has generated. The advantage of this system is that it requires sales representatives to sell in order to earn. The disadvantage is that it offers no security for the sales staff.

Salary-Plus-Commission or Bonuses.   The form of sales compensation used most frequently is the **salary-plus-commission,** which combines the stability of a salary with the performance aspect of a commission. A common split is 70% salary to 30% commission, although the split varies by industry and based on numerous other factors. Many organizations also pay salespeople salaries and then offer bonuses that are a percentage of the base pay, tied to how well the employee meets various sales targets or other criteria.

Sales Performance Metrics.   Successfully using variable sales compensation requires establishing clear performance criteria and measures. Figure 8-3 shows some of the possible sales metrics. Generally, no more than three sales performance measures should be used in a sales compensation plan. Consultants criticize many sales commission plans as being too complex to motivate sales representatives. Other plans may be too simple, focusing only on the salesperson's pay, not on organizational objectives. Many companies measure performance primarily by comparing an individual's sales revenue against established quotas. The plans would be better if the organizations used a variety of criteria, including obtaining new accounts and selling high-value versus low-value items that reflect marketing plans. A number of different criteria are commonly used

FIGURE 8-3 Sales Metric Possibilities

to determine incentive payments for salespeople and how they are part of determining sales effectiveness.[4]

. . . .

Employee Benefits

Benefits are costly for the typical U.S. employer, averaging 30% to 40% of payroll expenses. In highly unionized manufacturing and utility industries, they may be over 70% of payroll. At many employers, health insurance benefits are over 1/4 of total benefit costs. These numbers illustrate why benefits have become a strategic concern in HR management.

Benefits and HR Strategy

In the United States, a challenge for employers is how to best manage the balancing act between the growing costs of benefits and the use of those benefits in accomplishing organizational goals. For instance, organizations can choose to compete for or retain employees by providing different levels of base compensation, variable pay, and benefits. That is why benefits should be looked at as a vital part of the total rewards "package" when determining organizational strategies.

It is important that benefits be used to help create and maintain competitive advantages. Benefits should not be viewed merely as cost factors because they positively affect HR efforts. Employers may offer benefits to aid recruiting and retention and meet legal requirements. Also, some employers see benefits as reinforcing the company philosophy of social and corporate citizenship. Employers that provide good benefits are viewed more positively within a community and the industry by customers, civic leaders, current employees, and workers in other firms. Conversely, the employers who are seen as skimping on benefits, cutting benefits, or taking advantage of workers may be viewed more negatively.

The primary reasons executives see for offering benefits is to attract and retain talent and meet responsibilities to employees. According to a survey by an international consulting firm, 48% of executives saw benefits as extremely important to a company's competitive effectiveness and another 41% saw benefits as somewhat important. This survey and others confirm that benefits are viewed by both employers and employees as a part of being an "employer of choice" when attracting and retaining individuals.[5]

A major advantage of benefits is that they generally are not taxed as income to employees. For this reason, benefits represent a somewhat more valuable reward to employees than an equivalent cash payment. For example, assume that employee Clara Smith is in a 25% tax bracket. If Clara earns an extra $400, she must pay $100 in taxes on this amount (disregarding exemptions). But if her employer provides prescription drug coverage in a benefits plan, and she receives the $400 as payments for prescription drugs, she is not taxed on the amount, and she receives the value of the entire $400, not just $300. This feature makes benefits a desirable form of compensation to employees.

Benefits Design

Benefits plans can provide flexibility and choices for employees, or they can be standardized for all employees. Increasingly, employers are finding that providing employees with some choices and flexibility allows individuals to tailor their benefits to their own situations. However, the more choices available, the higher the administrative demands placed on organizations. A number of key decisions are part of benefits design:

- How much total compensation, including benefits, can be provided?
- What part of the total compensation of individuals should benefits constitute?
- Which employees should be provided which benefits?
- What expense levels are acceptable for each benefit offered?
- What is being received by the organization in return for each benefit?
- How flexible should the package of benefits be?

HR Technology and Benefits

The spread of HR technology, particularly Internet-based systems, has significantly changed the benefits administration time and activities for HR staff members. Internet-based systems are being used to communicate benefits information, conduct employee benefits surveys, and facilitate benefits administration.

Information technology also allows employees to change their benefits choices, track their benefits balances, and submit questions to HR staff members and external benefits providers. Use of the Internet for benefits enrollment has increased significantly. The greatest use has been to allow employees to sign up for, change, or update their benefits choices through Web-based systems. Previously, HR departments had to send out paper forms, hold numerous benefits meetings, and answer many phone calls from employees. The switch to on-line enrollment and communications has led to reductions in HR staff and benefits administration costs.

Benefits Measurement

The significant costs associated with benefits require that analyses be conducted to determine the payoffs for the benefits. With the wide range of benefits that are offered, numerous HR metrics can be used. Some examples are

- Benefits as a percentage of payroll (pattern over a multi-year period)
- Benefits expenditures per full-time equivalent (FTE) employee
- Benefits costs by employee group (full-time vs. part-time, union vs. non-union, office, management, professional, technical, etc.)
- Benefits administration costs (including staff time multiplied by the staff pay and benefits costs per hour)
- Health-care benefits costs per participating employee

Other metrics are used to measure the return on the expenditures for various benefits programs provided by employers. Some common benefits that employers track using HR metrics are workers' compensation, wellness programs, prescription drug costs, leave time, tuition aid, and disability insurance. The overriding point is that both benefits expenditures generally, as well as costs for individual benefits specifically, need to be measured and evaluated as part of strategic benefits management.

The most common means of health benefits cost control is cost sharing, which refers to having employees pay more of their benefits costs. Almost 60% of firms use this means. Other means of health-care cost control are using wellness programs, adding employee health education efforts, and changing prescription drug programs.[6]

Benefits Communication

Employees generally do not know much about the values and costs associated with the benefits they receive from employers. This ignorance is illustrated by a survey in which only 5% of HR executives identified that their employees appreciated their total compensation package. Over one-third stated that employees do not understand the value of benefits.[7]

Benefits communication and satisfaction of employees with their benefits are linked. Consequently, many employers have instituted special benefits communication systems to inform employees about the value of the benefits they provide. Employers can use various means, including videos, CDs, electronic alerts, newsletters, and employee meetings. All these efforts are done to ensure that employees are knowledgeable about their benefits. Some of the important information to be communicated includes the value of the plans offered, why changes have to be made, and the fundamental financial costs of the plans. When planning benefits communication efforts, it is important to consider factors such as the timing and frequency, the communication sources, and the specialized content.

Firms are using the Internet to provide statements. These statements often are used as part of a total rewards education and communication effort. Federal regulations under the Employee Retirement Income Security Act (ERISA) require that employees receive an annual pension-reporting statement, which also can be included in the personal benefits statement.

· ·

Types of Benefits

A wide range of benefits are offered by employers. Some are mandated by laws and government regulations, while others are offered voluntarily by employers as part of their HR strategies. Figure 8-4 shows how the typical employer dollar is spent on different types of benefits.

Government-Mandated Benefits

There are many mandated benefits that employers in the United States must provide to employees by law. Social Security and unemployment insurance are funded through a tax paid by the employer based on the employee's compensation. Workers' compensation laws exist in all states. In addition, under the Family and Medical Leave Act (FMLA), employers must offer unpaid leave to employees with certain medical or family difficulties. Other mandated benefits are funded in part by taxes, through Social Security. The Consolidated Omnibus Budget Reconciliation Act (COBRA) mandates that an employer continue to provide health-care coverage— albeit paid for by the employees—for a time after they leave the organization.

FIGURE 8-4 How the Typical Benefits Dollar Is Spent

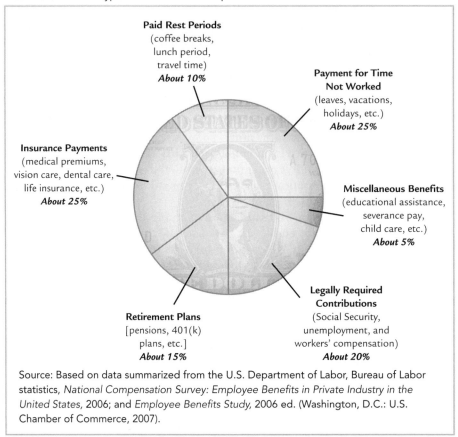

Paid Rest Periods
(coffee breaks,
lunch period,
travel time)
About 10%

**Payment for Time
Not Worked**
(leaves, vacations,
holidays, etc.)
About 25%

Insurance Payments
(medical premiums,
vision care, dental care,
life insurance, etc.)
About 25%

Miscellaneous Benefits
(educational assistance,
severance pay,
child care, etc.)
About 5%

Retirement Plans
[pensions, 401(k)
plans, etc.]
About 15%

**Legally Required
Contributions**
(Social Security,
unemployment, and
workers' compensation)
About 20%

Source: Based on data summarized from the U.S. Department of Labor, Bureau of Labor statistics, *National Compensation Survey: Employee Benefits in Private Industry in the United States*, 2006; and *Employee Benefits Study*, 2006 ed. (Washington, D.C.: U.S. Chamber of Commerce, 2007).

The Health Insurance Portability and Accountability Act (HIPAA) requires that most employees be able to obtain coverage if they were previously covered in a health plan and provides privacy rights for medical records.

A major reason for additional mandated benefits proposals is that federal and state governments would like to shift many of the social costs for health care and other expenditures to employers. This shift would relieve some of the budgetary pressures facing government entities that otherwise might have to raise taxes and/or cut spending.

More mandated benefits have been proposed for many other areas. These possibilities for which mandated coverage has been proposed but not adopted are as follows:

- Universal health-care benefits for all workers
- Child-care assistance
- Pension plan coverage that can be transferred by workers who change jobs
- Core benefits for part-time employees working at least 500 hours a year
- Paid time-off for family leave

FIGURE 8-5 Types of Benefits

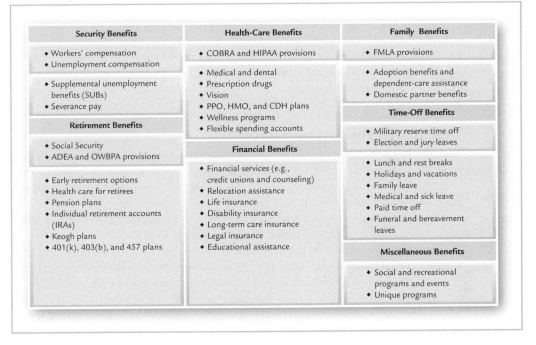

Voluntary Benefits

Employers voluntarily offer other types of benefits to help them compete for and retain employees. By offering additional benefits, organizations are recognizing the need to provide greater security and benefits support to workers with widely varied personal circumstances. In addition, as jobs become more flexible and varied, both workers and employers recognize that choices among benefits are necessary, as evidenced by the growth in flexible benefits and cafeteria benefit plans. Figure 8-5 lists several types of mandated and voluntary benefits. The following sections describe them by type.

Security Benefits

A number of benefits provide employee security. These benefits include some mandated by laws and others offered by employers voluntarily. The primary benefits found in most organizations include workers' compensation, unemployment compensation, and severance pay.

Workers' Compensation

Workers' compensation provides benefits to persons injured on the job. State laws require most employers to supply workers' compensation coverage by purchasing insurance from a private carrier or state insurance fund or by providing self-insurance. U.S. government employees are covered under the Federal Employees Compensation Act, administered by the U.S. Department of Labor.

The workers' compensation system requires employers to give cash benefits, medical care, and rehabilitation services to employees for injuries or illnesses occurring within the scope of their employment. In exchange, employees give up the right to pursue legal actions and awards. The costs to employers for workers' compensation average about 1.8% of total payroll, and cost about $0.47 per hour in wages per worker.[8]

Unemployment Compensation

Another benefit required by law is unemployment compensation, established as part of the Social Security Act of 1935. Because each U.S. state operates its own unemployment compensation system, provisions differ significantly from state to state. The tax is paid to state and federal unemployment compensation funds. The percentage paid by individual employers is based on "experience rates," which reflect the number of claims filed by workers who leave.

An employee who is out of work and is actively looking for employment normally receives up to 26 weeks of pay, at the rate of 50% to 80% of normal pay. Most employees are eligible. However, workers fired for misconduct or those not actively seeking employment generally are ineligible. Only about 40% of eligible people use the unemployment compensation system. This underutilization may be due both to the stigma of receiving unemployment and the complexity of the system, which some feel is simply not worth the effort.

Severance Pay

As a security benefit, severance pay is voluntarily offered by employers to individuals whose jobs are eliminated or who leave by mutual agreement with their employers. Employer severance pay provisions often provide severance payments corresponding to an employee's level within the organization and the person's years of employment. The Worker Adjustment and Retraining Notification Act (WARN) of 1988 requires that many employers give 60 days' notice if a mass layoff or facility closing is to occur. The act does not require employers to give severance pay.

Health-Care Benefits

Employers provide a variety of health-care and medical benefits, usually through insurance coverage. The most common plans cover medical, dental, prescription drug, and vision care expenses for employees and their dependents. Employers see controlling the increasing costs of health-care benefits as their most important concern.

Increases in Health Benefits Costs

For several decades, the costs of health care have escalated at rates well above those of inflation and changes in workers' earnings. As a result of these large increases, many employers find that dealing with health-care benefits is time consuming and expensive. This is especially frustrating for employers who have found that many employees seem to take their health benefits for granted. Consequently, a growing number of firms, particularly smaller ones, have asked, "Why are we offering these benefits anyway?" Two major groups of workers that have contributed to the increasing costs are uninsured workers and retirees.

Controlling Health-Care Benefits Costs

Employers offering health-care benefits are taking a number of approaches to controlling their costs. The most prominent ones are changing co-payments and employee contributions, using managed care, switching to mini-medical plans or consumer-driven health plans, and increasing health preventive and wellness efforts.

Changing Co-Payments and Employee Contributions. The co-payment strategy requires employees to pay a portion of the cost of insurance premiums, medical care, and prescription drugs. Requiring new or higher co-payments and employee contributions is the most prevalent cost-control strategy identified by many employers surveyed. For instance, employers who raise the per person deductible from $50 to $250 realize significant savings in health-care expenses due to decreasing employee usage of health-care services and prescription drugs.

These changes are facing significant resistance by employees, especially those who have had *first-dollar coverage*. With this type of coverage, all expenses, from the first dollar of health-care costs, are paid by the employee's insurance. Experts claim that when first-dollar coverage is included in a basic health plan, many employees see a doctor for even minor illnesses, which results in an escalation of the benefits costs.

Using Managed Care. Several other types of programs attempt to reduce health-care costs paid by employers. Managed care consists of approaches that monitor and reduce medical costs through restrictions and market system alternatives. Managed care plans emphasize primary and preventive care, the use of specific providers who will charge lower prices, restrictions on certain kinds of treatment, and prices negotiated with hospitals and physicians.

The most prominent managed care approach is the preferred provider organization (PPO), a health-care provider that contracts with an employer or an employer group to supply health-care services to employees at a competitive rate. Employees have the freedom to go to other providers if they want to pay the differences in costs. **Point-of-service plans** are somewhat similar, offering financial incentives to encourage employees to use designated medical providers.

Another managed care approach is a health maintenance organization (HMO), which provides services for a fixed period on a pre-paid basis. The HMO emphasizes both prevention and correction. An employer contracts with an HMO and its staff of physicians and medical personnel to furnish complete medical care, except for hospitalization. The employer pays a flat rate per enrolled employee or per enrolled family. The covered individuals may then go to the HMO for health care as often as needed. Supplemental policies for hospitalization are also provided. While HMOs remain widely used, a growing number of employers are focusing on other means to control the costs of health-care benefits.

Consumer-Driven Health Plans

Some employers are turning to "employee-focused" health benefits plans. The most prominent is a consumer-driven health (CDH) plan, which provides financial contributions to employees to help cover their own health-related expenses. Various surveys of companies have identified that a growing number of employers have switched to CDH plans, and that others are actively considering switching to these plans.

In these plans, which are also called **defined-contribution health plans**, an employer places a set amount into each employee's "account" and identifies a number of health-care alternatives that are available. Then individual employees select from those health-care alternatives and pay for part of the costs from their accounts.

There are two advantages to such plans for employers. One is that more of the increases in health-care benefits costs are shifted to employees, because the employer contributions need not increase as fast as health-care costs. Second, the focus of controlling health-care usage falls on employees, who may have to choose when to use and not use health-care benefits.

Health Savings Accounts. Health savings accounts (HSAs) are often combined with high-deductible insurance to cut employer costs. Components of an HSA include the following:

- Both employees and employers can make contributions to an account.
- Individual employees can set aside pre-tax amounts for medical care into an HSA.
- Unused amounts in an individual's account can be rolled over annually for future health expenses.
- Incentives are included to encourage employees to spend less on health expenses.

Health-Care Preventive and Wellness Efforts

Preventive and wellness efforts can occur in a variety of ways. Many employers offer programs to educate employees about health-care costs and how to reduce them. Newsletters, formal classes, and many other approaches are all designed to help employees understand why health-care costs are increasing and what they can do to control them. Many employers have programs that offer financial incentives to improve health habits. These wellness programs reward employees who stop smoking, lose weight, and participate in exercise programs, among other activities.

Health-Care Legislation

The importance of health-care benefits to employers and employees has led to a variety of federal and state laws being created. Some laws have been enacted to provide protection for employees who leave their employers, either voluntarily or involuntarily. To date, the two most important ones are COBRA and HIPAA.

COBRA Provisions.   The Consolidated Omnibus Budget Reconciliation Act (COBRA) requires that most employers (except churches and the federal government) with 20 or more employees offer extended health-care coverage to certain groups, as follows:

- Employees who voluntarily quit
- Widowed or divorced spouses and dependent children of former or current employees
- Retirees and their spouses whose health-care coverage ends

Compliance with COBRA regulations can be complex. For employers, the COBRA requirements mean additional paperwork and related costs. For example, firms must not only track the former employees but also notify their qualified dependents.

HIPAA Provisions.   The Health Insurance Portability and Accountability Act (HIPAA) of 1996 allows employees to switch their health insurance plans when they change employers, and to get new health coverage with the new company regardless of pre-existing health conditions. The legislation also prohibits group insurance plans from dropping coverage for a sick employee, and requires them to make individual coverage available to people who leave group plans.

One of the greatest impacts of HIPAA comes from its provisions regarding the privacy of employee medical records. These provisions require employers to provide privacy notices to employees. They also regulate the disclosure of protected health information without authorization.

....

Retirement Benefits

The aging of the workforce in many countries is affecting retirement planning for individuals and retirement plan costs for employers and governments. In the United States, the number of citizens at least 55 years or older will increase significantly in the next few years. Older citizens will constitute about 40% of the population in 2010. Simultaneously, the age of retirement will change for many people, as it has been doing for decades. With more people retiring earlier and living longer, retirement benefits are becoming a greater concern for employers, employees, and retired employees.

Unfortunately, most U.S. citizens have inadequate savings and retirement benefits for funding their retirements. Therefore, they are heavily dependent on employer-provided retirement benefits. But many employers with fewer than 100 workers do not offer retirement benefits. Therefore, individuals must rely on Social Security payments, which were not designed to provide full retirement income.

Social Security

The Social Security Act of 1935, with its later amendments, established a system providing *old-age, survivor's, disability,* and *retirement* benefits. Administered by the federal government through the Social Security Administration, this program provides benefits to previously employed individuals. Employees and employers share in the cost of Social Security through a tax on employees' wages or salaries.

Pension Plans

A pension plan is a retirement program established and funded by the employer and employees. Organizations are not required to offer pension plans to employees, and fewer than half of U.S. workers are covered by them. Small firms offer pension plans less often than do large ones.

Defined-Benefit Pension Plans. A "traditional" pension plan, in which the employer makes the contributions and the employee will get a defined amount each month upon retirement, is no longer the norm in the private sector. Through a **defined-benefit plan**, employees are promised a pension amount based on age and service. The employees' contributions are based on actuarial calculations on the *benefits* to be received by the employees after retirement and the *methods* used to determine such benefits. A defined-benefit plan gives employees greater assurance of benefits and greater predictability in the amount of benefits that will be available for retirement.

Defined-Contribution Pension Plans. In a defined-contribution plan, the employer makes an annual payment to an employee's pension account. The key to this plan is the *contribution rate;* employee retirement benefits depend on fixed contributions and employee earnings levels. Profit-sharing plans, employee stock ownership plans (ESOPs), and 401(k) plans are common defined-contribution plans. Because these plans hinge on the investment returns on the previous contributions, the returns can vary according to profitability or other factors. Therefore, employees' retirement benefits are somewhat less secure and predictable. But because of their structure, these plans are sometimes preferred by younger, shorter-service employees.

Employee Retirement Income Security Act

The widespread criticism of many pension plans led to passage of the Employee Retirement Income Security Act (ERISA) in 1974. The purpose of this law is to regulate private pension plans so that employees who put money into them or depend on a pension for retirement funds actually receive the money when they retire.

ERISA essentially requires many companies to offer retirement plans to all employees if they offer retirement plans to any employees. Accrued benefits must be given to employees when they retire or leave. The act also sets minimum funding requirements, and plans not meeting those requirements are subject to financial penalties imposed by the IRS. Additional regulations require that employers pay plan termination insurance to ensure payment of employee pensions should the employers go out of business. To spread out the costs of administration and overhead, some employers use plans funded by multiple employers.

Financial and Family Oriented Benefits

Employers may offer workers a wide range of special benefits that provide financial support to employees. Employers find that such benefits can be useful in attracting and retaining employees. Workers like receiving these benefits, which often are not taxed as income.

Insurance Benefits

In addition to health-related insurance, some employers provide other types of insurance. These benefits offer major advantages for employees because many employers pay some or all of the costs. Even when employers do not pay any of the costs, employees still benefit because of the lower rates available through group programs. The most common types of insurance benefits are life insurance, disability insurance, long-term care insurance, and legal insurance.

Financial benefits include a wide variety of items. A **credit union** sponsored by the employer provides saving and lending services for employees. **Purchase discounts** allow employees to buy goods or services from their employers at reduced rates. For example, a furniture manufacturer may allow employees to buy furniture at wholesale cost plus 10%, or a bank may offer employees use of a safe deposit box and free checking. Employee *thrift plans, savings plans,* or *stock investment plans* of different types may also be available.

Family-Oriented Benefits

Balancing family and work demands presents a major challenge to many workers at all levels of organizations. Therefore, employers have established a variety of family-oriented benefits. Since 1993, employers have also been required to provide certain benefits to comply with the Family and Medical Leave Act.

Family and Medical Leave Act.   The Family and Medical Leave Act (FMLA) covers all federal, state, and private employers with 50 or more employees who live within 75 miles of the workplace. Only employees who have worked at least 12 months and 1,250 hours in the previous year are eligible for leave under the FMLA. In 2008 additional FMLA changes where made for family members to take up to 26 work weeks to care for military members with medical problems.

FMLA Leave Provisions.   The law requires that typically employers must allow other eligible employees to take a total of 12 weeks' leave during any 12-month period for one or more of three situations:

- Birth, adoption, or foster care placement of a child
- Caring for a spouse, a child, or a parent with a serious health condition
- Serious health condition of the employee

Since the passage of the act, several factors have become apparent. First, a significant percentage of employees have been taking family and medical leave.

Numerous women and employees in the 25- to 34-year-old age group take more family and medical leave, primarily due to childbirth reasons.

Second, many employers have not paid enough attention to the law. Some employers are denying leaves or failing to reinstate workers after leaves are completed. Consequently, numerous lawsuits have resulted, many of which are lost by employers. Many employers' problems with the FMLA occur because of the variety of circumstances in which employees may request and use family leave.

Child-Care Assistance

Balancing work and family responsibilities is a major challenge for many workers. Whether single parents or dual-career couples, these employees often experience difficulty obtaining high-quality, affordable child care. Employers are addressing the child-care issue in the following ways:

- Providing referral services to help parents locate child-care providers
- Establishing discounts at day-care centers, which may be subsidized by the employer
- Arranging with hospitals to offer sick-child programs partially paid for by the employer
- Developing after-school programs for older school-age children, often in conjunction with local public and private school systems
- Offering on-site child-care centers

Time-off Benefits

Time-off benefits represent a significant portion of total benefits costs. Employers give employees paid time off for a variety of circumstances. Paid lunch breaks and rest periods, holidays, and vacations are common. These time-off benefits also include various leaves of absence.

Holiday and Vacation Pay

Most employers provide pay for a variety of holidays. U.S. employers commonly offer 10 to 12 holidays annually. Employers in many other countries are required to provide a significantly higher number of holidays, approaching 20 to 30 days in some cases. In both the United States and other countries, the number of holidays offered can vary depending on state/provincial laws and union contracts.

Paid vacations are a common benefit. Employers often use graduated vacation-time scales based on employees' lengths of service. Some organizations have a "use it or lose it" policy whereby accrued vacation time cannot be carried over from year to year. One survey found that workers on average forfeit three vacation days per year.

Some employers have policies to "buy back" unused vacation time. Other employers, such as banks, may have policies requiring employees to take a minimum number of vacation days off in a row. Regardless of the vacation policies used, employees are often required to work the day before and the day after vacation time off.

Sick Leave

Medical and sick leave are closely related. Many employers allow employees to miss a limited number of days because of illness without losing pay. Over 50% of all U.S. workers receive paid sick leave. But U.S. employers do not provide paid sick leave to as many workers percentagewise as do the employers in other developed countries.

Some employers allow employees to accumulate unused sick leave, which may be used in case of catastrophic illnesses. Others pay their employees for unused sick leave. A problem employers face is that only about 35% of unscheduled employee absences are due to illnesses. Some organizations have shifted emphasis to reward people who do not use sick leave by giving them well-pay—extra pay for not taking sick leave. Another approach is to use paid time off.

Paid-Time-Off Plans

A growing number of employers have made use of a paid-time-off (PTO) plan, which combines all sick leave, vacation time, and holidays into a total number of hours or days that employees can take off with pay. Studies have found that about 37% of all employers have PTO plans.[9] More importantly, many of those employers have found PTO plans to be more effective than other means of reducing absenteeism and in having time off scheduled more efficiently. Other advantages cited by employers with PTO plans are ease of administration and as an aid for recruiting and retention and for increasing employee understanding and use of leave policies.

NOTES

1. Kathy Gurchiek, "Incentive Programs Fall Short with Employees Survey Finds," *HR News,* December 16, 2004, *www.shrm.org/hrnews;* and Worldatwork Staff, "U.S. Companies Revise Variable Pay Plans for Non-Executive Workers," *Newsline,* November 3, 2004, *www.e-topics.com.*
2. Edward E. Lawler III, "Pay Practices in *Fortune 1000* Corporations," *WorldatWork Journal,* Fourth Quarter 2003, 45–54.
3. Stephen H. Wagner, Christopher P. Parker, and Neil D. Christiansen, "Employees that Think and Act Like Owners." *Personnel Psychology,* 56(2003), 847–871.
4. Jerry Colletti and Mary Fiss, "Sales Force Productivity Metrics," *http://Collettifiss.com/shortc.aspx.*

5. "Incorporate 'Employer of Choice' Goals into Strategic, Benefits Planing," *Best Practices in HR,* September 22, 2006, 3.
6. "Cost Control Is Shifting to a Long-Term View." *HR Focus,* September 2006, 1.
7. Few Employees Understand and Appreciate Their Total Compensation Package," *WorldatWork News,* November 29, 2006. For details go to *www.Charltonconsulting.com.*
8. U.S. Bureau of Labor Statistics, *www.bls.gov.*
9. George Faulkner, "Absent and Accounted For." *Human Resource Executive,* May 2. 2006, 56–57.

INTERNET RESOURCES

Halogen Software—For information on software and services to establish a pay-for-performance compensation system, link to this Website at: *halogensoftware.com*

Wilson Group—This firm provides consulting services on variable pay compensation systems. Visit their Website at: *www. wilsongroup.com*

SUGGESTED READINGS

Jerry S. Rosenbloom, *The Handbook of Employee Benefits: Design, Funding, and Administration*, 6th ed., (McGraw-Hill, 2005).

M. Michael Markowich, *Paid Time-Off Banks* (WorldatWork, 2007).

J. J. Martocchio, *Employee Benefits* 3rd ed. (McGraw Hill, 2007).

A. Bianchi, *Benefits Compliance: An overview for the HR professional*, (WorldatWork Press, 2008).

Risk Management and Employee Relations

HR—MEETING MANAGEMENT CHALLENGES

Employer protection activities are crucial to managing risks and maintaining an effective employee work environment. This chapter highlights the factors affecting risk management in organizations and how HR and managerial efforts must be addressed in organizations of all types. Key issues are

- Ensuring that worker health, safety, and security are consistently addressed
- Understanding why disaster preparation and recovery planning have grown
- Having employee relations and rights and responsibilities addressed by HR policies and practices.

The focus of HR managers on risk management and worker protection has grown significantly in the past several years. Previously, most HR efforts emphasized providing work environments that are safe, healthy, and secure. Risk management has a number of different facets beyond complying with safety and health regulations.

Risk Management

In the United States and most developed nations, the concept of using prevention and control to minimize or eliminate a wide range of risks in workplaces has been expanding. Effective risk management also is becoming a key component of strategic HR management.

Nature of Risk Management

Risk management involves responsibilities to consider physical, human, and financial factors to protect organizational and individual interests. For HR management, risk management includes a number of areas, as Figure 9-1 depicts. Its scope ranges from workplace safety and health to disaster preparation.

FIGURE 9-1 Risk Management Components

The nature and extent of risk management efforts are affected by a number of factors, including:

- Size and location of organizations
- Industry characteristics and demands
- Geographic and global location factors
- Government-mandated programs and requirements
- Strategic priorities of each organization
- Involvement and capabilities of HR professionals in the different risk management areas.

Nature of Health, Safety, and Security

The first emphasis in risk management in most organizations is health, safety, and security, which is discussed next. The terms **health**, **safety**, and **security** are closely related. The broader and somewhat more nebulous term is **health**, which refers to a general state of physical, mental, and emotional well-being. A healthy person is free from illness, injury, or mental and emotional problems that impair normal human activity. Health management practices in organizations strive to maintain the overall well-being of individuals.

Typically, **safety** refers to a condition in which the physical well-being of people is protected. The main purpose of effective safety programs in organizations is to prevent work-related injuries and accidents.

The purpose of **security** is protecting employees and organizational facilities. With the growth of workplace violence and other risk management concerns, security has become an even greater concern for both employers and employees alike. For some employers now, security issues include protecting employees from terrorist attacks, loss of electric service, bomb threats, and hostage situations.

Current State of Health, Safety, and Security

In the United States, about 4.2 million non-fatal injuries and illnesses occur at work annually. Specific rates vary depending on the industry, job type, etc. The number of workplace injuries varies by employer size also, with smaller employers having more injuries per employee. The three major causes of injury (overextending, falling, and bodily reaction) were responsible for over 40% of the direct costs of injuries. Accident costs have gone up faster than inflation because of the rapid increase in medical costs, even though the total number of accidents has been decreasing for some time.[1]

Globally, safety and health laws and regulations vary from country to country, ranging from virtually non-existent to more stringent than those in the United States. The importance placed on health, safety, and security relates somewhat to the level of regulation and other factors in each country.

....

Legal Requirements for Safety and Health

Employers must comply with a variety of federal and state laws when developing and maintaining healthy, safe, and secure workforces and working environments. Three major legal areas are workers' compensation legislation, the Americans with Disabilities Act, and child labor laws.

Workers' Compensation

Workers' compensation laws in some form are on the books in all states today. Under these laws, employers contribute to an insurance fund to compensate employees for injuries received while on the job. Premiums paid reflect the accident rates of the employers, with employers that have higher incident rates being assessed higher premiums.

Workers' compensation coverage has been expanded in many states to include emotional impairment that may have resulted from physical injury, as well as job-related strain, stress, anxiety, and pressure. Some cases of suicide have also been ruled to be job related, with payments due under workers' compensation.

Workers' compensation costs have become a major issue for many employers. These costs usually represent from 2% to 10% of payroll for most employers. The major contributors to increases have been higher medical costs and litigation expenses. However, the frequency of workers' compensation claims for lost time has decreased some in all industry groups. Many of the safety and health management suggestions discussed later in this chapter can contribute to reducing workers' compensation costs.

Americans with Disabilities Act and Safety Issues

Employers sometimes try to return injured workers to "light-duty" work in order to reduce workers' compensation costs. However, under the Americans with Disabilities Act (ADA), when making accommodations for injured employees through light-duty work, employers may undercut what are really essential job functions. Also, making such accommodations for injured employees for a period of time may require employers to make similar accommodations for job applicants with disabilities.

Child Labor Laws

Safety concerns are reflected in restrictions affecting younger workers, especially those under the age of 18. Child labor laws, found in Section XII of the Fair Labor Standards Act (FLSA), set the minimum age for most employment at 16 years. For "hazardous" occupations, 18 years is the minimum.

In addition to complying with workers' compensation, ADA, and child labor laws, most employers must comply with the Occupational Safety and Health Act of 1970. This act has had a tremendous impact on the workplace.

··

Occupational Safety and Health Act

The Occupational Safety and Health Act of 1970 (OSHA) was passed "to assure so far as possible every working man or woman in the Nation safe and healthful working conditions and to preserve our human resources." Every employer that is engaged in commerce and has one or more employees is covered by the act. Farmers having fewer than 10 employees are exempt. Employers in specific industries, such as coal mining, are covered under other health and safety acts. Federal, state, and local governments are covered by separate statutes and provisions.

OSHA Enforcement Standards

To implement OSHA regulations, specific standards were established to regulate equipment and working environments. A number of provisions have been recognized as key to employers' efforts to comply with OSHA. Two basic ones are as follows:

- *General duty*: The act requires that the employer has a "general duty" to provide safe and healthy working conditions, even in areas where OSHA standards have not been set. Employers who know or reasonably should know of unsafe or unhealthy conditions can be cited for violating the general duty clause.
- *Notification and posters*: Employers are required to inform their employees of safety and health standards established by OSHA. Also, OSHA posters must be displayed in prominent locations in workplaces.

Hazard Communication.   OSHA established process safety management (PSM) standards that focus on hazardous chemicals. As part of PSM through a risk management program, hazard communication standards require manufacturers, importers, distributors, and users of hazardous chemicals to evaluate, classify, and label these substances. Employers also must make available information about hazardous substances to employees, their representatives, and health professionals.

This information is contained in material safety data sheets (MSDSs), which must be kept readily accessible to those who work with chemicals and other substances. The MSDSs also indicate antidotes or actions to be taken should someone come in contact with the substances.

Bloodborne Pathogens.   OSHA has issued a standard regarding exposure to hepatitis B virus (HBV), human immunodeficiency virus (HIV), and other bloodborne pathogens. This regulation was developed to protect employees who regularly are exposed to blood and other such substances from contracting AIDS and other serious diseases. Regulations require employers with the most pronounced risks to have written control and response plans and to train workers in following the proper procedures.

Personal Protective Equipment.   One goal of OSHA has been to develop standards for personal protective equipment (PPE). These standards require that employers analyze job hazards, provide adequate PPE to employees in hazardous jobs, and train employees in the use of PPE items. Common PPE items include safety glasses, hard hats, and safety shoes. If the work environment presents hazards or if employees might have contact with hazardous chemicals and substances on the job, then employers are required to provide PPE to all those employees.

Ergonomics and OSHA

Ergonomics is the study and design of the work environment to address physiological and physical demands placed on individuals. In a work setting, ergonomic studies look at such factors as fatigue, lighting, tools, equipment layout, and placement of controls.

For a number of years, OSHA has focused on the large number of work-related injuries due to repetitive stress, repetitive motion, cumulative trauma disorders, carpal tunnel syndrome, and other causes. OSHA has approached ergonomics concerns by adopting voluntary guidelines for specific problem industries and jobs, gone after industries with serious ergonomic problems, and given employers tools for identifying and controlling ergonomics hazards. Among the industries receiving guidelines are nursing homes, poultry processors, and retail grocery stores.

OSHA Recordkeeping Requirements

Employers are generally required to maintain a detailed annual record of the various types of injuries, accidents, and fatalities for inspection by OSHA representatives and for submission to the agency. Many organizations must complete OSHA Form 300 to report workshop accidents and injuries. Four types of injuries or illnesses are defined by the Occupational Safety and Health Act. They are as follows:

- *Injury- or illness-related deaths*: fatalities at workplaces or caused by work-related actions
- *Lost-time or disability injuries*: job-related injuries or disabling occurrences that cause an employee to miss regularly scheduled work on the day following the accident

- *Medical care injuries*: injuries that require treatment by a physician but do not cause an employee to miss a regularly scheduled work turn
- *Minor injuries*: injuries that require first aid treatment and do not cause an employee to miss the next regularly scheduled work turn

OSHA Inspections

The Occupational Safety and Health Act provides for on-the-spot inspections by OSHA representatives, called compliance officers or inspectors. In *Marshall v. Barlow's, Inc.*, the U.S. Supreme Court held that safety inspectors must produce a search warrant if an employer refuses to allow an inspector into the plant voluntarily. The Court also ruled that an inspector does not have to show probable cause to obtain a search warrant. A warrant can easily be obtained if a search is part of a general enforcement plan.[2]

OSHA inspection has been criticized because since the agency has so many work sites to inspect, many employers have only a relatively small chance of being inspected. Some suggest that many employers pay little attention to OSHA enforcement efforts for this reason. Employers, especially smaller ones, continue to complain about the complexity of complying with OSHA standards and the costs associated with penalties and with making changes required to remedy problem areas.

....

Safety Management

Well-designed and well-managed safety programs can pay dividends in reduced accidents and associated costs, such as workers' compensation and possible fines. Further, accidents and other safety concerns usually decline as a result of management efforts that emphasize safety. Often, the difference between high-performing firms with good occupational safety records and other firms is that the former have effective safety management programs. Successful safety management includes several components highlighted next.

Organizational Commitment and a Safety Culture

At the heart of safety management is an organizational commitment to a comprehensive safety effort that should be coordinated at the top level of management and include all members of the organization. Support by management and continuing management/employee relations are two key aspects affecting the extent of occupational accidents.[3] Three approaches are used by employers in managing safety, as Figure 9-2 shows. Successful programs may use all three in dealing with safety issues.

Safety Policies, Discipline, and Recordkeeping

Designing safety policies and rules and disciplining violators are important components of safety efforts. Frequently reinforcing the need for safe behavior and frequently supplying feedback on positive safety practices are also effective ways

FIGURE 9-2 Approaches to Effective Safety Management

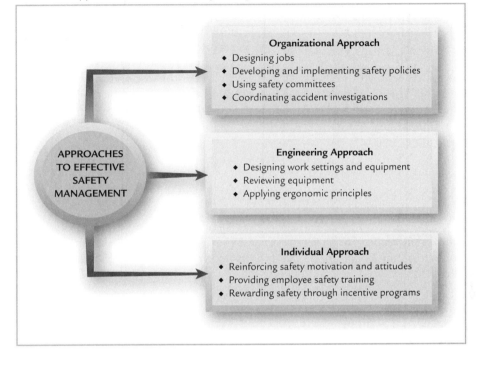

of improving worker safety. Such safety-conscious efforts must involve employees, supervisors, managers, safety specialists, and HR staff members.

For policies about safety to be effective, good recordkeeping about accidents, causes, and other details is necessary. Without records, an employer cannot track its safety performance, compare benchmarks against other employers, and may not realize the extent of its safety problems.

Safety Training and Communication

Good safety training reduces accidents. Safety training can be done in various ways. Regular sessions with supervisors, managers, and employees are often coordinated by HR staff members. Communication of safety procedures, reasons why accidents occurred, and what to do in an emergency is critical. Without effective communication about safety, training is insufficient. To reinforce safety training, continuous communication to develop safety consciousness is necessary.

Safety Committees

Employees frequently participate in safety planning through safety committees, often composed of workers from a variety of levels and departments. A safety committee generally meets at regularly scheduled times, has specific responsibilities for conducting safety reviews, and makes recommendations for changes necessary to avoid future accidents. Usually, at least one member of the committee comes from the HR department.

Inspection, Investigation, and Evaluation

It is not necessary to wait for an OSHA inspector to check the work area for safety hazards. Inspections may be done by a safety committee or by a safety coordinator regularly. Problem areas should be addressed immediately in order to keep work productivity at the highest possible levels. Also, OSHA inspects organizations with above-average rates of lost workdays more frequently. When accidents occur, they should be investigated by the employer's safety committee or safety coordinator. Identifying why an accident occurred is useful; taking steps to prevent similar accidents from occurring is even more important.

....

Employee Health

Employee health problems are varied—and somewhat inevitable. They can range from minor illnesses such as colds to serious illnesses related to the jobs performed. Employers face a variety of workplace health issues, some of which are discussed next.

Substance Abuse

Use of illicit substances or misuse of controlled substances, alcohol, or other drugs is called substance abuse. The millions of substance abusers in the workforce cost global employers billions of dollars annually, although recently there has been a decline in illegal drug use by employees. In the United States, the incidence of substance abuse is greatest among young single men. Also, blue-collar workers are more likely than white-collar workers to abuse substances.

Employers' concerns about substance abuse stem from the ways it alters work behaviors, causing increased tardiness, increased absenteeism, a slower work pace, a higher rate of mistakes, and less time spent at the work station. Alcohol testing and drug testing are used by many employers, especially following an accident or some other reasonable cause. Some employers also use random testing programs.

The Americans with Disabilities Act (ADA) affects how management can handle substance abuse cases. Current users of *illegal* drugs are specifically excluded from the definition of *disabled* under the act. However, those addicted to *legal* substances (alcohol, for example) and prescription drugs are considered disabled under the ADA. Also, recovering substance abusers are considered disabled under the ADA.

To encourage employees to seek help for their substance abuse problems, a *firm-choice option* can be offered, whereby the employee has a choice between help and discipline. Treatment options and consequences of further unsatisfactory performance are clearly discussed, including what the employer will do. Confidentiality and follow-up are critical when employers use the firm-choice option.

Emotional/Mental Health

Many individuals today are facing work, family, and personal life pressures. A variety of emotional/mental health issues arise at work that must be addressed by employers. It is important to note that emotional/mental illnesses such as schizophrenia and depression are considered disabilities under the ADA. Employers should be cautious when using disciplinary policies if employees diagnosed with such illnesses have work-related problems.

Depression is a common emotional/mental health concern. The effects of depression are seen at all organizational levels, from warehouses and accounting offices to executive suites. Often, employees who appear to be depressed are guided to employee assistance programs and helped with obtaining medical treatment.

Workplace Air Quality

A number of employees work in settings where air quality is a health issue. Poor air quality may occur in "sealed" buildings (where windows cannot be opened) and when airflow is reduced to save energy and cut operating costs. Also, inadequate ventilation, as well as airborne contamination from carpets, molds, copy machines, adhesives, and fungi, can cause poor air quality and employee illnesses. One major contributor to air quality problems is smoking in workplaces.

Smoking at Work

Arguments and rebuttals characterize the smoking-at-work controversy, and statistics abound. A multitude of state and local laws deal with smoking in the workplace and in public places. In response to health studies, complaints by non-smokers, and resulting state laws, many employers have instituted no-smoking policies throughout their workplaces. Some employers also offer smoking cessation workshops as part of health promotion efforts.

Health Promotion

Employers concerned about maintaining a healthy workforce must move beyond simply providing healthy working conditions and begin promoting employee health and wellness in other ways. Health promotion efforts can range from providing information and increasing employee awareness of health issues to creating an organizational culture supportive of employee health enhancements.

Wellness Programs. Wellness programs are designed to maintain or improve employee health before problems arise by encouraging self-directed lifestyle changes. Such programs emphasize healthy lifestyles and environment, including reducing cholesterol and other heart disease risks and individualized exercise programs and follow-up.

Employee Assistance Programs. One method organizations use as a broad-based response to health issues is an employee assistance program (EAP), which provides counseling and other help to employees having emotional, physical, or other personal problems. In such a program, an employer contracts with a counseling agency. Employees who have problems may then contact the agency, either voluntarily or by employer referral, for assistance with a broad range of problems. Counseling costs are paid for by the employer, either in total or up to a pre-established limit.

Security Concerns at Work

Traditionally, when employers have addressed worker health, safety, and security, they have been concerned about reducing workplace accidents, improving workers' safety practices, and reducing health hazards at work. However, in the past decade, providing security for employees has become increasingly important. Heading the list of security concerns is workplace violence.

Workplace Violence

Worldwide violence in workplaces is increasing with actions involving workplace fatality in many different industries. Specifically regarding employees, there are a number of warning signs. A person with some of these signs and characteristics may cope for years until a trauma pushes the individual over the edge. A profound humiliation or rejection, the end of a marriage, the loss of a lawsuit, or termination from a job may make a difficult employee turn violent.

Management of Workplace Violence.   The increase in workplace violence has led many employers to develop policies and practices for preventing and responding to workplace violence. One aspect of HR policies is to identify how workplace violence is to be dealt with in conjunction with disciplinary actions and referrals to EAPs. Training of managers and others is crucial, as well as creating a *violence response team* composed of security personnel, key managers, HR staff members, and selected employees.

Security Management

An overall approach to security management is needed to address a wide range of issues, including workplace violence. Often, HR managers have responsibility for security programs or work closely with security managers or consultants. Also crucial is providing adequately trained security personnel in sufficient numbers.

A key part of security involves controlling access to the physical facilities of the organization. Yet another part of security centers on controlling access to computer systems. This concern is magnified when individuals are terminated or leave an organization. HR staff must coordinate with information technology staff to change passwords, delete access codes, and otherwise protect company information systems.[4]

Employee Screening and Selection

A key facet of providing security is screening job applicants. HR management is somewhat limited on what can be done, particularly regarding the use of psychological tests and checking of references. However, firms that do not screen employees adequately may be subject to liability if an employee commits crimes later. When selecting employees, employers must be careful to use only valid, job-related screening means and to avoid violating federal EEO laws and the Americans with Disabilities Act.

....

Disaster Preparation and Recovery Planning

During the past several years, a number of significant disasters have occurred. Some have been natural disasters, others where firms have been damaged by fires and explosions or terrorism. All of these situations have led to HR management having an expanded role in disaster planning.

Disaster Planning

For disaster planning to occur properly, three components must be addressed by HR, as depicted in Figure 9-3. Imagine that a hurricane destroys the work facility were employees work, as well as many of their homes. Or an explosion or terrorist attack prohibits workers from getting to their workplaces. Those situations illustrate why each of the components has human dimensions to be addressed.

Organizational Assessment.   A crucial part of organizational assessment is to establish a disaster planning team, often composed of representatives from HR, security, information technology, operations, and other areas. The purpose of this team is to conduct an organizational assessment of how various disasters might affect the organization and its employees. Then a disaster recovery plan is developed to identify how the organization will respond to different situations.

FIGURE 9-3 Disaster Planning Components

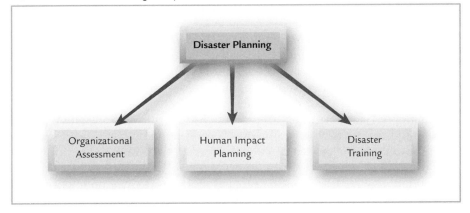

Human Impact Training.   A number of areas are part of human impact planning. Such items as having backup databases for numerous company details, including employee contact information, are vital. Who will take responsibilities for various duties and how these efforts will be coordinated must be identified.

Disaster Training.   All of the planning efforts may be wasted if managers and employees are not trained on what to do when disasters occur. This training covers a wide range of topics. But this training is not sufficient without conducting exercises for managers and employees to use the training.

A significant worldwide concern is the occurrence of environmental risks. One such concern during the past few years has been the spread of Avian flu, a virus that has occurred throughout the world, especially in Asia. The global nature of business travel has increased the likelihood of the spread of this or another deadly virus.

· ·

Employee Relations

Three very interrelated HR issues are considered part of employee relations: *employee rights,* *HR policies,* and *discipline,* and they change and evolve as laws and societal values change.

Employee Rights and Responsibilities

There are three related and important issues in managing human resources: employee rights, HR policies and rules, and discipline. These areas may seem separate, but they definitely are not. The policies and rules that an organization enacts help to define employees' rights at that employer, as well as constrain those rights (sometimes inappropriately or illegally). Similarly, discipline for those who fail to follow policies and rules is often seen as a fundamental right of employers. Employees who feel that their employers have taken inappropriate action can challenge that action—both inside and outside the organization—using an internal dispute resolution process or through a variety of external legal means.

Rights generally do not exist in the abstract. Instead, they exist only when someone is successful in demanding their application. **Rights** are powers, privileges, or interests that belong to a person by law, nature, or tradition.

Rights are offset by **responsibilities**, which are obligations to perform certain tasks and duties. Employment is a reciprocal relationship in that both sides have rights and obligations. The reciprocal nature of rights and responsibilities suggests that both parties to an employment relationship should regard the other as having rights and should treat the other with respect.

Employees' **statutory rights** are the result of specific laws or statutes passed by federal, state, or local governments. Various federal, state, and local laws have granted employees certain rights at work, such as equal employment opportunity, collective bargaining, and workplace safety. These laws and their interpretations also have been the subjects of a considerable number of court cases.

Employment Contracts.   An employment contract is a formal agreement that outlines the details of employment. Written employment contracts are often very detailed. Traditionally, employment contracts have been used mostly for executives and senior managers, but the use of employment contracts is filtering down the organization to include highly specialized professional and technical employees who have scarce skills.

Employment contracts may include non-compete agreements, which prohibit individuals who leave an organization from working with an employer in the same line of business for a specified period of time. A non-compete agreement may be presented as a separate contract or as a clause in an employment contract.

Implied Contracts.   The idea that a contract (even an implied or unwritten one) exists between individuals and their employers affects the employment relationship. The rights and responsibilities of the employee may be spelled out in a job description, in an employment contract, in HR policies, or in a handbook, but often they are not. When the employer fails to follow up on the implied promises, the employee may pursue remedies in court.

Rights Affecting the Employment Relationship

As employees increasingly regard themselves as free agents in the workplace—and as the power of unions declines in the United States—the struggle between individual employee and employer "rights" is heightening. Several concepts from law and psychology influence the employment relationship: employment-at-will, wrongful or constructive discharge, just cause, due process, and distributive and procedural justice.

Employment-at-Will.   Employment-at-will (EAW) is a common-law doctrine stating that employers have the right to hire, fire, demote, or promote whomever they choose, unless there is a law or a contract to the contrary. Conversely, employees can quit whenever they want and go to another job under the same terms. An employment-at-will statement in an employee handbook usually contains wording such as the following:

> *This handbook is not a contract, express or implied, guaranteeing employment for any specific duration. Although we hope that your employment relationship with us will be long term, either you or the Employer may terminate this relationship at any time, for any reason, with or without cause or notice.*

Wrongful Discharge.   Employers who run afoul of EAW restrictions may be guilty of wrongful discharge, which is the termination of an individual's employment for reasons that are illegal or improper. Some state courts have recognized certain non-statutory grounds for wrongful-discharge suits. Additionally, courts generally have held that unionized workers cannot pursue EAW actions as at-will employees because they are covered by the grievance arbitration process. Employers should take several precautions to reduce wrongful-discharge liabilities.

Having a well-written employee handbook, training managers, and maintaining adequate documentation are key.

Closely related to wrongful discharge is **constructive discharge**, which is deliberately making conditions intolerable to get an employee to quit. Under normal circumstances, an employee who resigns rather than being dismissed cannot later collect damages for violation of legal rights. An exception to this rule occurs when the courts find that the working conditions were made so intolerable as to *force* a reasonable employee to resign. Then, the resignation is considered a discharge.

Just Cause.   **Just cause** is reasonable justification for taking employment-related action. A "good reason" or just cause for disciplinary actions such as dismissal can usually be found in union contracts, but not in at-will situations. The United States has different just-cause rules than do some other countries. Even though definitions of **just cause** vary, the overall concern is fairness. To be viewed by others as *just*, any disciplinary action must be based on facts in the individual case.

Due Process.   Due process, like just cause, is about fairness. Due process is the requirement that the employer use a fair process to determine if there has been employee wrongdoing and that the employee have an opportunity to explain and defend his or her actions. Figure 9-4 shows some factors to be considered when evaluating just cause and due process. How HR managers address these factors determines whether the courts perceive employers' actions as fair.

Alternative Dispute Resolution.   Disputes between management and employees over different work issues are normal and inevitable, but how the parties resolve their disputes can become important. Formal grievance procedures and lawsuits provide one method. Another means is arbitration, a process that uses a neutral third party to make a decision, thereby eliminating the necessity of using the court system.

FIGURE 9-4 Criteria for Evaluating Just Cause and Due Process

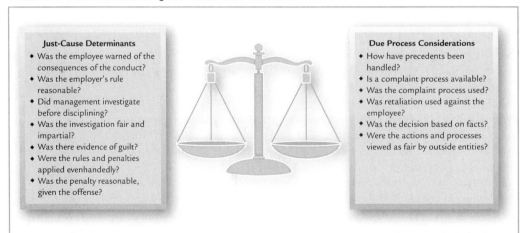

Just-Cause Determinants
- Was the employee warned of the consequences of the conduct?
- Was the employer's rule reasonable?
- Did management investigate before disciplining?
- Was the investigation fair and impartial?
- Was there evidence of guilt?
- Were the rules and penalties applied evenhandedly?
- Was the penalty reasonable, given the offense?

Due Process Considerations
- How have precedents been handled?
- Is a complaint process available?
- Was the complaint process used?
- Was retaliation used against the employee?
- Was the decision based on facts?
- Were the actions and processes viewed as fair by outside entities?

Some firms use **compulsory arbitration**, which requires employees to sign a pre-employment agreement stating that all disputes will be submitted to arbitration, and that employees waive their rights to pursue legal action until the completion of the arbitration process. Continuing pressure from state courts, federal employment regulatory commissions, and additional cases have challenged the fairness of compulsory arbitration in some situations. Requiring arbitration as a condition of employment is legal. In other situations, however, exceptions have been noted, so a legal check of where compulsory arbitration as part of ADR is allowed should be done before adopting the practice.

Some employers allow their employees to appeal disciplinary actions to an internal committee of employees. This panel reviews the actions and makes recommendations or decisions. Panel members are specially trained volunteers who sign confidentiality agreements, after which the company empowers them to hear appeals.

Balancing Employee and Employer Rights

Employees join organizations in the United States and some other countries with certain rights, including *freedom of speech, due process, and protection against unreasonable search and seizure.* Although the U.S. Constitution grants these and other rights to citizens, over the years, laws and court decisions have identified limits on them in the workplace.

Employees' Free Speech Rights

The right of individuals to freedom of speech is protected by the U.S. Constitution. However, that freedom is *not* an unrestricted one in the workplace. Three areas in which employees' freedom of speech have collided with employers' restrictions are controversial views, blogs and wikis, and whistle-blowing. Questions of free speech arise over the right of employees to advocate controversial viewpoints at work.

Individuals who report real or perceived wrongs committed by their employers are called whistle-blowers. The reasons why people report actions that they question vary and are often individual in nature. Whistle-blowers are less likely to lose their jobs in public employment than in private employment because most civil service systems follow rules protecting whistle-blowers. However, no comprehensive whistle-blowing law fully protects the right to free speech of both public and private employees.

Privacy Rights and Employee Records.   Recordkeeping and retention practices are a provision in the Americans with Disabilities Act (ADA): As interpreted by attorneys and HR practitioners, this provision requires that all medical-related information be maintained separately from all other confidential files.

Additionally, it is important that specific access restrictions and security procedures for employee records be established. These restrictions and procedures are designed to protect the privacy of employees and to protect employers from potential liability for improper disclosure of personal information. Personnel files and records should usually be maintained for three years. However, different types of records should be maintained for shorter or longer periods of time based on various legal and regulatory standards.

Workplace Monitoring

The commonplace monitoring of e-mail and voice mail is only one way employers watch the workplace. In the United States, the right of protection from unreasonable search and seizure protects an individual against activities of the government only. Thus, employees of private-sector employers can be monitored, observed, and searched at work by representatives of the employer. In addition, several court decisions have reaffirmed the principle that both private-sector and government employers may search desks, files, lockers, and computer files without search warrants if they believe that work rules were violated. Also, many employers have developed and disseminated Internet use policies.

Whether on or off the job, unethical or illegal employee behavior can be a serious problem for organizations. Employee misconduct may include illegal drug use, falsification of documents, misuse of company funds, disclosure of organizational secrets, workplace violence, employment harassment, and theft. Workplace investigations can be conducted internally or externally.

Monitoring of E-Mail and Voice Mail.   Employers have a right to monitor what is said and transmitted through their e-mail and voice-mail systems, despite employees' concerns about free speech. Advances in information and telecommunications technology have become a major issue for employers regarding employee privacy. The use of e-mail and voice mail increases every day, along with employers' liability if they improperly monitor or inspect employees' electronic communications. Many employers have specialized software that can retrieve deleted e-mail, and even record each keystroke made on their computers.

Substance Abuse and Drug Testing.   Employee substance abuse and drug testing have received a great deal of attention. Concern about substance abuse at work is appropriate given that absenteeism, accident/damage rates, health-care expenses, and theft/fraud are higher for workers using illegal substances or misusing legal substances such as drugs and alcohol.

The U.S. Supreme Court has ruled that certain drug-testing plans do not violate the Constitution. Unless state or local law prohibits testing, employers have a right to require applicants or employees to submit to a drug test. Where employers conduct drug testing of current employees, they use one of three policies: (1) random testing of everyone at periodic intervals, (2) testing only in cases of probable cause, or (3) testing after accidents.

HR Policies, Procedures, and Rules

HR policies, procedures, and rules greatly affect employee rights (just discussed) and discipline (discussed next). Where there is a choice among actions, **policies** act as general guidelines that focus organizational actions. Policies are general in nature, whereas **procedures** and **rules** are specific to the situation. The important role of policies requires that they be reviewed regularly.

Procedures provide customary methods of handling activities and are more specific than policies. For example, a policy may state that employees will be given vacations according to years of service, and a procedure establishes a specific method for authorizing vacation time without disrupting work.

Rules are specific guidelines that regulate and restrict the behavior of individuals. They are similar to procedures in that they guide action and typically allow no discretion in their application. Rules reflect a management decision that action be taken—or not taken—in a given situation, and they provide more specific behavioral guidelines than do policies.

Employee Handbooks

Often policies, procedures, and rules are provided in employee handbooks. An employee handbook can be an essential tool for communicating information about workplace culture, benefits, attendance, pay practices, safety issues, and discipline.[5] When preparing handbooks, management should consider legal issues, readability, and use.

To communicate and discuss HR information, a growing number of firms are distributing employee handbooks electronically using an intranet, which enables employees to access policies in employee handbooks at any time. It also allows changes in policies to be made electronically rather than distributed as paper copies.

Employee Discipline

The earlier discussion about employee rights provides an appropriate introduction to the topic of employee discipline, because employee rights often are a key issue in disciplinary cases. Discipline is a form of training that enforces organizational rules.

The disciplinary system can be viewed as an application of behavior modification to a problem or unproductive employee. The best discipline is clearly self-discipline. Most people can usually be counted on to do their jobs effectively when they understand what is required at work. Yet some find that the prospect of external discipline helps their self-discipline. One approach is positive discipline.

Positive Discipline Approach.   The positive discipline approach builds on the philosophy that violations are actions that can usually be corrected constructively without penalty. In this approach, managers focus on using fact-finding and guidance to encourage desirable behaviors, rather than using penalties to discourage undesirable behaviors.

Progressive Discipline Approach.   Progressive discipline incorporates steps that become progressively more stringent and are designed to change the employee's inappropriate behavior. Figure 9-5 shows a typical progressive discipline

FIGURE 9-5 Progressive Discipline Process

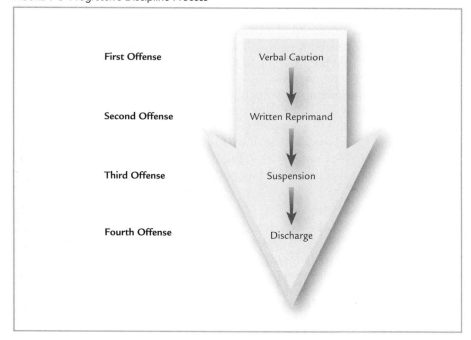

process; most progressive discipline procedures use verbal and written repri-
mands and suspension before resorting to dismissal.

The final stage in the disciplinary process is termination. Both the positive
and the progressive approaches to discipline clearly provide employees with
warnings about the seriousness of their performance problems before dismissal
occurs. Terminating workers because they do not keep their own promises is
more likely to appear equitable and defensible to a jury.

NOTES

1. Occupational Safety and Health Administration, *www.osha.gov.*

2. *Marshall v. Barlow's Inc.*, 98 S. Ct. 1816
(1978).

3. J. C. Wallace, Eric Popp, and Scott Mondore,
"Safety Climate as a Mediator Between
Foundation Climates and Occupational
Accidents: A Group-Level Investigation,"
Journal of Applied Psychology, 91 (2006),
681–668.

4. Will Strother, "A Security Primer," *SHRM
White Paper, www.shrm.org/hrtx.*

5. W. S. Hubbartt, "Ten Reasons to Write (or
Revise) Your Employee Handbook," *SHRM
White Paper*, February 2006, 1–6.

INTERNET RESOURCES

Occupational Safety and Health Administration—Access to OSHA regulations for compliance, newsroom, and much more can be found at the OSHA home page by linking to their Website at *www.osha.gov*

Institute for a Drug-Free Workplace—This Website provides employers with information on a drug-free workplace including the state and federal laws regarding drug testing. Link to their Website at *http://drugfreeworkplace.org*

SUGGESTED READINGS

Lisa Guerin and Amy Delpo, *Create Your Own Employee Handbook*, 3rd ed., (Nolo, 2007).

Liz Guthridge and Kathryn Mckee, *Leading People Through Disasters*. (Barrett-Koehler Publishers, 2006).

Gerald Lewis, *Organizational Crisis Management*, (Auerbach, 2006).

Mark Moran, *OSHA Answer Book Kit*, (Safety Certified, 2006).

CHAPTER 10

Labor Relations

HR—MEETING MANAGEMENT CHALLENGES

Even though union membership has been changing in the U.S., labor relations must be considered as an important part of HR considerations. The future of employer-union relations may be evolving as political and work environment changes affect HR. Key issues are

- Why the state of unions in the U.S. has been changing
- How a number of legal requirements affect employer HR policies and practices
- Establishing means to resolve employee complaints and grievances

Whether or not the CTWF efforts will offset the continuing decline in union membership will take several years to determine. But if not successful, union membership in the United States is likely to continue to represent a diminishing part of the U.S. workforce.

The changing nature of unions and unionization efforts will be interesting to observe during the next decade. How the economic and workforce changes affect employers and unions will be major factors. Even though fewer workers have chosen to be union members than in the past, employers and HR professionals still need to have an understanding of the system of laws, regulations, court decisions, and administrative rulings related to the nature of unions. This is important because unions remain an alternative for employees in the event of poor HR management.

Union-Management Labor Relations

A **union** is a formal association of workers that promotes the interests of its members through collective action. Why employees join unions and why employers resist unionization are part of understanding the current state of unionization in the United States.

Why Employees Unionize

Over the years employees have joined unions for two general reasons: (1) they are dissatisfied with how they are treated by their employers and (2) they believe that unions can improve their work situations. If employees do not receive what they perceive as fair treatment from their employers, they may turn to unions for help obtaining what they believe is equitable. As Figure 10-1 shows, the major factors that can trigger unionization are issues of compensation, working environment, management style, and employee treatment.

The primary determinant of whether employees unionize is management. Reasonably competitive compensation, a good working environment, effective management and supervision, and fair and responsive treatment of workers all act as antidotes to unionization efforts. Unionization results when employees feel disrespected, unsafe, underpaid, and unappreciated, and see a union as a viable option. Once unionization occurs, the union's ability to foster commitment from members and to remain as their bargaining agent depends on how well the union succeeds in providing services that its members want.

Why Employers Resist Unions

Employers usually would rather not have to deal with unions because doing so constrains what managers can and cannot do in a number of areas. Generally, union workers receive higher wages and benefits than do non-union workers. In turn, unions sometimes can be associated with higher productivity, although management must find labor-saving ways of doing work to offset the higher labor

FIGURE 10-1 Factors Leading to Employee Unionization

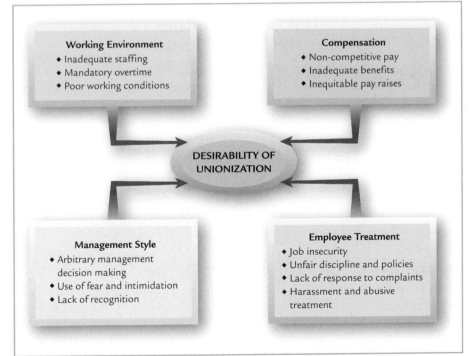

costs. Some employers pursue a strategy of good relations with unions. Others may choose an aggressive, adversarial approach.

Union Membership Globally

As the world economy becomes more integrated, unions worldwide are facing changes. The percentage of union membership varies significantly from country to country. In some countries, unions either do not exist at all or are relatively weak. In other countries, unions are closely tied to political parties. For instance, in Italy and France, national strikes occur regularly to protest proposed changes in government policy on retirement, pension programs, and regulations regarding dismissal of employees. Some countries require that firms have union or worker representatives on their boards of directors. This practice, which is called **co-determination**, is present in some European countries.

The union movement in the United States has some approaches different from those used in other countries. In the United States, the key emphases have been the following:

- Economic issues
- Organization by kind of job and employer
- Collective agreements as "contracts"
- Competitive relations

Union Membership in the United States

The statistics on union membership tell a disheartening story for organized labor in the United States during the past several decades. Unions represented over 30% of the workforce from 1945 to 1960. But by 2006, unions in the United States represented less than 12% of all civilian workers and only 7.4% of the private-sector workforce. Even more disheartening for the unions, the actual number of members has declined in most years even though more people are employed than previously. Of the approximately 130 million U.S. workers, only about 15.4 million belong to a union.[1]

But within those averages, some unions have prospered. In the past several years, certain unions have organized thousands of janitors, health-care workers, cleaners, and low-paid workers using publicity, pickets, boycotts, and strikes.

Reasons for U.S. Union Membership Decline

Several general reasons have contributed to the decline of unions: deregulation, foreign competition, a larger number of people looking for jobs, and a general perception by firms that dealing with unions is expensive compared with non-union alternatives. Also, management at many employers has taken a much more activist stance against unions than during the previous years of union growth.

Therefore, unions are not seen as necessary by many workers, even though those workers enjoy the results of past union efforts to influence legislation.

Geographic Changes. During the past decade, job growth in the United States has been the greatest in states located in the South, the Southwest, and the Rocky Mountains. Most of these states have little tradition of unions, "employer-friendly" laws, and relatively small percentages of unionized workers.

Industrial Changes. Much of the decline of union membership can be attributed to the shift in U.S. jobs from industries such as manufacturing, construction, and mining to service industries. There is a small percentage of union members in wholesale/retail industries and financial services, the sectors in which many new jobs have been added, whereas the number of industrial jobs continues to shrink. Figure 10-2 reveals that non-governmental union members are heavily concentrated in transportation, utilities, and other "industrial" jobs.

Workforce Changes. Many of the workforce changes discussed in earlier chapters have contributed to the decrease in union representation of the labor force. The decline in many blue-collar jobs in manufacturing has been especially significant, and the primary growth in jobs in the U.S. economy has been in

FIGURE 10-2 Union Membership by Industry

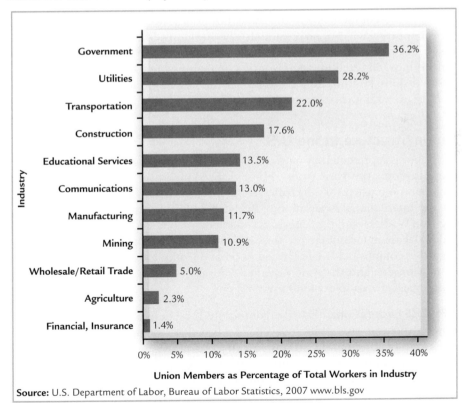

Source: U.S. Department of Labor, Bureau of Labor Statistics, 2007 www.bls.gov

technology, financial, and other service industries where union membership has typically been much lower. Also, in the past, unions have not been as successful in organizing female workers as they have been in organizing male workers.[2]

Public-Sector Unionism

Unions have had significant success with public-sector employees. The government sector (federal, state, and local) is the most highly unionized part of the U.S. workforce, with 36% of government workers represented by unions. Local government workers at 42% have the highest unionization percentage of any group in the U.S. workforce.[3]

Unionization of state and local government employees presents some unique problems and challenges. More than 30 states have laws prohibiting work stoppages by public employees. These laws also identify a variety of ways to resolve negotiation impasses, including arbitration. But unions still give employees in these areas greater security and better ability to influence decisions on wages and benefits than non-union workers have.

Union Targets for Membership Growth

To attempt to counteract the overall decline in union membership, unions are focusing on a number of industries and types of workers. Some unions target more addition of members in the retail, hospitality, home health care, and other service industries. Also, professionals who have turned to unionization include engineers, physicians, nurses, and teachers. On the other end of the labor scale, unions have targeted low-skill workers, many of whom have lower-paying, less desirable jobs. Janitors, building cleaners, nursing home aides, and meatpacking workers are examples of groups targeted by unions.

Union Structure in the U.S.

U.S. labor is represented by many different unions. But regardless of size and geographic scope, two basic types of unions developed over time. In a **craft union**, members do one type of work, often using specialized skills and training. Examples are the International Association of Bridge, Structural, Ornamental and Reinforcing Iron Workers, and the American Federation of Television and Radio Artists. An **industrial union** includes many persons working in the same industry or company, regardless of jobs held. The United Food and Commercial Workers, the United Auto Workers, and the American Federation of State, County, and Municipal Employees are examples of industrial unions.

AFL-CIO Federation.   Labor organizations have developed complex organizational structures with multiple levels. The broadest level is the federation, which is a group of autonomous unions. A federation allows individual unions to work together and present a more unified front to the public, legislators, and members. The most prominent federation in the United States is the AFL-CIO, which is a confederation of unions currently representing about 10 million workers.

However, the establishment of the Change to Win Federation (CTWF) in 2005 meant that seven unions with about 6 million members left the AFL-CIO. The primary reason for the split was a division between different unions about how to stop the decline in union membership, as well as some internal organizational leadership and political issues. Prominent unions in the CTWF are the Teamsters, the Service Employees International Union, and the United Food and Commercial Workers.

Like companies, unions find strength in size. In the past several years, about 40 mergers of unions have occurred, and a number of other unions have considered merging. For smaller unions, these mergers provide financial and union-organizing resources. Larger unions can add new members to cover managerial and administrative costs without spending funds to organize non-union workers to become members.

Local Unions.   Local unions typically have business agents and union stewards. A **business agent** is a full-time union official who operates the union office and assists union members. The agent runs the local headquarters, helps negotiate contracts with management, and becomes involved in attempts to unionize employees in other organizations. A **union steward** is an employee who is elected to serve as the first-line representative of unionized workers. Stewards address grievances with supervisors and generally represent employees at the work site.

. . . .

Basic Labor Laws: "National Labor Code"

The right to organize workers and engage in collective bargaining offers little value if workers cannot freely exercise it. Historical evidence shows that management has consistently developed practices calculated to prevent workers from using this right. Over a period of many years, the federal government has taken legislative action to both hamper unions and protect them.[4] For example, the Railway Labor Act (RLA) of 1926 represented a shift in government regulation of unions. As a result of a joint effort between railroad management and unions to reduce transportation strikes, this act gave railroad employees unionization rights.

Three more acts were passed over a period of almost 25 years, and constitute what has been labeled the "National Labor Code": (1) the Wagner Act, (2) the Taft-Hartley Act, and (3) the Landrum-Griffin Act. Each act was passed to focus on some facet of the relations between unions and management. Figure 10-3 indicates the primary focus of each act. Another piece of legislation, the Civil Service Reform Act, also affect governmental aspects of union/management relations.

Wagner Act (National Labor Relations Act)

The National Labor Relations Act, more commonly referred to as the Wagner Act, was an outgrowth of the Great Depression. With employers having to close or cut back their operations, workers were left with little job security. Unions

FIGURE 10-3 National Labor Code

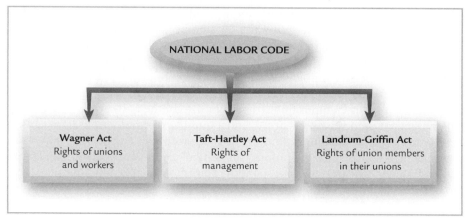

stepped in to provide a feeling of solidarity and strength for many workers. The Wagner Act declared, in effect, that the official policy of the U.S. government was to encourage collective bargaining. Specifically, it established the right of workers to organize unhampered by management interference through unfair labor practices.

Unfair Labor Practices. To protect union rights, the Wagner Act prohibited employers from utilizing unfair labor practices. Five of those practices are identified as follows:

- Interfering with, restraining, or coercing employees in the exercise of their right to organize or to bargain collectively
- Dominating or interfering with the formation or administration of any labor organization
- Encouraging or discouraging membership in any labor organization by discriminating with regard to hiring, tenure, or conditions of employment
- Discharging or otherwise discriminating against an employee because he or she filed charges or gave testimony under the act
- Refusing to bargain collectively with representatives of the employees

National Labor Relations Board. The Wagner Act established the National Labor Relations Board as an independent entity to enforce the provisions of the act. The NLRB administers all provisions of the Wagner Act and of subsequent labor relations acts. The primary functions of the NLRB include conducting unionization elections, investigating complaints by employers or unions through its fact-finding process, issuing opinions on its findings, and prosecuting violations in court. The five members of the NLRB are appointed by the President of the United States and confirmed by the U.S. Senate.

Taft-Hartley Act (Labor-Management Relations Act)

The passage in 1947 of the Labor-Management Relations Act, better known as the Taft-Hartley Act, was accomplished as a means to offset the pro-union Wagner Act by limiting union actions. Therefore, it was considered to be pro-management and became the second part of the National Labor Code. The new law amended or qualified in some respect all the major provisions of the Wagner Act and established an entirely new code of conduct for unions. The Taft-Hartley Act forbade unions from engaging in a series of unfair labor practices, much like those management was prohibited from engaging in.

The Taft-Hartley Act also established the Federal Mediation and Conciliation Service (FMCS) as an agency to help management and labor settle labor contract disputes. The act required that the FMCS be notified of disputes over contract renewals or modifications if they were not settled within 30 days after the designated date.

National Emergency Strikes.   The Taft-Hartley Act allows the President of the United States to declare that a strike presents a national emergency. A national emergency strike is one that would impact an industry or a major part of it in such a way that the national economy would be significantly affected. Over the decades national emergencies have been identified in the railroad, airline, and other industries.

Right-to-Work Provision.   One specific provision of the Taft-Hartley Act, Section 14(b), deserves special explanation. This section allows states to pass laws that restrict compulsory union membership. Accordingly, some states have passed **right-to-work laws**, which prohibit requiring employees to join unions as a condition of obtaining or continuing employment. The laws were so named because they allow a person the right to work without having to join a union. The nature of union/management relations is affected by the right-to-work provisions. The Taft-Hartley Act generally prohibits the closed shop, which is a firm that requires individuals to join a union before they can be hired.

In states with right-to-work laws, employers may have an *open shop*, which indicates workers cannot be required to join or pay dues to a union. Consequently, in many of the right-to-work states, individual membership in union groups is significantly lower.

In states that do not have right-to-work laws, there may be a number of different types of arrangements. Three of the different types of "shops" are as follows:

- *Union shop*: Requires that individuals join the union, usually 30 to 60 days after being hired.
- *Agency shop*: Requires employees who refuse to join the union to pay amounts equal to union dues and fees in return for the representation services of the union.
- *Maintenance-of-membership shop*: Requires workers to remain members of the union for the period of the labor contract.

Landrum-Griffin Act (Labor-Management Reporting and Disclosure Act)

The third segment of the National Labor Code, the Landrum-Griffin Act, was passed in 1959. Because a union is supposed to be a democratic institution in which union members vote on and elect officers and approve labor contracts, the Landrum-Griffin Act was passed in part to ensure that the federal government protects the democratic rights of those members. The law appointed the U.S. Secretary of Labor to act as a watchdog of union conduct.

Civil Service Reform Act of 1978

Passed as part of the Civil Service Reform Act of 1978, the Federal Service Labor-Management Relations statute made major changes in how the federal government deals with unions. The act also identified areas subject to bargaining and established the Federal Labor Relations Authority (FLRA) as an independent agency similar to the NLRB. The FLRA, a three-member body, was given the authority to oversee and administer union/management relations in the federal government and to investigate unfair practices in union organizing efforts.

Unionization Process

The typical union organizing process is outlined in Figure 10-4. The process of unionizing an employer may begin in one of two primary ways: (1) a union targeting an industry or a company, or (2) employees requesting union representation. In the first case, the local or national union identifies a firm or an industry in which it believes unionization can succeed. The logic for targeting is that if the union succeeds in one firm or a portion of the industry, then many other workers in the industry will be more willing to consider unionizing.

In the second case, the impetus for union organizing occurs when individual workers at an employer contact a union and express a desire to unionize. The employees themselves—or the union—may then begin to campaign to win support among the other employees.

Organizing Campaign

Like other entities seeking members, a union usually mounts an organized campaign to persuade individuals to support its efforts. As would be expected, employers respond to unionization efforts by taking various types of actions. As part of union prevention, many employers have a written "no-solicitation" policy to restrict employees and outsiders from distributing literature or soliciting union membership on company premises. Employers without such a policy may be unable to prevent those acts. Union prevention efforts that may be conducted by consultants or done by management and outside labor attorneys include:

- Holding mandatory employee meetings.
- Distributing anti-union leaflets at work and mailing anti-union letters to employees' homes.
- Providing and using anti-union videos, e-mails, and other electronic means.

FIGURE 10-4 Typical Unionization Process

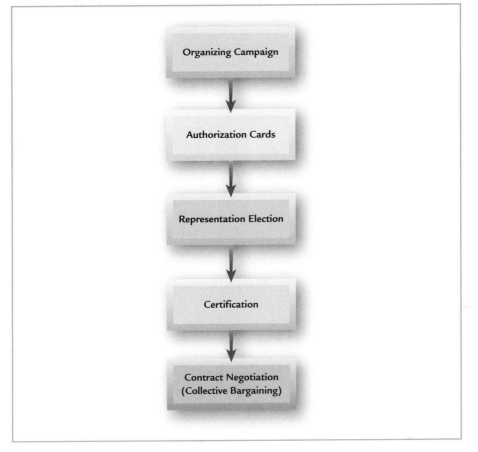

The persuasion efforts by unions can take many forms, including personally contacting employees outside work, mailing materials to employees' homes, inviting employees to attend special meetings away from the company, and publicizing the advantages of union membership. The purpose of all this publicity is to encourage employees to sign authorization cards.

Authorization Cards

A union authorization card is signed by an employee to designate a union as her or his collective bargaining agent. At least 30% of the employees in the targeted group must sign authorization cards before an election can be called. Union advocates have lobbied for changing laws so that elections are not needed if over 50% of the eligible employees sign authorization cards.

In reality, the fact that an employee signs an authorization card does not necessarily mean that the employee is in favor of a union; it means only that the employee would like the opportunity to vote on having a union. Employees who do not want a union might sign authorization cards because they want management to know they are disgruntled or to avoid upsetting a co-worker advocating unionization.

Employers and some politicians argue that eliminating elections violates the personal secrecy and democracy rights of employees. The extent of legislative changes will depend on the political composition of the U.S. Congress and Presidential reactions to such efforts.

Representation Election

An election to determine if a union will represent the employees is supervised by the NLRB for private-sector organizations and by other legal bodies for public-sector organizations. If two unions are attempting to represent employees, the employees will have three choices: union A, union B, and no union.

Bargaining Unit.   Before any election, the appropriate bargaining unit must be determined. A bargaining unit is composed of all employees eligible to select a single union to represent and bargain collectively for them. Employees who constitute a bargaining unit have mutual interests in the following areas:

- Wages, hours, and working conditions
- Traditional industry groupings for bargaining purposes
- Physical location and amount of interaction and working relationships between employee groups
- Supervision by similar levels of management

Supervisors and Union Ineligibility.   Provisions of the National Labor Relations Act exclude supervisors from wipeout protection when attempting to vote for or join unions. As a result, supervisors cannot be included in bargaining units for unionization purposes, except in industries covered by the Railway Labor Act. But who qualifies as a supervisor is not always clear. The NLRB expanded its definition to identify a supervisor as any individual with authority to hire, transfer, discharge, discipline, and use independent judgment with employees.[5]

Unfair Labor Practices.   Employers and unions engage in a number of activities before an election. Both the Wagner Act and the Taft-Hartley Act place restrictions on these activities. Once unionizing efforts begin, all activities must conform to the requirements established by applicable labor laws. Both management and the union must adhere to those requirements, or the results of the effort can be appealed to the NLRB and overturned. Appendix C highlights some of the legal and illegal actions managers must be aware of during unionization efforts.

Election Process.   If an election is held, the union need receive only a *majority of the votes*. For example, if a group of 200 employees is the identified bargaining unit, and only 50 people vote, only 26 (50% of those voting plus 1) need to vote yes for the union to be named as the representative of all 200 employees. If either side believes that the other side used unfair labor practices, the election results can be appealed to the NLRB. If the NLRB finds evidence of unfair practices, it can order a new election. If no unfair practices were used and the union obtains a majority in the election, the union then petitions the NLRB for certification.

Certification and Decertification

Official certification of a union as the legal representative for designated private-sector employees is given by the NLRB, or for public-sector employees by an equivalent body. Once certified, the union attempts to negotiate a contract with the employer. The employer must bargain; refusing to bargain with a certified union constitutes an unfair labor practice.

When members no longer wish to be represented by the union, they can use a decertification process whereby a union is removed as the representative of a group of employees. Employees attempting to oust a union must obtain decertification authorization cards signed by at least 30% of the employees in the bargaining unit before election may be called. If a majority of those voting in the election want to remove the union, the decertification effort succeeds. Current regulations prohibit employers from initiating or supporting decertification because it is a matter between employees and unions, and employers must stay out of the process.

· ·

Collective Barganing and Contract Negotiation

Collective bargaining, the last step in unionization, is the process whereby representatives of management and workers negotiate over wages, hours, and other terms and conditions of employment. This give-and-take process between representatives of the two organizations attempts to establish a formal contract that will govern the employer-union management relation for several years.

Collective Bargaining Issues

A number of issues can be addressed during collective bargaining. Although not often listed as such in the contract, management rights and union security are two important issues subject to collective bargaining.

Virtually all labor contracts include management rights, which are rights reserved so that the employer can manage, direct, and control its business. By including such a provision, management attempts to preserve its unilateral right to make changes in areas not identified in a labor contract.

A major concern of union representatives when bargaining is the negotiation of **union security provisions**, which are contract clauses to help the union obtain and retain members. A growing type of union security in labor contracts is the *no-layoff policy*, or *job security guarantee*. One union security provision is the *dues checkoff*, which provides for the automatic deduction of union dues from the payroll checks of union members. The dues checkoff makes it much easier for the union to collect its funds; without it, the union must collect dues by billing each member separately.

The NLRB has defined collective bargaining issues in three ways. The categories it has used are mandatory, permissive, and illegal.

Issues identified specifically by labor laws or court decisions as subject to bargaining are mandatory issues. If either party demands that issues in this category be subject to bargaining, then that must occur. Generally, mandatory issues relate to wages, benefits, nature of jobs, and other work-related subjects.

Issues that are not mandatory and that relate to certain jobs are permissive issues. For example, the following issues can be bargained over if both parties agree: benefits for retired employees, product prices for employees, or performance bonds.

A final category, illegal issues, includes those issues that would require either party to take illegal action. Examples would be giving preference to union members when hiring employees or demanding a closed-shop provision in the contract. If one side wants to bargain over an illegal issue, the other side can refuse.

Collective Bargaining Process

The collective bargaining process consists of a number of stages: preparation and initial demands, negotiations, settlement or impasse, and strikes and lockouts. Throughout the process, management and labor deal with the terms of their relationship.

Preparation and Initial Demands.   Both labor and management representatives spend considerable time preparing for negotiations. Employer and industry data concerning wages, benefits, working conditions, management and union rights, productivity, and absenteeism are gathered. If the organization argues that it cannot afford to pay what the union is asking, the employer's financial situation and accompanying data become all the more relevant. However, the union must request such information before the employer is obligated to provide it. Typical bargaining includes initial proposals of expectations by both sides.

Continuing Negotiations.   After taking initial positions, each side attempts to determine what the other side values highly so that the best bargain can be struck. Provisions in federal law require that both employers and union bargaining representatives negotiate in good faith. In good-faith negotiations, the parties agree to send negotiators who can bargain and make decisions, rather than people who do not have the authority to commit either group to a decision. To be more effective, meetings between the parties should be conducted professionally and address issues, rather than being confrontational. Refusing to bargain, scheduling meetings at absurdly inconvenient hours, or other conflicting tactics may lead to employers or unions filing complaints with the NLRB.

Settlement and Contract Agreement. After reaching an initial agreement, the bargaining parties usually return to their respective constituencies to determine if the informal agreement is acceptable. A particularly crucial stage is ratification of the *labor agreement*, which occurs when union members vote to accept the terms of a negotiated labor agreement. Before ratification, the union negotiating team explains the agreement to the union members and presents it for a vote. If the members approve the agreement, it is then formalized into a contract. Figure 10-5 lists typical items in labor agreements.

Bargaining Impasse. Regardless of the structure of the bargaining process, labor and management do not always reach agreement on the issues. If they reach an impasse, then the disputes can be taken to conciliation, mediation, or arbitration.

Conciliation and Mediation. When an impasse occurs, an outside party such as the Federal Mediation and Conciliation Service may help the two deadlocked parties to continue negotiations and arrive at a solution. In **conciliation**, the third party assists union and management negotiators to reach a voluntary settlement, but makes no proposals for solutions. In **mediation**, the third party helps the negotiators reach a settlement. Sometimes, *fact-finding* helps to clarify the issues of disagreement as an intermediate step between mediation and arbitration.

In **arbitration**, a neutral third party makes a decision. Arbitration can be conducted by an individual or a panel of individuals. Fortunately, in many situations,

FIGURE 10-5 Typical Items in a Labor Agreement

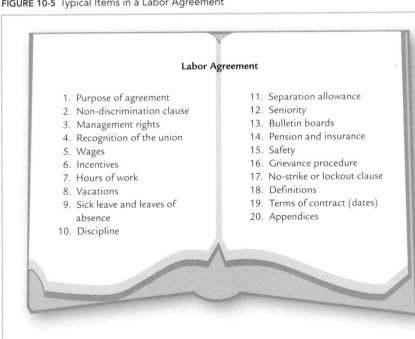

Labor Agreement

1. Purpose of agreement
2. Non-discrimination clause
3. Management rights
4. Recognition of the union
5. Wages
6. Incentives
7. Hours of work
8. Vacations
9. Sick leave and leaves of absence
10. Discipline
11. Separation allowance
12. Seniority
13. Bulletin boards
14. Pension and insurance
15. Safety
16. Grievance procedure
17. No-strike or lockout clause
18. Definitions
19. Terms of contract (dates)
20. Appendices

agreements are reached through negotiations without the need for arbitration.[6] When disagreements continue, strikes or lockouts may occur.

Strikes and Lockouts. The adversarial relationship that naturally exists between unions and management may lead to strikes and lockouts. However, such conflicts are relatively rare.

If a deadlock cannot be resolved, an employer may revert to a lockout—or a union then may revert to a strike. During a strike, union members refuse to work in order to put pressure on an employer. Often, the striking union members picket or demonstrate against the employer outside the place of business by carrying placards and signs. In a lockout, management shuts down company operations to prevent union members from working. This action may avert possible damage or sabotage to company facilities or injury to employees who continue to work. It also gives management leverage in negotiations.

As a result of the decline in union power, work stoppages due to strikes and lockouts are relatively rare. In a recent year only 22 strikes and lockouts occurred. Over three-fourths of the work stoppages ended within 20 days. Management retains and sometimes uses its ability to simply replace workers who strike. Workers' rights vary depending on the type of strike that occurs.

Union/Management Cooperation

Typically management resists union efforts and has had limited cooporation with unions. But in a number of firms, including South West Airlines, Union management coporation is present.

Unions in some situations have encouraged workers to become partial or complete owners of the companies that employ them. Unions have been active in helping members put together employee stock ownership plans to purchase all or part of some firms.[7] Such programs have been successful in some situations but have caused problems in others.

· ·

Grievance Management

Unions know that employee dissatisfaction is a potential source of trouble for employers, whether it is expressed or not. Hidden dissatisfaction grows and creates reactions that may be completely out of proportion to the original concerns. Therefore, it is important that dissatisfaction be given an outlet. A **complaint**, which is merely an indication of employee dissatisfaction, is one outlet. Complaints often are made by employees who are not represented by unions. If an employee is represented by a union, then a complaint becomes a **grievance**, which is a complaint formally stated in writing.

Management should be concerned with both complaints and grievances, because both indicate potential problems within the workforce. Without a grievance procedure, management may be unable to respond to employee concerns because managers are unaware of them. Therefore, a formal grievance procedure provides a valuable communication tool for the organizations, whether a union is present or not.[8]

Grievance Procedures

Grievance procedures are formal channels of communication designed to resolve grievances as soon as possible after problems arise. First-line supervisors are usually closest to a problem. However, these supervisors are concerned with many other matters besides one employee's grievance, and may even be the subject of an employee's grievance. To receive the appropriate attention, grievances go through a specific process for resolution.

Grievance procedures can vary in the number of steps they include. Figure 10-6 shows a typical grievance procedure, which consists of the following steps:

1. The employee discusses the grievance with the union steward (the representative of the union on the job) and the supervisor.
2. The union steward discusses the grievance with the supervisor's manager and/or the HR manager.
3. A committee of union officers discusses the grievance with appropriate company managers.
4. The representative of the national union discusses the grievance with designated company executives or the corporate industrial relations officer.
5. If the grievance is not solved at this stage, it goes to arbitration. An impartial third party may ultimately dispose of the grievance.

FIGURE 10-6 Steps in a Typical Grievance Procedure

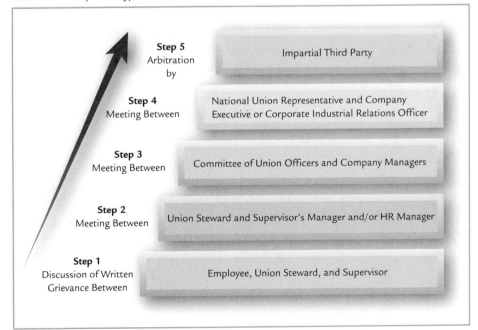

Step 5
Arbitration
by

Impartial Third Party

Step 4
Meeting Between

National Union Representative and Company Executive or Corporate Industrial Relations Officer

Step 3
Meeting Between

Committee of Union Officers and Company Managers

Step 2
Meeting Between

Union Steward and Supervisor's Manager and/or HR Manager

Step 1
Discussion of Written
Grievance Between

Employee, Union Steward, and Supervisor

Grievance arbitration is a means by which a third party settles disputes arising from different interpretations of a labor contract. This process should not be confused with contract or issues arbitration, discussed earlier, in which arbitration is used to determine how a contract will be written. The U.S. Supreme Court has ruled that grievance arbitration decisions issued under labor contract provisions are enforceable. Grievance arbitration includes more than 50 topic areas, with discipline and discharge, safety and health, and security issues being most prevalent.

NOTES

1. U.S. Bureau of Labor Statistics, "Union Members in 2006," January 25, 2007, *www.bls.gov/pub/news.release.*

2. J. R. B. Halbesleben and M. R. Buckley, "The Effect of Economic Conditions on Union Membership of Men and Women: A Quantitative and Historical Analysis," *Journal of Management History,* 12 (2006), 293.

3. U.S. Bureau of Labor Statistics, *www.bls.gov.*

4. Joseph Adler, "The Past as Prologue? A Brief History of the Labor Movement in the United States," *Public Personnel Management,* 34 (2006), 311.

5. Allen Smith, "NLRB's Expansive Definition of 'Supervisor' Could Cut Union Strength," *SHRM News,* October 14, 2006, *www.shrm.org/hrnews.*

6. "Major Work Stoppages," *Bureau of Labor Statistics News,* March 2, 2006, *www.bls.gov/cba.*

7. Jacquelyn Yates, "Unions and Employee Ownership: A Road to Economic Recovery?" *Industrial Relations,* 45 (2006), 709.

8. Lawrence Nurse and Dwayne Devonish, "Grievance Management and Its Links to Workplace Justice," *Employee Relations,* 29 (2007), 89.

INTERNET RESOURCES

National Labor Relations Board—For information on workplace rights and other issues, visit the NLRB's Website at: *http//www.nlrb.gov*

Federal Mediation and Conciliation Service— This Website provides information on the services and resources available through the agency of the United States Government that handles arbitration and mediation of labor disputes and contract negotiations. Visit their site at: *http://www.fmcs.gov <http://thomsonedu.com/Mathis.>*

SUGGESTED READINGS

Philip M. Dine, *State of the Unions,* (McGraw-Hill, 2008).

Mark Ethridge, *Grievances,* (New South Books, 2006).

William M.Holly, Kenneth M. Jennings, and Roger S. Wolters, *The Labor Relations Process,* 9th ed. (Thomson Learning, 2008).

David Prosten, *The Union Steward's Complete Guide,* (Union Communication Services, 2006).

Internet Resources

HR-RELATED INTERNET LINKS

American Arbitration Association
http://www.adr.org

Academy of Management
http://www.aom.pace.edu

American Federation of Labor/Congress of
Industrial Organizations (AFL-CIO)
http://www.aflcio.org

American Institute for Managing Diversity
http://www.aimd.org

American Psychological Association
http://www.apa.org

American Society for Industrial Security
http://www.asisonline.org

American Society for Payroll Management
http://www.aspm.org

American Society for Training and
Development
http://www.astd.org

Australian Human Resource Institute
http://www.ahri.com.au

CPR Institute for Dispute Resolution
http://www.cpradr.org

Employee Benefit Research Institute
http://www.ebri.org

Employment Management Association
http://www.shrm.org/ema

Foundation for Enterprise Development
http://www.fed.org

Hong Kong Institute of Human Resource
Management
http://www.hkihrm.org

Human Resource Certification Institute
http://www.hrci.org

Institute of Personnel and Development (UK)
http://www.ipd.co.uk

International Association for Human Resource
Information Management
http://ihrim.org

International Association of Industrial Accident
Boards and Commissions
http://www.iaiabc.org

International Foundation of Employee Benefit
Plans (IFEBP)
http://www.ifebp.org

International Personnel Management
Association
http://www.ipma-hr.org

International Personnel Management
Association Assessment Council
http://ipmaac.org

Labor and Employment Relations Association
www.lera.uiuc.edu

National Center for Employee Ownership
http://www.nceo.org

National Health Information Research Center
http://www.nhirc.org

Society for Human Resource Management
http://www.shrm.org
Union Resource Network
http://www.unions.org

Workforce Management
http://www.workforce.com
World at Work
http://www.worldatwork.org

SELECTED GOVERNMENT INTERNET LINKS

Bureau of Labor Statistics
http://www.bls.gov
Census Bureau
http://www.census.gov
Department of Labor
http://www.dol.gov
Economic Statistics Briefing Room
http://www.whitehouse.gov/fsbr/esbr.html
Employment and Training Administration
http://www.doleta.gov
Equal Employment Opportunity Commission
http://www.eeoc.gov
FedStats
http://www.fedstats.gov
National Institute of Environmental Health Sciences
http://www.niehs.nih.gov
National Institute for Safety and Health (NIOSH)
http://www.cdc.gov/niosh/homepage.html

National Labor Relations Board
http://www.nlrb.gov
Occupational Safety and Health Administration
http://www.osha.gov
Office of Personnel Management
http://www.opm.gov
Pension and Welfare Benefits Administration
http://www.dol.gov/ebsa/welcome.html
Pension Benefit Guaranty Corporation
http://www.pbgc.gov
Small Business Administration
http://www.sba.gov
Social Security Administration
http://www.ssa.gov
Training Technology Resource Center
http://www.ttrc.doleta.gov
U.S. House of Representatives
http://www.house.gov
U.S. Senate
http://www.senate.gov

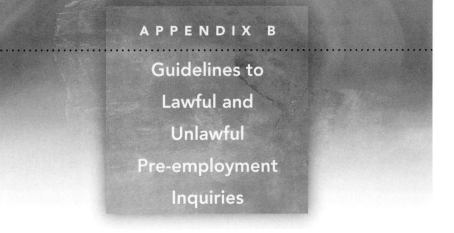

Guidelines to Lawful and Unlawful Pre-employment Inquiries

Subject of Inquiry	It May Not Be Discriminatory to Inquire About ...	It My Be Discriminatory to Inquire About ...
1. Name	a. Whether applicant has ever worked under a different name	a. The original name of applicant whose name has been legally changed b. The ethnic association of applicant's name
2. Age	a. If applicant is over the age of 18 b. If applicant is under the age of 18 or 21 if that information is job related (e.g., for selling liquor in a retail store)	a. Date of birth b. Date of high school graduation
3. Residence	a. Applicant's place of residence b. Alternative contact information	a. Previous addresses b. Birthplace of applicant or applicant's parents c. Length lived at current and previous addresses
4. Race or color		a. Applicant's race or color of applicant's skin
5. National Origin and Ancestry		a. Applicant's lineage, ancestry, national origin, parentage, or nationality b. Nationality of applicant's parents or spouse
6. Sex and Family Composition		a. Sex of applicant b. Marital status of applicant c. Dependents of applicants or child-care arrangements d. Whom to contact in case of emergency

(continued)

Subject of Inquiry	It May Not Be Discriminatory to Inquire About ...	It My Be Discriminatory to Inquire About ...
7. Creed or Religion		a. Applicant's religious affiliation b. Applicant's church, parish, mosque, or synagogue c. Holidays observed by applicant
8. Citizenship	a. Whether the applicant is a U.S. citizen or has a current permit/visa to work in the U.S.	a. Whether applicant is a citizen of a country other than the U.S. b. Date of citizenship
9. Language	a. Language applicant speaks and/or writes fluently, if job related	a. Applicant's native tongue b. Language used at home
10. References	a. Names of persons willing to provide professional and/or character references for applicant b. Previous work contacts	a. Name of applicant's religious leader b. Political affiliation and contacts
11. Relatives	a. Names of relatives already employed by the employer	a. Name and/or address of any relative of applicant b. Whom to contact in case of emergency
12. Organizations	a. Applicant's membership in any professional, service, or trade organization	a. All clubs or social organizations to which applicant belongs
13. Arrest Record and Convictions	a. Convictions, if related to job performance (disclaimer should accompany)	a. Number and kinds of arrests b. Convictions, unless related to job requirements and performance
14. Photographs		a. Photographs with application, with resume, or before hiring
15. Height and Weight		a. Any inquiry into height and weight of applicant, except where a BFOQ exists
16. Physical Limitations	a. Whether applicant has the ability to perform job-related functions with or without accommodation	a. The nature or severity of an illness or physical condition b. Whether applicant has ever filed a workers' compensation claim c. Any recent or past operations, treatments, or surgeries and dates

Subject of Inquiry	It May Not Be Discriminatory to Inquire About ...	It My Be Discriminatory to Inquire About ...
17. Education	a. Training applicant has received, if related to the job b. Highest level of education applicant has attained, if validated that having certain educational background (e.g., high school diploma or college degree) is needed to perform the specific job	a. Date of high school graduation
18. Military	a. Branch of the military applicant served in and ranks attained b. Type of education or training received in military	a. Military discharge details b. Military service records
19. Financial Status		a. Applicant's debts or assets b. Garnishments

Legal Do's and Don'ts for Managers during the Unionization

Do (legal)

- Tell employees about current wages and benefits and how they compare with those in other firms
- Tell employees that the employer opposes unionization
- Tell employees the disadvantages of having a union (especially cost of dues, assessments, and requirements of membership)
- Show employees articles about unions and relate negative experiences elsewhere
- Explain the unionization process to employees accurately
- Forbid distribution of union literature during work hours in work areas
- Enforce disciplinary policies and rules consistently and appropriately

Don't (illegal)

- Promise employees pay increases or promotions if they vote against the union
- Threaten employees with termination or discriminate when disciplining employees
- Threaten to close down or move the company if a union is voted on
- Spy on or have someone spy on union meetings
- Make a speech to employees or groups at work within 24 hours of the election (before that, it is allowed)
- Ask employees how they plan to vote or if they have signed authorization cards
- Encourage employees to persuade others to vote against the union (such persuasion must be initiated solely by employees)

Glossary

A

administrative Focusing on HR clerical administration and recordkeeping.

applicant tracking An approach that takes an applicant all the way from a job listing to performance appraisal results.

arbitration Process that uses a neutral third party to make a decision.

auditory learners Those who learn best by listening to someone tell them about the training content.

B

balanced scorecard An effective approach to the measurement of the strategic performance of organizations, including their HR departments.

base pay The basic compensation that an employee receives, usually as a wage or a salary.

behavior-based information Focuses on specific behaviors that lead to job success.

benchmark jobs Jobs that are found in many other organizations. Often these jobs are performed by individuals who have similar duties that require similar KSAs.

benchmarking Comparing specific measures of performance against those in other organizations.

benefit Indirect reward given to an employee or a group of employees for organizational membership.

bonus A one-time payment that does not become part of the employee's base pay.

burden of proof What individuals who file suit against employers must prove in order to establish that illegal discrimination has occurred.

business agent Full-time union official who operates the union office and assists union members.

C

career planning Identifies paths and activities for individual employees as they move within the organization.

checklist A list of statements or words from which raters check statements most representative of the characteristics and performance of employees.

co-determination Some countries require that firms have union or worker representatives on their boards of directors.

collective bargaining Process whereby representatives of management and workers negotiate over wages, hours, and other terms and conditions of employment.

compa-ratio Pay level divided by the midpoint of the pay range.

compensatory approach Scores from individual predictors are added and combined into an overall score, thereby allowing a higher score on one predictor to offset, or compensate for, a lower score on another. The combined index takes into consideration performance on all predictors.

compensatory time-off Compensatory hours given to an employee in lieu of payment for extra time worked.

complaint Indication of employee dissatisfaction.

compressed workweek Schedule in which a full week's work is accomplished in fewer than five 8-hour days.

compulsory arbitration A process in which the employees sign a pre-employment agreement stating that all disputes will be submitted to arbitration and those employees waive their rights to pursue legal action until the completion of the arbitration process.

conciliation The third party assists union and management negotiators to reach a voluntary settlement, but makes no proposals for solutions.

constructive discharge Process of deliberately making conditions intolerable to get an employee to quit.

continuance commitment factors The decisions to remain with or leave an organization are reflected in employee absenteeism and turnover statistics.

contrast error Tendency to rate people relative to others rather than against performance standards.

Cost-of-living adjustment (COLA) A common pay-raise practice adjustments that are tied to changes in the Consumer Price Index (CPI) or some other general economic measure.

craft union Union whose members do one type of work, often using specialized skills and training.

credit union Union that provides saving and lending services for employees.

critical incident method The manager keeps a written record of both highly favorable and unfavorable actions performed by an employee during the entire rating period.

cultural awareness To see and accept the differences in people with widely varying cultural backgrounds.

cultural compatibility The extent to which such factors as decision-making styles, levels of teamwork, information-sharing philosophies, the formality of the two organizations, etc., are similar.

D

data Factual pieces of information regarding observed actions or consequences.

defined-benefit plan Employees are promised a pension amount based on age and service.

defined-contribution health plans A plan in which an employer places a set amount into each employee's "account" and identifies a number of health-care alternatives that are available.

differential piece-rate system One piece-rate wage for units produced up to a standard output and a higher piece-rate wage for units produced over the standard.

different-size reward Employers vary individual rewards depending on such factors as contribution to group/team results, current pay, years of experience, and skill levels of jobs performed.

direct compensation A tangible component of a compensation program, whereby the employer exchanges monetary rewards for work done and performance results achieved.

discrimination Recognizing differences among items or people.

distributive justice The perceived fairness in the distribution of outcomes.

dues check off Union security provision which provides automatic deduction of union dues from the payroll checks of union members.

duty A larger work segment composed of several tasks that are performed by an individual.

E

Economic value added (EVA) Net operating profit of a firm after the cost of capital is deducted.

employee engagement The extent to which an employee is willing and able to contribute.

employer career websites Convenient recruiting places on an employer's website where applicants can see what jobs are available and apply.

encapsulated development A situation when an individual learns new methods and ideas, but returns to a work unit that is still bound by old attitudes and methods.

entitlement philosophy Assumes that individuals who have worked another year are entitled to pay increases, with little regard for performance differences.

essay method The manager writes a short essay describing each employee's performance during the rating period.

essential job functions Fundamental job duties.

evaluation The way the feedback system reacts to the facts and it requires performance standards.

extrinsic rewards Rewards that are tangible and take both monetary and non-monetary forms.

F

fact-finding An intermediate step between mediation and arbitration to clarify the issues of disagreement.

firm-choice option The employee is offered a choice between help and discipline.

forced distribution method The method in which ratings of employees' performance are distributed along a bell-shaped curve.

Full-time equivalents (FTEs) A measure equal to one person working full-time for a year.

G

goal sharing The system of sharing with employees greater-than-expected gains in profits and/or productivity.

graphic rating scale Allows the rater to mark an employee's performance on a continuum.

grievance Complaint formally stated in writing.

grievance arbitration Means by which a third party settles disputes arising from different interpretations of a labor contract.

H

halo effect A rater scores an employee high on all job criteria because of performance in one area.

health General state of physical, mental, and emotional well-being.

horns effect A low rating on one characteristic leads to an overall low rating.

Human Resource (HR) management Designing management systems to ensure that human talent is used effectively and efficiently to accomplish organizational goals.

I

inactivity rate The percentage of time lost to absenteeism.

incidence rate The number of absentees per 100 employees each day.

industrial union Many persons working in the same industry or company, regardless of jobs held.

informal appraisal Evaluation communicated through conversation on the job, over coffee, or by on-the-spot discussion of a specific occurrence.

internal mobility A system that tracks prospects in the company and matches them with jobs as they come open.

intrinsic rewards Praise for completing a project or meeting performance objectives.

J

job analysis Systematic way of gathering and analyzing information about the content, context, and human requirements of jobs.

job description Identifies the tasks, duties, and responsibilities of a job.

job design Organizing tasks, duties, responsibilities, and other elements into a productive unit of work.

job duties Important elements in a given job.

job satisfaction A positive emotional state resulting from evaluating one's job experiences.

job specifications Identify what KSAs a person needs to do the job, not necessarily the current employee's qualifications.

just cause Reasonable justification for taking employment-related action.

L

law of effect States that people tend to repeat responses that give them some type of positive reward and to avoid actions associated with negative consequences.

legal awareness Focuses on the legal implications of discrimination.

M

mediation The third party helps the negotiators reach a settlement.

motivation The desire within a person causing that person to act.

multiple hurdles A minimum cutoff is set on each predictor, and each minimum level must be "passed." For example, a candidate for a sales representative job must achieve a minimum education level, a certain score on a sales aptitude test, and a minimum score on a structured interview to be hired.

N

negligent hiring Occurs when an employer fails to check an employee's background, and the employee later injures someone on the job.

negligent retention Occurs when an employer becomes aware that an employee may be unfit for employment, but continues to employ the person, and the person injures someone.

O

objective measures Can be observed.

open shop Firm in which workers are not required to join or pay dues to a union.

operational and employee advocate Managing most HR activities in keeping with the strategy that has been identified by management and serving as employee "champion."

organizational commitment The degree to which employees believes in and accept organizational goals and desire to remain with the organization.

P

pay compression Occurs when the pay differences among individuals with different levels of experience and performance become small.

pay grades Groupings of individual jobs having approximately the same job worth.

pay survey Collection of data on compensation rates for workers performing similar jobs in other organizations.

performance appraisal Process of determining how well employees do their job relative to a standard and communicating that information to the employee.

performance management Series of activities designed to ensure that the organization gets the performance it needs from its employees.

performance philosophy Requires that compensation changes reflect performance differences.

performance standards The expected levels of performance, labeled benchmarks or goals or targets, depending on the approach taken.

point-of-service plans Financial incentives to encourage employees to use designated medical providers.

policies General guidelines that focus organizational actions.

pre-supervisor training The training to provide realistic job previews of what supervisors will face and to convey to individuals that they cannot just rely on their current job skills and experience in their new positions.

prevailing wage The rate paid for a job by a majority of the employers in the appropriate geographic area.

primacy effect The opposite of recency effect which occurs when a rater gives greater weight to information received first.

procedural justice The perceived fairness of the process and procedures used to make decisions about employees, including their pay.

procedures Provide customary methods of handling activities and are more specific than policies.

purchase discounts Employees buy goods or services from their employers at reduced rates.

Q

quid pro quo Sexual harassment in which employment outcomes are linked to the individual granting sexual favors.

R

ranking method Lists all employees from highest to lowest in performance.

rater bias Occurs when a rater's values or prejudices distort the rating.

recency effect When a rater gives greater weight to recent events when appraising an individual's performance.

recruiting The process of generating a pool of qualified applicants for organizational jobs.

red-circled employee Incumbent who is paid above the range set for the job.

replacement costs Includes recruiting and advertising expenses, search fees, HR interviewer and staff time and salaries, employee referral fees, relocation and moving costs, supervisor and managerial time and salaries, employment testing costs, reference checking fees, pre-employment medical expenses, etc.

re-recruiting Recruitment of former employees and former applicants for the organization.

responsibilities Obligations to perform certain tasks and duties.

results-based information Considers employee accomplishments.

resume mining A software approach to getting the best resumes for a fit from a big database.

Return on investment (ROI) A calculation showing the value of expenditures for HR activities.

reverse discrimination When a person is denied an opportunity because of preferences given to protected-class individuals who may be less qualified.

rights Powers, privileges, or interests that belong to a person by law, nature, or tradition.

right-to-work laws State laws that prohibit requiring employees to join unions as a condition of obtaining or continuing employment.

rules Specific guidelines that regulate and restrict the behavior of individuals.

S

safety Condition in which the physical well-being of people is protected.

salary-only approach An approach used when an organization emphasizes serving and retaining existing accounts, over generating new sales and accounts.

salary-plus-commission The form of sales compensation which combines the stability of a salary with the performance aspect of a commission.

same-size reward All the members receive the same payout, regardless of job level, current pay, seniority, or individual performance differences.

security Protection of employees and organizational facilities.

selection Process of choosing individuals with qualifications needed to fill jobs in an organization.

self-efficacy Person's belief that he or she can learn the training program content.

sensitivity training To sensitize people to the differences among them and how their words and behaviors are seen by others.

separation costs Includes HR staff and supervisor time and salaries to prevent separations, exit interview time, unemployment expenses, legal fees for separations challenged, accrued vacation, continued benefits, etc.

separations Departures from the organization.

sequencing The career approach for women to work hard before children arrive, plateau or step off the career track when children are younger, and go back to career-focused jobs that allow flexibility when they are older.

severity rate The average time lost per absent employee during a specified period of time.

sexual harassment Actions that are sexually directed, are unwanted, and subject the worker to adverse employment conditions or create a hostile work environment.

shift differential A form of additional pay provided by the employers for working in the evening or night shift.

shift work A commonly used work schedule design.

statutory rights Rights based on laws or statutes passed by federal, state, or local government.

stock option plan Gives employees the right to purchase a fixed number of shares of company stock at a specified exercise price for a limited period of time.

straight commission system A sales representative receives a percentage of the value of the sales he or she has made.

strategic Helping to define the strategy relative to human capital and its contributing to organizational results

strategic business partner The role of HR as "having a seat at the table," and contributing to the strategic directions and success of the organization.

subjective measures Require judgment on the part of the evaluator.

systematic appraisal Used when the contact between a manager and employee is formal, and a system is in place to report managerial impressions and observations on employee performance.

T

tactile learners Learners who get their hands on the training resources and use them.

talent management Concerned with enhancing the attraction, development, and retention of key human resources.

task A distict, identifiable work activity composted of motions.

team sharing The system of sharing with employees greater-than-expected gains in profits and/or productivity

technical competencies The specific knowledge and skills that the employees have.

telecommute Working via electronic computing and telecommunications equipment.

total rewards Are the monetary and non-monetary rewards provided to employees in order to attract, motivate, and retain them.

training Process whereby people acquire capabilities to perform jobs.

trait-based information Identifies a character trait of the employee—such as attitude, initiative, or creativity—and may or may not be job related.

U

union A formal association of workers that promotes the interests of its members through collective action.

union security provisions Contract clauses to help the union obtain and retain members.

union steward Employee elected to serve as the first-line representative of unionized workers.

V

variable pay Compensation linked directly to individual, team, or organizational performance.

violence response team Security personnel, key managers, HR staff members, and selected employees are grouped together to develop policies and practices for preventing and responding to workplace violence.

visual learners Those who think in pictures and figures and focus on the purpose and process of the training.

Index